ECONOMIC PLANNING IN TRANSITION

Economic Planning in Transition

Socio Economic Development and Planning in Post-Socialist and Capitalist Societies

Edited by
JÅNOS KOVÅCS
Institute of Economics
Hungarian Academy of Sciences
and
BRUNO DALLAGO
Department of Economics
University of Trento

Dartmouth
Aldershot · Brookfield USA · Hong Kong · Singapore · Sydney

© J. Kovács, B. Dallago, 1990

Published by

Dartmouth Publishing Company
Gower House, Croft Road, Aldershot,
Hants. GU11 3HR, England

Dartmouth Publishing Company
Old Post Road, Brookfield, Vermont 05036,
USA

ISBN 1 85521 113 0

Printed in Great Britain by
Billing & Sons Ltd, Worcester

Contents

PREFACE

The origin of the present book was research on «The role of planning in preparing the strategy of socio-economic development», which began in 1985 under the direction of Prof. János Kovács and financed by the Hungarian Academy of Sciences. The central core of the research group comprised 7 people at the Department of Theory of Planning of the Institute of Economics, Hungarian Academy of Sciences. The research group also included 18 researchers from outside the Department: 9 of these were foreigners, from both the East and the West.

The aim of the research project was to evaluate the role of socio-economic planning in present-day societies in order to gain ideas and experience for use in the process of modernization of the Hungarian planning system. To this end it was considered important to compare Hungarian practice with experiences obtained in other countries of both the East and the West. The idea of a conference on the topic arose from the desire to test the results gained from the research project in an international environment, where the participants in the research project could discuss and compare their findings with other experts, from both Hungary and abroad, who had not taken part in the project.

This book sets out the main results of the international conference, which was organized in Budapest by the Institute of Economics of the Hungarian Academy of Sciences on March 14-16, 1989.

A number of organizations and people contributed to the implementation of the research project and the organization of the conference. Without pretending to be able to thank everybody involved, we would like first of all to express our gratitude to the Hungarian Academy of Sciences, the Department of Economics, University of Trento (Italy) and to the various foundations (OTKA, TSI) which financed a large part of the research project. We wish to express our thanks to UNESCO for having contributed morally and financially to the success of the international conference. Our appreciation goes to Mr T.H. Yoo for his personal participation in the conference on behalf of UNESCO. The National Commission of UNESCO for Hungary also made a major effort to promote the international meeting.

Among the people who most contributed to the success of the conference and the publication of the present book particular mention should be made of three researchers at the Institute of Economics, Hungarian Academy of Sciences: Mrs. I. Virág who helped to prepare the whole research program, Mrs. I. Maltinszky who as secretary took on a leading role in the organization of the conference, and Mr. G. Tenyi whose participation in the editorial work was a great help in

7

the preparation of the papers for publication. A. Belton and Mrs. A. Cava in Italy were responsible respectively for the language editing of the original manuscripts and for preparing the camera-ready version.

Finally, we wish to thank all participants in the conference and authors of the present book for their kind permission to publish their papers and their readiness in following the editors' requirements. All these factors enabled us to present the state of research and thinking on planning and development which prevailed in late 1989 in a fast-changing world.

Budapest, March 1990

About the authors

Báger, Gusztáv
Professor of Economics, Head of Department,
National Planning Office, Budapest

Belousov, Pavel
Head of Department, Academy of Social Sciences,
Central Committee CPSU, Moscow

Bod, Péter A.
Head of Department, Institute of Planning,
National Planning Office of Hungary, Budapest

Dallago, Bruno
Associate Professor of Economics, University of Trento,
Trento

Dyba, Karel
Senior Research Fellow, Institute of Prognoses,
Czechoslovak Academy of Sciences, Prague

Gadó, Ottó
Professor of Economics, Adviser of Ministry of Finance,
Former Vice President of National
Planning Office, Budapest

Hall, John B.
Assistant Professor, Portland State University,
Portland

Hoós, János
Professor of Economics, President of Statistical Office,
Former President of National Planning Office,
Budapest

Huszár, Józsefné
Head of Department, Institute of Planning,
National Office of Planning, Budapest

Jezek, Tomas
Senior Research Fellow, Institute of Prognoses,
Czechoslovak Academy of Sciences, Prague

Karpinsky, Andrzej
Deputy Secretary for Scientific Research,
Polish Academy of Sciences, Warsaw

Kigyóssy, Éva
Research Fellow, Central Institute of Economics,
Academy of Sciences of the GDR, Berlin

Kiglics, István
Research Fellow, Institute for Economic Planning,
National Planning Office, Budapest

Kysilka, Pavel
Senior Research Fellow, Institute of Economics,
Czechoslovak Academy of Sciences, Prague

Kornek, Martin
Assistant Professor,
High School of Economics, Berlin

Kovács, János
Professor of Economics, Head of Department,
Institute of Economics, HAS Budapest

Nikiforov, Veselin
Professor of Economics,
Member of the Bulgarian Academy
of Sciences, Sofia

Schmidt, Adám
Emeritus Professor of Economics,
Former Head of Department,
Institute of Economics, HAS Budapest

Semjén, András
Senior Research Fellow,
Institute of Economic Planning,
National Planning Office, Budapest

Senjur, Marjan
Professor of Economics, University of Ljubljana
Ljubljana

Sirotkovic, Jakov
Professor of Economics,
President of Yugoslav Academy
of Sciences and Arts, Zagreb

Stacewicz, Janusz
Institute of Economics,
Polish Academy of Sciences, Marsaw

Tényi, György
Research Fellow,
Institute of Economics, HAS Budapest

FOREWORD

Unesco was pleased to initiate the idea for this Conference and make a modest contribution to its organization in Budapest in 1989, effectively assured by the Institute of Economics, Academy of Sciences of Hungary. Unesco's contribution was, within its Programme of Participation, linked with Programme VIII.1. 'Study and Planning of Development' the objective of which is to elucidate the concept of development and elaborate the methods of planning of development.

After forty-five years, during which two different economic and social systems coexisted with difficulty, the calling of the conference of experts in development planning to review the existing economic planning system and examine the future one in Eastern Europe was a positive action, in view of socio-economic reforms in this region.

This meeting provided, in fact, an excellent occasion for frank and open international debate which enabled the participants to draw some historical lessons on the relationship between the socio-economic system, socio-economic planning and the political system. The interest in comparing the planning experiences in twelve countries was great and allowed identification of some common factors for the success and failure of socio-economic planning.

It was only after many years of failure in many countries that people started to realize that economic planning is not a simple quantitative instrument to illustrate the preferences of power but a dynamic institutional process which permits the achievement of socio-economic goals. In fact, Professor Jan Tinbergen, Nobel Prize-Winner in Economics, came to Canada in 1968 to speak on development and planning. He had already presented a clear notion on the nature of development planning. He spoke on 'planning as a process designed to reflect socio-economic objectives, organizing the adequate consultations of groups concerned and undertaking the efficient procedure of planning'.

It appears to me that three levels of integration are necessary: a) political system, b) socio-economic system, and c) development planning. There are many examples of development planning as a simple forecasting exercise without being linked to the real political decision-making process. Contradictory examples indicate that although economic plan is approved by supreme political authorities, it ignores real market mechanisms and is consequently deprived of real efficiency.

11

When Professor Wassily Leontief, Nobel Prize-Winner in Economics, came to Unesco this year to speak on development, he convinced me that development planning will be a dead letter if a certain level of education is not achieved. In this regard, he mentioned the experience of Korean Development.

I was not surprised to hear during the conference that traditional central planning systems cannot be maintained. Among the criticisms against traditional central planning systems, the reformers seemed to insist on the following:

a) economic policies for planning did not sufficiently take into account market mechanisms;
b) regulations of planning were not articulated adequately with micro-economic management;
c) governments were not always able to link efficiently development planning to capital overheads such as efficient human resources development.

It appears that the road to success of development planning opens in three directions:

a) redefine the nature of development planning;
b) evaluate the role of the market in planning;
c) efficient management of economic development.

By organizing and publishing the proceedings of this conference, the Institute of Economics, the Academy of Sciences of Hungary, has contributed greatly to providing an interesting international forum in Eastern Europe on the role of development planning for the year 2000.

Tae-Ho Yoo
UNESCO

INTRODUCTION (*)

by
János Kovács

and
Bruno Dallago

The role of planning has been much debated among scholars and policy makers in both the West and the East, with an intensity that has varied considerably through time. In general, commitment to planning is directly correlated to the economic performance of the country (or group of countries) concerned, but varies according to the economic system and the prevailing coordinating mechanism. In the Soviet-type economies the role of planning is stressed when the economy is performing well, but is criticized after a prolonged period of stagnation and depression (depending also on the socio-political situation). In the West the role of planning is often invoked in periods of deep economic slump or when radical and wide transformations are deemed to be necessary.

There is no doubt that – since the October Revolution – the fortunes of planning have never been as low as at present. A prolonged boom in Western economies and a persistent profound crisis in the East have radically challenged the role of macroeconomic (nation-wide) planning in most countries.

This situation reveals that, in spite of the results of the theoretical debate involving policy-makers, the public at large and also a large number of scholars, macroeconomic (nation-wide) plan and market are still seen as mutually incompatible. The most recent move in this direction is presently under way in some East European countries where a considerable number of policy-makers and scholars propose creating a new allocation and coordinating mechanism for the economy based on the market and *not* on the plan. More precisely, they propose abolishing macroeconomic planning as a means of resources allocation and reducing it to little more than the simple collection of information and elaboration of studies and research. Macroeconomic coordination should be left, they argue, to the operation of the market alone.

The aim of this book is to challenge this new conventional wisdom by showing that in Soviet-type economies macroeconomic planning is necessary – together with a true market – as the engine of transformation in the economic system, although it must change its nature radically. An attempt will be made to delineate the fundamental prerequisites and features of such planning. The book also shows that much misunderstanding arises from identification of one particular type of planning (namely the direct or administrative planning) with macroe-

---

(*) Although this introduction is the result of a joint effort by the authors, parts 1 and 2 were written by Bruno Dallago, parts 3, 4 and 5 by János Kovács.

conomic planning *tout court*.

1. Types of macroeconomic (nation-wide) planning

The term 'planning' means different things to different people. Since this is also the case of other terms, such as 'market', a clear definition and a specification of the components of such an activity are required before its role is analyzed. First, a distinction must be drawn between planning and similar but nevertheless different types of activities, such as simple forecasts, policies and government intervention (M. Bornstein, 1975b, pp. 1-3). Planning and plans usually comprise such activities, although they may also exist without planning. Macroeconomic (nation-wide or national economic) planning is defined here as a conscious government activity whose purpose is to bring about a desired situation of the economy after a given period of time. This activity includes socio-political control (by society's representatives: government, parliament, political parties, etc.) over the economy, the preparation of studies on the present situation of the economy and its 'spontaneous' evolution, the drawing up of a picture of a desired state of an economy at a future point in time, and the utilization of various means (instruments, policies, orders, etc.) to bring about this desired state (see also H.S. Levine, 1971, p. 140). Such a definition allows us to group together various types of planning activity, defined according to the degree of compulsoriness of the plan itself for microeconomic agents. The plan is the result of such planning activity and usually takes the form of a publicized document.

Planning can be grouped under the following four headings (for a rather similar classification see E.S. Kirschen, 1974, pp. 299-306). They are discussed in an order that reflects the increasing importance of the planning agency (government):

a. *indicative planning*: the aim of planning activity is to draw up documents (plans) outlining the governments forecast for the desired development of the economy and containing decisions on government expenditure and the investment and current expenditure of state-owned enterprises. The specific target of the plan is therefore coordination of the allocation of state resources to this end. There is no direct attempt to govern the decisions of private economic agents (enterprises). However, the announcement of macroeconomic and growth targets and targets for the activity of state agencies and state-owned enterprises is intended to create an environment that influences the decisions of private enterprises. Broadly speaking, indicative planning may be said to influence a non-state economy through a demand-pull effect.

b. *regulative planning*: the explicit aim of planning activity is not only to allocate state resources and to coordinate and decide the activity of the state sector, but also actively to influence the decisions and activity of the private sector. To achieve this target, the government gives incentives (often *ex ante*, through private finance and credit) to private agents in order to induce them to cooperate in plan implementation. On some occasions, the government and/or state enterprises stipulate contracts among themselves. In this kind of planning activity, the government acts as the overall coordinator

14

of the nation's economic activity.

c. *indirect planning*: the government formulates its strategy and priorities in a plan and devises the means, instruments and parameters actively to induce economic agents (enterprises) to implement it. Not only is the allocation of centralized resources tied to plan implementation, but the establishment of government controlled ("market") parameters (price formation, interest rate and credit, taxes, exchange rate, etc.) also serves the same purpose. No punishment accrues to those agents that do not implement the plan; however, in this case they have to forego the (usually economic) advantages deriving from plan implementation (bonuses for managers and employees; priorities in state resources allocation for those enterprises implementing or overimplementing plan targets, etc.). This means that a certain amount of state-owned resources is distributed *ex post* by the government to reward those people and agents that have implemented the plan. These resources therefore influence the economy in the following plan period. To achieve successful implementation, this type of planning requires not only that economic agents actively cooperate, but also that economic parameters are established by the government at the right values (to keep the market in equilibrium and to incentivate agents to implement the plan).

d. *direct (administrative, dirigist, command) planning*: the plan is the document embodying the government's strategy and priorities, the instruments (generally administrative orders) to implement it and the way (structure, quantities) in which state resources have to be allocated. To facilitate the issuing of plan orders and the control of their implementation, plan targets may be expressed in physical units. Plan implementation is compulsory for enterprises: to this end the government can use both economic and administrative (orders) and also political means. If economic agents fulfil the plan targets, they receive economic or moral rewards. However, if they do not implement the plan, they are punished in economic or other terms.

There are some similarities among these various types of planning, such as the procedures used to draw up plans and their reliance on the collection and publication of information. However, there are also substantial differences, and on these depends the specific content of each type of planning: these differences concern in particular the systemic environment, the mode of implementation (e.g. via incentives or orders) and the microeconomic behaviour on which planning relies and which is generated by the plan implementation process (D.M. Nuti, 1986, pp. 243-244). These basic differences mean that the utilization of each type of planning is limited by various factors, in particular by systemic ones. Planning can also be used – as an element of major reforms – to change or transform the economic system itself. However, it is true that, historically, planning has proved to be more a factor in conservation of the existing economic system that a means for its reform.

2. Limits and advantages of planning

Planning in itself – i.e. independently of its specific types and features – has many limitations but also many advantages. The balance between these limitations and advantages depends on the type and role of planning in the economy, on specific features (scientific basis, coordination among the various agencies involved in planning, importance of incentives in its implementation, etc.) of the plan, and on the relationship (cooperative or conflictual) between government and economic agents.

Theoretical discussion and analysis of the working of economies with planning have proved that the latter suffer from many limitations. At the same time, however, various advantages of planning have been stressed and shown to exist. The main limits and advantages are as follows:

a. *Economic calculation, information and control.* The Austrian school (von Mises, Hayek and others) pointed out in different ways that the planning of economy is suboptimal and irrational. According to the traditional interpretation of von Mises' thought, socialism is theoretically impossibile because it would belong to the realm of irrationality. In fact, rational economic calculation in socialism is impossible, because of the lack of prices reflecting relative scarcities. This is due to the fact that in the market of production goods both demand and supply come from the state. Therefore, prices are fixed arbitrarily by the state and this prevents an economically rational allocation of resources (cf. L. von Mises, 1920, 1922).

On the other hand, the advantages of planning were emphasized by many classics of socialist thought. However, in the celebrated socialist calculation debate of the 1930s the stress was more on the capacity of planning to imitate the working of the free competitive market than on the intrinsic advantages of planning. In fact, F.M. Taylor in 1929 and H.D. Dickinson in 1933 and 1939, in further developing E. Barone's classical argument (published in 1908), proved the theoretical feasibility of socialism. They were soon followed by O. Lange and others. Lange demonstrated that a ministry of production can identify equilibrium prices through a process of "trial and error" – by varying prices in order to preserve an equilibrium in the market between demand and supply – thus playing the role of the Walrasian auctioneer (O. Lange, 1936).

After that, the argument of the theoretical unfeasibility found no further support. However, in various contributions (1935a, 1935b, 1945) F.A. Hayek challenged not the theoretical but the practicability of socialism. In his view, even if the rational use of resources in socialism is theoretically possible through a process of trial and error, it is impracticable because central planners would have to collect and process such an enormous mass of information that no office could cope with it. The Austrians' criticism focused on socialism – defined as a socio-economic system based on the state ownership of production means – rather than on planning itself. However, because in their view it is interference in the unconstrained working of a free market that prevents the economy from reaching its optimum position, the argument can easily be extended to planning.

In the 1960s the Soviet school of linear programming and optimal planning

(L.V. Kantorovich, 1965; V.V. Novozhilov, 1969; and others) applied linear programming not only to the problem of combining available productive resources in a factory to maximize production, but also to the problem of optimal macroeconomic planning in a socialist economy. According to them, a successful centrally-planned economy should utilize a system of prices – so-called 'shadow prices' – derived from solving linear programming problems, including a social rate of discount similar to an interest rate.

One fundamental criticism of the market as a mechanism of economic calculation acts in favour of planning: it has been stressed that the market solves only *private* calculation. Welfare economics and economic policy in general have proposed various correctives to the working of market (taxes, subsidies). However, planning is *per sé* – in principle – a mechanism for *social* calculation which can be used without correctives. It should also be stressed that planning helps in the collection, elaboration, coordination and circulation of information: therefore, it greatly facilitates the formation of a macroeconomic vision of the economy and reduces transaction costs.

b. *Motivations, incentives, coordination.* According to M. Dobb (1969, pp. 204-205 of the Italian edition), Hayek's "retreat" from von Mises' position shifted the emphasis onto a very different set of questions: the institutional structures of a socialist economy, systems of information and control, motivation and incentives to economic activity. These are all largely unsolved problems in planning. As pointed out by Hayek (1935b), the practicability of socialism is not merely a technical question but a genuinely political-economic one. It has to do with the nature of the motivations of economic agents, who are often unwilling to cooperate with the planning agency and transmit false or wrong information to avoid risk and to defend their autonomy and their pursuit of specific interests. Moreover, because in a planned economy the collection of information is not left to the free working of a competitive market, it is organized bureaucratically and is, by its very nature, slow.

The problems of contrasting interests within the center, between the center and economic agents, and the lack of incentives to production and work have been stressed, among others, by O. Sik (1967). For instance, if the plan gives priority to a certain sector or activity, economic agents operating in that sector soon realize the importance of their activity for the government. Since agents are risk-free, because of the institutional solutions adopted, this may give them an opportunity to gain extra advantages in ways not envisaged by the plan (bargaining, lobbying, etc.). As a consequence, the flow of information from enterprises to planners easily becomes distorted and incomplete. However, planning also has well-known advantages, in the sense that it may help to coordinate the activity of economic agents and may stimulate cooperation among economic agents and between them and government agencies; it produces a rational and efficient allocation of centralized (state) resources and a coordinated state intervention in the economy; it improves the coordination and forecasting of long-run economic processes (e.g. educational training, development of energy sources, coordination of research activity). All these facts and potentialities may represent an additional source of motivation and incentive (e.g. through a demand-pull

17

effect or by guaranteeing energy resources) for economic agents – private, co-operative and state-owned alike.

c. *Rivalry and competition.* D. Lavoie (1985), a follower of the Austrian school, roundly criticizes the standard account of the socialist calculation debate and has recently pointed out that the most detrimental consequence of planning is that it eliminates rivalry (intended as dynamic, dialectical competition – as distinct from the non-rivalrous, static notion of neoclassical economists) among economic agents. This has adverse effects on both the transmission of information and the efficiency of production. Therefore, contrary to the conclusions reached by the neoclassical "market socialism" position (E. Barone, F. Taylor, O. Lange, and others), planning is in fact incompatible with the market, since they are fundamentally alternative coordination mechanisms which, if combined, would interfere with the operation of each other.

However, Lavoie forgets that competition may sometimes be harmful (e.g. certain types of monopolistic price or non-price competition to achieve closer control over the market, or when competition prevents economic agents from fully exploiting economies of scale). Competition may also be less efficient than cooperation: in such cases planning can be of great utility in regulating the market.

d. *Entrepreneurship, uncertainty, expectations.* A further problem has been pointed out by J.A. Schumpeter (1942). He stressed the importance of entrepreneurship and predicted the fall of capitalism and the rise of socialism on the basis of the routinization of innovation, which entails the vanishing of the role of the entrepreneur. However, his idea of socialism was that of a bureaucratic society directed by the center (A. Vercelli, 1989). The recent experience both of the Western countries (positive) and of the Eastern European countries (negative) has shown the fundamental importance of entrepreneurship even in modern economies. The process of economic development is in reality unbalanced (non-equilibrating), but planning tends by its nature towards balance and equilibrium and is incapable of planning innovation fully and of replacing entrepreneurship effectively.

However, planning can usefully help to improve the environment for entrepreneurship. In particular, by working out and advertising a general (and even a detailed) framework for the economy in the next period, it helps the formation of expectations and reduces uncertainty. This is particularly important for long-term investments, but may also favour short-run processes.

e. *Property rights.* Planning interferes to a certain extent in property rights, in particular when planning takes place in an economy based on the private ownership of production means. In order to assert plan targets, property rights have to be attenuated to some extent, and this may have negative consequences on the agent's motivations and behaviour.

However, directly or through a better flow of information, the use of coordination, etc., may in certain circumstances help to overcome the isolation among economic agents caused by property rights (private ownership) and atomistic organizational forms (small enterprises, local monopolies, etc.). In the case of state-owned enterprises, it favours communication among them and may help to overcome limits and obstacles posed by bureaucratic behaviour, which is largely independent of planning.

f. *Budget constraint.* J. Kornai's work indicates that planning contributes – together with other factors – to the softening of the budget constraint (J. Kornai, 1980). The consequences of this on motivations and the behaviour of economic agents generate a situation of shortage. In these circumstances not only does economic calculation become difficult, but incentives to work and production also become largely ineffective and the "perverse" behaviour of economic agents proliferates. However, Kornai's criticism appears to concern direct planning in a Soviet-type economy and not other types. Moreover, it seems to relate most closely to the absence of economic and financial autonomy of enterprises – which absolves them from any responsibility and risk deriving from their activity.

However, planning may prove to be an irreplaceable instrument in achieving a general hardening of the economic agents' budget constraint and may also be used to vary the agents' budget constraint selectively.

g. *Type of goods.* One problem implicit in applied analyses of planning – though one rarely touched on in theoretical debates – is the efficacy of planning in relation to the types of goods considered. Although, there is a substantial literature on "market failures" in the case of public goods and externalities, "planning failures" appear to refer basically to private goods. In this sense, too, both plan and market are coordinating mechanisms of limited scope and validity.

h. *Freedom and democracy.* Last but not least, there may be consequences for freedom and democracy. As pointed out by various authors (e.g. C. Bettelheim, 1975; F. Hayek, 1960 pp. 45-46, 1944; S. Ricossa, 1989), the necessity to develop plans gives rise to a group of specialists and bureaucrats, who may become extremely powerful and whose democratic control by the rest of society may be difficult. If this is the case, this group may impose its allocation, production and consumption preferences on the rest of society.

However, planning may give the economy and the society a more general and better coordinated perspective ("social preferences") which assigns a fairer (greater) weight to economically disadvantaged individuals. It may also stabilize the political situation and favour the freedom of society's members and democracy by reducing or eliminating unemployment and by promoting economic and socio-political equality.

From what has been said so far, it appears that the issues concern not so much planning in itself as its institutional organization and democratic control. From a theoretical point of view, one may also conclude that neither market nor planning are perfect and universal coordinating mechanisms. This raises a further problem: can plan and market co-exist so that they can mutually reinforce their advantages and correct their weaknesses? This book attempts to give an answer to this question based on the experiences of various countries.

19

3. The experience of the past and the road to the future

It is not surprising that, in such a large company and on such a controversial topic, there are many points of view. Certainly it is not only planning which becomes debatable but the range itself of government intervention in the economy.

A widely shared belief among this book's authors (including the editors), although expressed in a broad variety of opinions, is that government intervention should be planned, but substantial changes should be made to both the role and the nature of planning. This is necessary not only to improve planning methods and techniques, but above all to bring fruitful cooperation with the market. These is necessary not only to improve planning methods and techniques, but above all to bring fruitful cooperation with the market. These requirements are even more pressing now that, since 1989, the situation has changed so dramatically in all the countries of Central and Eastern Europe.

In the first part of the book the theoretical problems of planning are analyzed. A clear and interesting taxonomy of "concurrents" and "relatives" of planning is set out by A. Schmidt. He starts from the observation that there is a multiplicity of coordinating mechanisms for social activities and actions. From this it follows that planning cannot manage everything; but Schmidt also shows that planning is necessary, together with its concurrents and relatives. Dealing with methodological questions related to a new shape of central planning, J. Stacewicz delineates a new philosophy of central planning. Particularly important in his view is a clear definition of the role of the various types of central planning: under the present conditions, central planning should be used as a tool to design a way of implementing the concept of national development. This approach entails concentrating attention on development problems and tasks in perspective planning, on the reallocation and increase of resources in medium term planning, and on shaping streams of goods and money in short term planning. A radical criticism of the traditional planning system is made by P.A. Bod. In his view there is no basis for a distinction between "micro" and "macro" under traditional planning, in which any production or distribution decision forms part of an integral decision procedure covering the whole economy. This system has to be changed rapidly: bureaucratic, market-substituting coordination has gradually to hand over its functions to market coordination. This requires the adoption of a completely new type of planning. The last paper in the first section, by J. Kovács, deals with the future of plan and market. After reviewing the evolution of both market and planned economies, and pointing out that many other regulators exist apart from those traditionally considered by central planning or in the working of a pure market, Kovács concludes that the world is proceeding towards an organic unity of plan and regulated market.

The second section comprises three chapters presenting the traditional way of planning. In spite of their defence of traditional planning, the papers in this section do not spare their criticism of it and make proposals for its improvement. The main idea behind Belousov's paper is that the lower levels of the planning hierarchy should take on a stronger operative role in order to allow higher levels to concentrate on less detailed and indirect regulation (based in particular on a government contract system and financial regulators). The paper by K. Kornek, although basically content with the traditional planning system in the GDR, sees the more extensive use of "commodity-money relations" as a useful improvement. Also V. Nikiforov expects a remedy for the illnesses of planned economy (which he criticises sharply) to come, not from the introduction of market relations but from a specially constructed indicator and a stronger position of endusers.

Critics of the traditional planning system have been assembled in the third section. The idea common to the papers included in this section is that the experiences of Central and East European countries prove that reform restricted to the planning system is not viable and that what is needed is a reform that also embraces the governmental-political system and property relations. A sharp, discernible line of division identifies transitions from directive and indirect planning into regulative or indicative planning. The drawbacks and advantages of planning can be clarified in academic debates. However, choices need political decisions based on policy makers' preferences. Moreover, a planned economy presumes power relations, a social hierarchy and individual behaviour that differ from those of a market economy. The paper by Mrs. Huszár sets the ideologic ideal of planned economy against its practical realisation. The topic addressed by K. Dyba and T. Jezek is whether the cautious reform introduced in the late 1980s in Czechoslovakia led to indirect bureaucratic control or instead to a true market economy. The same question is raised by P. Kysilka, who analyses the reasons why previous Czechoslovakian reform endeavours failed. A special feature of the Yugoslavian economic system is that the power relation between central management and the sphere of self-management is unstable; it is always possible to shift towards a fully-fledged planned economy or towards pure market relations. The interesting history of this conflict is presented by J. Sirotkovic. The other Yugoslavian author, M. Senjur, maintains that the state has to renounce interference in investment and structural adjustment decisions of economic agents, and that it has to promote saving and investment through monetary and fiscal policy. The state has a more direct role only in the energy sector, in agriculture and in the reallocation of investments.

Planning is not a monopoly of socialist countries. In fact substantial and often successful planning activity has also taken place in various market economies, albeit in a different context. Therefore, in evaluation of the prospects for reform of the planning system in Central and Eastern Europe, it is important to analyse the planning experiences of market economies. This analysis is provided in section four, where experiences of planning in a limited sample of market economies are considered. The evidence of these developed capitalist economies shows the existence of barriers to forecasting and indicative planning in a situation where the attitude of economic agents is preponderantly competitive and non co-operative. In such cases - where there are few limits on property rights - planning organs are not powerful enough to enforce co-ordination and cooperation among economic agents. In some countries, for example the Federal Republic of Germany (see the paper by É. Kigyóssy) or Italy (see B. Dallago), the state engages only in short-term, fragmented activity which does not add up to a real nation-wide plan. A particular case is that of France, where since World War II there have been large fluctuations in the importance of planning, as illustrated in G. Tényi's paper. This results from the fact that macroeconomic planning gains in importance when – as a result of a crisis in the previous economic and political elite – a power vacuum opens up and social forces striving for reorganisation and modernization of the economy gain substantial power in the government bureaucracy. This is even more the case of Japan, where central management and the traditional spirit of consensus arose after World War II (when the previous organising centers of the economy disintegrated) in central planning. This is discussed in I. Kiglics's paper. Somewhat different has been the role of planning in Scandinavian countries, as presented by the study of A. Semjén of Norway, where social problems have recently gained prominence in planning activity beyond short-term planning. This is reflected in the whole attitude of planning: the plan does not contain distinct economic and social chapters but investigates social problems from the point of view how much they contribute to the realisation of a solidaristic society. The source of a standing role for planning is a clear division of labour between regulated market and planning competence. The paper by J. Hall analyzes the double task facing South-Korea: escaping from the blind alley of dependent development, and taking advantage of the cost-reducing possibilities of late, follower-type industrialization. An important role has been played in this process by strong, directive, investment-resource-centralising state management, co-ordinated by medium-term (five year) plans. High priority is given to infrastructure and to export. As in the case of Japan, in recent years the importance of government regulation has receded, in parallel with structural reinforcement of the economy.

4. The new paradigm of planning and the preconditions of reform

The fifth section of the book comprises four papers specifically dealing with the necessity of achieving a new paradigm of nation-wide economic planning, and specifying the requirement of such a transition as well as the main characteristics of the new paradigm. According to A. Karpinski, the emphasis should shift from the formal characteristics of planning to the shaping of strategy and of long-term structure. Instead of determining actual plan indicators, planning activity should formulate development mechanisms and principles regulating the firms' activity. This new type of planning should restrict itself to strategic problems. O. Gadó analyzes the Hungarian experience of planning, regulation and deregulation, and concentrates his attention of the third of these. In Gadó's view, deregulation is needed to do away with governmental overregulation resulting from a distortion in ownership relations. A precondition of deregulation is to develop market relations and, in accordance with these, ownership relations; and also to modify the interests of economic units and the aims of state management. According to J. Hoós, who deals with planning reform in Hungary, yearly plan calculations intended to exert regular controls on macroeconomic processes should be replaced by easily accessible analyses which forecast processes. The strategic and social policy character of long-term planning should be reinforced. Technical-methodological conditions of the new type of planning are dealt with by G. Báger. The range of those participating in the drawing up of plan conceptions (experts, pressure groups) should widen, and the role of Parliament should increase. Alternative development conceptions must be elaborated and the simple allocation of resources should be replaced by a systems approach addressing at human values.

References

Barone, E. (1908), 'Il ministro della produzione nello stato collettivista', *Giornale degli economisti*, September, pp. 267-93 and October, pp. 391-414 (Engl. transl. 'The Ministry of Production in the Collectivist State', in Hayek, F.A., 1935c, pp. 245-90)

Bettelheim, C. (1975), *Economic Calculation and Forms of Property: An Essay on the Transition between Capitalism and Socialism*, Monthly Review Press, New York

Bornstein, M. (1975a) (ed.), *Economic Planning, East and West*, Ballinger, Cambridge, Mass., 1975

Bornstein, M. (1975b), 'Introduction', in Bornstein, M. (1975a), pp. 1-21

Dickinson, H.D. (1933), 'Price Formation in a Socialist Community', *Economic Journal*, June, pp. 237-50

Dickinson, H.D. (1939), *Economics of Socialism*, Oxford University Press, Oxford

Dobb, M. (1969), *Welfare Economics and the Economics of Socialism*, Cambridge University Press, Cambridge

Eckstein, A. (1971) (ed.), *Comparison of Economic Systems. Theoretical and Methodological Approaches*, University of California Press, Berkeley, 1971

Hayek, F. (1935a), The Nature and History of the Problem, reprinted in Hayek, F. (1948), pp. 119-47

Hayek, F. (1935b), The Present State of the Debate, reprinted in Hayek, F. (1948), pp. 148-80

Hayek, F. (1935c) ed., *Collectivist Economic Planning: Critical Studies on the Possibilities of Socialism*, Routledge & Sons, London

Hayek, F. (1944), *The Road to Serfdom*, University of Chicago Press, Chicago

Hayek, F. (1945), The Use of Knowledge in Society, *American Economic Review*, vol 35, September, pp. 519-30, reprinted in Hayek, F. (1948), pp. 77-91

Hayek, F. (1948), *Individualism and Economic Order*, University of Chicago Press, Chicago

Hayek, F. (1960), *The Constitution of Liberty*, The University of Chicago Press, Chicago

Jossa, B. (1989) (ed.), *Teoria dei sistemi economici*, UTET, Turin

Kantorovich, L.V. (1965), *The Best Use of Economic Resources*, Harvard University Press, Cambridge, Mass.

Kirschen, E.S. (1974) (ed.), *Economic Policies Compared. West and East*, North-Holland, Amsterdam – American Elsevier, New York, vol. 1

Kornai, J. (1980), *A hiány*, KJK, Budapest (Engl. trans. *Economics of Shortage*, North Holland, Amsterdam, 1980)

Lange, O. (1936), 'On the Economic Theory of Socialism', *The Review of Economic Studies*, October 1936 and February 1937, reprinted with modifications in Lippincott, B.E. (1938)

Lavoie, D. (1985), *Rivalry and Central Planning. The Socialist Calculation Debate Reconsidered*, Cambridge U.P., Cambridge

Levine, H.S. (1971), 'On Comparing Planned Economies (A Methodological

Inquiry)', in Eckstein, A. (1971), pp. 137-160

Lippincott, B.E. (1938) ed., *On the Economic Theory of Socialism*, Philadelphia and McGraw-Hill, New York, 1964, pp. 55-143

Mises, L. von (1920), 'Die Wirtschaftsrechnung in sozialistischen Gemeinwesen', *Archiv für Sozialwissenschaft und Sozialpolitik*, vol. 47, April, pp. 86-121 (Engl. translation: 'Economic Calculation in the Socialist Commonwealth' in Hayek, F. (1935c), pp. 87-103

Mises, L. von (1922), *Die Gemeinwirtschaft*, G. Fischer, Jena (Engl. translation: *Socialism: An Economic and Sociological Analysis*, Jonathan Cape, London, 1936; 2nd ed.: Yale University Press, New Haven, Conn., 1951)

Novozhilov, V.V. (1969), *Problems of Measuring Outlays and Results under Optimal Planning*, International Arts and Sciences Press, New York

Nuti, D.M. (1986), 'Information, Expectations and Economic Planning', in AISSEC, *III Convegno scientifico annuale*, Nuova immagine editrice, Siena, pp. 231-250

Ricossa, S. (1989), 'Socialismo, liberalismo e liberismo', in Jossa, B. (1989), pp. 53-76

Schumpeter, J.A. (1942), *Capitalism, Socialism and Democracy*, Harper & Brothers, New York

Sik, O. (1967), *Plan and Market under Socialism*, International Arts and Sciences Press, White Plains, N.Y.

Taylor, F.M. (1929), 'The Guidance of Production in a Socialist State', in *American Economic Review*, March, reprintend in Lippincott, B.E. (1938), pp. 41-54

Vercelli, A. (1989), 'Un riesame critico della teoria schumpeteriana della 'transizione' al socialismo', in Jossa, B. (1989), pp. 265-293

PART I
THEORETICAL PROBLEMS
OF PLANNING

Adam Schmidt

Plans, their relatives
and their concurrents

1. Plan and Market

Earlier, in socialist countries planning and plans held a central position and enjoyed high esteem in science, politics and practice. Later this situation changed
and the prestige of planning suffered more or less heavy losses. Even now the
discussion over the problem of 'plan versus market' is still going on between
planners and market advocates. In parenthesis it could be remarked that – in my
opinion – the answer to the question can not be other than one word: both. Any-
how, we are presently witnessing several symptoms of planning in the de-
scending branch, in spite of the rather significant development in planning methods, techniques and institutions. Taking into account the theme of our conference the fundamental question can be formulated as follows: what is the place
(role) of planning among the possible bases for social and economic activities,
especially in the field of development? We might approach the question from
two sides – first looking for the 'concurrents' of planning, second for its
'relatives'.

2. Concurrents of planning

Our starting point consists in the phenomenon of multiplicity of bases for human
and social activities and actions. This multiplicity of bases is worthy of thorough
research, but here a short enumeration should suffice. Without any attempt at
scientific systematization we mention only the most apparent and/or more
general bases as follows:
- tradition and tradition-originated customs;
- imitation, using various patterns;
- improvisations, followed by rush decisions;
- danger situations, generating evasion or escape;
- guidance-indicating directions (cf. indicative planning);
- command-containing orders (cf. directive planning);
- planning in the strict sense of the word, resulting in (indicative or directive)
  plans;

27

- market with its forces and events.

The above enumeration can not be regarded as complete and exhaustive; some other basis may exist too. But for us the above items are the most important.

It seems plans are not the sole bases for any activity. There are other 'concurrent' bases, some of them rather important ones, sometimes more important than plans. And here the question emerges: what can, what could be the adequate – and acceptable – relation between plans and their concurrents? It is probable that various types of relations exist and therefore some selection of them is necessary.

Some possibilities of selection are as follows from the viewpoint of planners:
- neglecting;
- suppression;
- acceptance;
- cooperative adoption;
- incorporation

of other bases are the most important variants.

For the sake of concretization and illustration some instances may be mentioned. For example, tradition or customs can be neglected by planners and advisers (in LDCs a rather frequent incident); even harmless customs can be suppressed, mainly in dogmatic-dictatorial systems; direction indicating the acceptance of professional guidance; incorporation of imitation patterns, perhaps somewhat perfected and improved; cooperation of plans and markets, and so on. Planners must not forget the existence of several other useful activity bases.

3. The fundamental principle of planning.

The basic principle of planning can be formulated in a simple and summary sentence: in a rational world everybody is planning, more or less. This sentence may serve also a maxim for practice. Formally the principle is quite simple, but its content and sense raise several questions. First: is there a world which is indeed rational? Second: supposing that everybody is planning, what is the outcome of these activities, a chaos of plans? Third: is it sensible to speak of plans instead of plan systems or hierarchy of plans?

In order to answer the above questions, we have to acknowledge that the world is not entirely rational – and must not be such. But the field of problems we are dealing with belongs to the world of rationality or should belong to it. The result of various planning activities must not be a chaotic disorder of fully independent and even contradictory separate plans; one of the most important tasks of planning consists in the realization of a system of connected and harmonized plans. The hierarchy of plans is not (only) a scientific notion but a fact of real life. In socialist planned economies there is the national plan on the highest level of plan hierarchy ('this above all') but also the plans of organizations, enterprises and even of individuals have to find some place in the plan hierarchy. And not only in socialist economies is the existence of plan hierarchy an indubitable reality. In capitalist countries the individual economic and other plans of contractors, outworkers, employees, workers, households and so on depend mainly on the plans of enterprises, big firms, multinational corporations (and on the state budget, of course); that is, also a kind of plan hierarchy. Without some planning and some possibly rational plans, the life of actors in society may become a series of random events.

In parenthesis: when stressing the importance of system, hierarchy and harmony of plans it can be added that among the factors of plan harmonization in a broad sense also the – present and future – market deserves mention.

We have to underline that planning can not be and is not a solitary, independent activity. And here we could introduce – or better reiterate – the notion of future building. (The term itself was coined about twenty years ago.) Planning can be regarded as a very important but not the sole activity of future building: in the latter framework it (planning) has some prominent 'relatives', relations. We may have a look at them.

4. Future building: the relatives of planning.

The notion of future building could be defined as the entirety of activities aimed at solving problems relating to the (mainly more distant) future that contains peculiar elements of novelty. The activities in question have characteristc features: with regard to them various types of future building can be distinguished. The main types of activities within the realm of future building are the following:

1. General 'fields', namely
   a) future research;
   b) policy;
   c) planning.
2. Special 'strips', for instance
   a) scientific research and technical development, i.e. R&D activity;
   b) education and training;
   c) technical planning in the strict sense.
3. A special 'point' of future building:
   legislation.

The notion of the above items can be explained shortly in some sentences: future research is aimed at the cognition, reconnaissance, exploration, analysis and evaluation of the future; it comprises prognostics, futurology, prospective future research, with their products as forecasts, prognoses, projections, so-called future pictures. Its importance consists in the fact that it yields bases for other activities of future building. Policy (politics) in this context and in the sense of long term activity is the selection, application and enforcement of aims and tasks as well as means and methods for achieving these aims. To define the notions of planning and plan seems superfluous here.

Scientific research is aimed at attaining novel knowledge; development is destined to give new content to the future by practical application of research findings. Education and training – beyond the mere reproduction and transfer of knowledge – indirectly shapes the man of the future. Technical planning on the other hand, especially when based on the results of the technical development mentioned above, shapes the objects of the technical world, from great cities to small gadgets. Legislation can be characterized as a formative and finalizing activity of future building.

all these activities are more or less connected, and it is an item of elementary wisdom that the activities mentioned should be harmonized. Unfortunately, experience shows us that in the sphere of future building the connection between the various types of activity is far from being perfect or at least satisfactory. Therefore we are not entitled to speak of future building as a fact; it is now generally (only) a theoretical concept.

Both theoretically and practically, first an inquiry into the problems of the so-called 'general fields' seems necessary. Therefore we now shall deal with some questions of relations and interrelations between future research, policy and planning. From our point of view these problems have prime importance, conceding that concerning special issues other ones may be even more important.

5. Connections between fields of future building

For brevity's sake we have to content ourselves with a rather sketchy and schematic treatment of the problem of (inter) relations of the above fields of future research.

First some remarks on the trinity of general field activities. Historically, without doubt the policy has been the oldest, even with its special provinces. Concerning planning, it is only a superstition that it originated in socialist states. Planning is a general (and social) activity – cf. above part 3 – and some kinds of planning already existed in capitalist countries; in some sense state budgets are plans too and several other nation-wide or even international programmes could be mentioned. But it is true indeed that planning in centrally planned economies, resulting in obligatory plan commands, has been a feature of socialist countries for a rather long period. Later, more and more socialist countries substituted this kind of planning for a modified type, with more indicative than directive plans. In socialist planned economies future research arrived lastly in the general field of future building. In our country even ten or fifteen years ago speaking about futurology was a heresy; now planning is unthinkable without certain prognoses, forecasts, future pictures.

And here the question emerges: what is the time relation and especially what is the adequate order (of succession) of the activities mentioned. In our opinion they are partly simultaneous, partly following each other. It is possible to elaborate a rough scheme of possible orders of succession, comprising them as order types, as follows:

Types of succession order

Fields	A	All		fields			B Without 2		C Without 3
Policy=1	1	1	2	2	3	3	1	3	1
Future research=2	2	3	1	3	1	2	3	1	-
Planning=3	3	2	3	1	2	1	-	-	-

NB. In an iterative future building process the type of succession order may change.

It should be emphasized that in the case of future building close connections exist (have to exist) between the fields enumerated above. The activities may stand in cause and effect, action-reaction, feedback-response relations, while nearly all fields of activity repetitions, modifications, changes, etc. may occur, giving place for iterations. But the actors, especially planners, have to arrive at a final stage; planning must not be a permanent process of modifications. The dilemma of some stability vs. being up to date may bring many headaches to central planners, mainly in the case of overdetailed, exhaustive and rigid obligatory plans, leaving no proper place for the real economic and social actors.

6. Socio-economic development and planning.

Among the general fields of future building long run social and economic development strategy belongs to the realm of policy. The strategy in question can be defined and understood as the complex system of ends, means and ways concerning social-economic development. From the above treatment it follows that the strategy has to be an important part of the country's policy. In the framework of future building its realization needs several conditions and preconditions. Among them – from our point of view – the activity of planning deserves special attention. Planning, resulting in various plans, has to play an important role regarding realization of the objectives of the strategy.

According to other views, strategy could be intepreted as policy and planning together. Even in this case it is first of all policy!

The whole system could be sketched as follows:

		Perspective	
	Development strategy	l.t.planning m.t.planning	- l.t.plans Realizing - m.t.plans actions
General policy	Development tactics	s.t.planning operative planning	- s.t.plans Realizing - op.plans actions

Abbreviations: l.t.= long term; m.t.= medium term;
s.t.= short term; op.= operative

It is useful to point out that in the problem sphere of social and economic development not only the horizontal, but also the vertical relations and connections are of great interest.

To the above may be added some words of caution. As regards social, economic – and technical – development, planning and plans are extremely important. But in and from the process of development neither heuristic ideas nor spontaneous initiatives should be excluded. They must not be against plans but might complete them. Activities, as we may remember, have more possible bases...

7. Concluding remarks

The role of planners on the stage of the economic and social development theatre deserves high esteem – when they play their role with success. But in any case their responsibility is very great. They are responsible in the first place for lacking or bad plans, with no or harmful impact on the development process – even if the decisions about concrete actions are those of the government or parliament. On the other hand, real and steady development is due – partly or eventually mainly – to planning and planners without doubt.

Janusz Stacewicz

Central planning
at the crossroads

1. Methodological dilemmas

At the present moment, central planning is spoken of and written about differently. For some it still is the 'novelty of the epoch', creating new possibilities of organizing an economizing society and, for others, it is a hardly specific category 'suspended somewhere between Being and Nonbeing'. Between these extreme approaches there is a whole gamut of possible ways of considering this; of which apparently closest to reality is the perception of the present status of central planning as a *sui generis* transitional state between traditional states and those that should result from contemporary expectations.

Fundamentally, the sources of such a situation are methodological problems related to a new form of central planning. Thus, although there is almost general agreement as to what it should not be, at the same time there are no accepted views of its required range, character, procedure and the institutional solutions which would implement it.

As a result, old solutions and habits of thinking. whose role in the final shape of planner determinations still appear to be dominant, are superimposed upon new ones which are not ultimately concretized. Therefore, the current nature of central planning is still determined by traditional, formal and informal patterns of planner thinking and action, conceived as historically shaped ways of formulating and solving planner problems, resulting from a specific manner of understanding the economic process on the national scale.

These patterns derive from the traditional concept of central planning related to the allocation system. As the years passed, this system underwent gradual evolution. At the same time there were attempts to 'rationalize' it by using so called mathematical economic methods. Great hopes were placed on the concept of 'optimal planning', which led to the treatment of the problem of macroeconomic choice as a task of mathematical programming. It was believed for many years that the solution of the thus formulated problem of central planning was just a matter of better computer technology. However, it turned out that there were fundamental theoretical and methodological difficulties related, for example, to the interpretation and the use of so called dual prices, and above all to the formulation of the macroeconomic criterion of choice. Because of these difficulties, despite many years of experiments, this approach to improved central planning never went beyond experimental applications, apart from its usefulness in solving specific analytical problems. [1]

Disappointments over the idea of 'optimal planning' and the difficulties arising over the functioning of the traditional economic system brought a gradual evolution of the concept of central planning. It moved towards 'socialization' of the choice of development aims, changes in the nature of the plan and 'economization' of planner calculations and instrumentation. The character of central planning evolved towards so-called 'planning for oneself', i.e., planning adapted to the real decisionmaking competence of a given level, which in the case of central planning would mean strategic planning. Although the sense of strategic planning has not yet been defined unambiguously, it seems that today it should be understood as the formulation of the concept of development of the country and the design of its implementation.

However, planning practice deviates greatly from this ideal, since it is dominated by patterns of thinking connected with medium and short-term planning. [2] These patterns are diversified in character. One can speak of institutional patterns which determine the organizational shape of central planning. There are methodological patterns which define its procedures. There are, finally, cognitive patterns related to the 'image of the world' of the central planner.

The institutional and methodological patterns have already been the objects of numerous discussions and elaborations. Let us then have a look in greater detail at cognitive patterns, since there is a great deal to indicate that it is precisely here that one should seek the basic sources of difficulties. Let us then formulate the hypothesis that the basic cause of the current difficulties in central planning is an inadequate 'image of the world', i.e., the economy on the national scale, preventing the proposal of appropriate solutions.

2. Cognitive sources of difficulties

Central planning is a specific form of interference with reality. Such interference is always based on certain images of the nature of the shaped reality, irrespective of whether they are fully realized by the actors. These images are formed through a cognitive process, a specific case of which is scientific cognition. The result of scientific cognition is a theory, i.e. a consistent set of judgments creating the framework of description and the basis for understanding reality, and prediction of the results of development trends occurring in it.

A theory is usually contained within a specific paradigm, i.e. a certain pattern for conducting science, universally accepted by the scientific community; a pattern from which there follows the choice of research problems, the applied methods, and hence the results obtained. [3]

The observed paradigm defines then the 'view of the world' achievable over a given period via scientific cognition in the sense defined above. In the last centuries, and in many disciplines until today, such a paradigm, or the observed pattern of conducting science, was that of mechanistic-reductionist type.

The paradigm was derived from classic Newtonian physics and linked with the cognitive successes to which it led. These successes entailed that this approach to reality and the related methodology became synonymous with scientific cognition, which should be worked towards in social sciences as well.

However, this approach involved certain assumptions, which should be accepted, concerning the nature of the studied reality, in particular the measurability of phenomena, the continuity of the processes taking place and stationariness, i.e. the time-constant nature of the structure and parameters of the constructed models. In economics the acceptance of such assumptions made it possible to construct many models falling within the so-called theory of general equilibrium. The way of thinking that derived from this theory, involving in particular the treatment of the dynamic equilibrium of the economic system as a sequence of balanced states, dominated all the significant aspects of planner thought. What is meant here in particular was the way of perceiving macroeconomic reality, the language of macroeconomics, the way of formulating the problems of macroeconomic choice and also the planner procedures serving to implement this choice. [4]

It should be pointed out in this connection that the assumptions underlying macro-economic patterns of thinking are justified only for objects able to function in an equilibrium state but which are not developing. For development is change, whereas the mechanistic way of description requires the assumption of the constant nature of the structure and parameters of the models in time. In other words, the mechanistic approach is not able to describe reality in which development processes are under way, and it is exactly this feature that is specific to socio-economic reality, especially today.

In connection with the above, the dilemma arises whether one should use a traditional 'scientific' approach, but which does not coincide with reality, or whether one should look for another, risking the objection of 'nonscientificity' from the point of view of the old paradigm. However, this dilemma was, fortunately, solved in the philosophy of science, in connection with the crisis of the so called scientism at the turn of the 19th and 20th centuries. [5] This crisis brought about the formation of a new pattern of conducting science, i.e. the holistic-evolutionist paradigm which gradually replaced the formerly dominant mechanistic pattern.

The new paradigm can be considered from the ontological, epistemological and ethical point of view, i.e. from the point of view of the image of the world to which it leads, the postulated patterns of cognition and their consequences for the human criteria of value. [6]

From the ontological point of view it meant departure from the image of the world as a gigantic mechanism towards the image of the world as a process of cosmic evolution. It involved the conviction that real existence was due to the process as a whole, and all the rest is only a temporarily isolated, relative aspect of reality.

From the epistemological point of view, the new paradigm led to the methodological postulate of the 'systems approach'. Since its consequence was the perception of the world as an organized complexity, the ontological and epistemological aspects of the new paradigm were mutually complementary.

The new image of the world had also essential ethical consequences, since it led to the rehabilitation of altruistic attitudes, signifying that they were given at least an equal rank as traditionally emphasized selfish or utilitarian attitudes.

The new pattern of conducting science and the resultant image of the world had essential consequences from the point of view of perceiving the way of working in economics. It led towards economics which could be called holistic and humanistic. Such economics would have essential practical significance, in connection with a change in the way of seeing the rationality of economy. This would also mean the necessity to take a new look at central planning, which would be one of the ways of implementing this rationality.

3. Towards holistic and humanistic economics

From the point of view of economic theory, the consequences of the new paradigm were on its method, the way of understanding its object, and range and the way in which economics treats man.

The methodological consequences can be reduced to the postulated use of the holistic, systemic approach. [7] Although this postulate has long been formulated in economics, in practical research its application did not as a rule go beyond verbal declarations, or just attempts at 'smuggling in' the old mechanistic methodology as a new term.

The postulate of the systemic approach should have specific consequences from the point of view of understanding the object and range of economics. In the light of remarks about process philosophy it should denote that at present this object is the economic process on the scale of the whole country, insofar as it cannot be considered more broadly in global terms. This process should be considered in complementary synchronic and diachronic approaches leading to the distinguishing of economic growth, and the pointing out of their interdependencies.

The new paradigm should also lead to a change in the way of treating man by economics. This would mean giving up the concept of 'economic man' for 'multi-dimensional', complete man. Accordingly, economic activity would be only a specific case of human actions based on criteria of value resulting from the accepted view of the world and the related way of perceiving the sense of existence.

Thus, the holistic-humanistic economics would significantly deviate from traditional, specialized approaches to the problem of economy, such as the microeconomics of an enterprise, techno-economic production economics, or the macroeconomics of the production and distribution of the social product.

Traditional thinking on the economics of the enterprise was connected with orientation towards the financial result. The purposefulness of investment is determined by the relation between the rate of profit and the interest rate – since if the expected rate of profit is higher than the interest rate, it is profitable to take the risk of investment, renouncing in this way the gains which would have derived from keeping the assets in the bank.

Thinking in terms of techno-economic production economics means addressing the efficiency of the production process, measured by the productivity of the resources invested or the rate of investments required by the production. The purposefulness of investments is determined here by the expected technical improvement in the economy with respect to earlier applications.

Finally, thinking in macroeconomic terms of the production and distribution of the social product means orientation towards balanced growth, measured by the rate of increase of the social product in conditions close to general equilibrium of the system. Thus, in this case, the purposefulness of investments is determined by the possibility of gaining a higher rate of economic growth, on the assumption that this does not cause an essential deterioration of the economic equilibrium.

All the above-mentioned approaches are insufficient from the point of view of the holistic-evolutionist approach. This does not mean that they are useless, but that they are only specific cases of economic thinking, useful in solving narrow, specialist, specifically defined problems. What arises in this connection is the problem of understanding the rationality of the economy in contemporary conditions. For the handbook 'principle of economic rationality' or the related concept of 'hierarchy of goals' are no longer sufficient. Rationality turns out to be a relative category, depending on the approach to the problem of economy. [8]

In the light of these considerations one can distinguish various kinds of rationality: microeconomic rationality (of the enterprise manager), where the rate of profit is the criterion of rationality; techno-economic rationality (on the engineering level), where the criterion of rationality is the productivity of resources; and macroeconomic rationality (of the economic politician), where the criterion of rationality is the rate of balanced growth.

These patterns of rational thinking and acting in economy evolve towards social rationality where the quality of life is the criterion of rationality. Social rationality, as an expression of a new approach to economy, should become, with the passage of time, the superior rationality. This would have essential significance for economic theory and practice in contemporary conditions, since the quality of life is an integrating criterion in contrast to specialized criteria of enterprise managers, engineers and economic politicians which disintegrate.

4. The Concept of the Development of the Country as the Basis for Rational Economy

These different criteria of rationality can lead to divergent evaluations of desired allocation directions, and thus to a conflict of interest among the acting subjects. This conflict cannot be resolved in a simple, unambiguous way within available institutional solutions. [9] Moreover, they can be camouflaged, meaning that the true, deciding actions are not public. As a result, allocation decisions may result from the current system of forces the observation of which does not have to mean at all that they are proper from the general public point of view.

Accordingly, it is necessary to find a way of publicly elaborating a social compromise in terms of desired allocation directions. In contemporary conditions this can be the process of formulating the concept of the development of the country.

The potential differences in evaluation of the desired allocation directions resulting from the application of different criteria of rationality entail elaborating a 'hierarchical order of preferences' on the set of rationality criteria. The working out of such an order would mean the unambiguous determination of the relations between technical, microeconomic, macroeconomic and social criteria of rationality. In present conditions such an order of preferences should result from a socially accepted vision of the future, expressed precisely through the concept of the development of the country.

The logic of formulation of such a concept imposes unique relations among the above criteria of rationality. They should occur in the process in the following order:

- social criteria (identification and evaluation of development problems),
- techno-economic criteria (identification of the necessary undertakings and development tasks),
- macro-economic criteria (choice of permissible tasks and determination of their metaregulatory consequences).

The formulation of the concept of development thus understood would then entail the formation of an unambiguous reference basis to microeconomic decisions through the mapping of the hierarchical order of preferences on the set of criteria of social, techno-economic and macroeconomic rationality – i.e. the rational answer of society to the challenges of development which it faces.

The concept of the development of the country would emerge from a set of diversified diagnostic, prognostic and evaluating premises. At the same time it would involve multiple implementation conditioning of the techno-economic, macroeconomic and instrumental-systemic nature. It should be pointed out that both the premises and the circumstances of implementation of the concept of development are 'spatial in dimension'. This applies to most development problems and tasks and also to the potential instrumentation of the development programmes. This fact has essential methodological consequences. In the case of the identification and social evaluation and choice of development problems, it means the necessity for reflecting regional diversification in diagnostic-prognostic studies and in procedures of social evaluation – and thus in development scenarios. In turn, in the formulation of development tasks it is necessary to take into account their potential localization and spatial effects, and thus the spatial diversification of development programmes. Finally, in elaborating the instrumentation of development programmes, it is also necessary to differentiate instruments regionally, encouraging or discouraging the undertaking of given forms of techno-economic activities in a given area.

5. Central Planning as a Tool for Designing the Way of Implementing the Development Concept

In the process of formulation and implementation of the concept of a country's development, decisions of diversified nature are undertaken. They are 'cognitive' decisions, related to the identification of the current situation and the prediction of the course of development processes; socio-political decisions related to the evaluation and choice of problems to be undertaken; techno-economic decisions connected with the identification of development tasks; macroeconomic decisions related to the choice of permissible tasks; instrumental decisions connected with the implementation of tasks; and systemic decisions connected with a possible remodelling of the economic system.

From the 'workshop' point of view these decisions can be divided into three sets, namely:

- a set of pre-planning decisions (cognitive and socio-political);
- a set of planning decisions in the proper sense of the term (techno-economic and macro-economic);
- a set of post-planning decisions (instrumental decisions in the sense of implementation tools).

This means that in present conditions central planning should be used as a tool for designing implementation of the concept of national development. Such an approach to the role of central planning makes it possible to define precisely the functions of the basic kinds of central plans.

Therefore, the prospective plan should identify the basic development problems on the national scale, pointing out the resulting tasks and defining their expected general economic effects.

The medium-term plan should include the concept of reallocation of resources between continued tasks and new ones, showing its metaregulatory consequences.

Finally, the short-term plan should include the current instrumentation of shaping streams of goods and money, resulting from the determinations featured in earlier planner elaborations.

Such an approach signifies concentration of attention on the development problems and tasks in perspective planning, in reallocation and increasing of resources in medium-term planning, and in shaping the streams of goods and money in short-term planning. This makes it possible to define clearly the relation between central planning and the economy process on the national scale.

As mentioned, this problem can be considered from the point of view of its structural, functional and developmental aspects. Moreover, these aspects are interdependent. In the previous, traditional approach, each of these aspects was connected with a certain kind of state interference – respectively, restructuration, metaregulation and shaping of development process. On the other hand, these methodological proposals entail treatment of central planning as a tool for integrated shaping of the development on a national scale. This means that distinct forms of interference, traditionally treated as separate, should form a consistent sequence of actions in which the concept of shaping development processes would be the starting point, metaregulation and possible systemic changes the tools for shaping flows of goods and money, but structural changes the cumulative effect of these actions rather than the object of a separate 'restructuration' policy.

References

[1] Czerwinski, Z. et al., *Modelowanie i planowanie wzrostu gospodarki narodowej* (Modelling and Planning of Growth of National Economy), PWN, Warszawa, 1982, p. 73.

[2] Karpinski, A., *40 lat planowania w Polsce* (40 Years of Planning in Poland), PWN, Warszawa, 1966.

[3] Kuhn, T. S., *Struktura rewolucji naukowych* (The Structure of Scientific Revolution), PWN, Warszawa, 1966.

[4] Stacewicz, J., *Dylematy kierowania rozwijajaca sie gospodarka* (Managing Dilemmas of Developing Economy), Monografie i Opracowania SGPIS no. 168, Warszawa, 1985, p. 133.

[5] Amsterdamski, S., *Pomiedzy historia a metoda* (Between History and Method), PIW, Warszawa, 1983, p. 110.

[6] Capra, F., *Punkt zwrotny* (The Turning Point), PIW, Warszawa, 1987.

[7] Dopfer, K. (ed.), *Ekonomia w przyszlosci* (Economics in the Future), PWN, Warszawa 1982, p. 19.

[8] Stacewicz, J., *Racjonalnosc gospodarowania a wspolczesne wyzwania rozwojowe* (The Rationality of Allocation and Contemporary Development Challenges), PWN, Warszawa, 1988, p.13.

[9] Arrow, K. J., *Granice organizacji* (The Limits of Organization), PWN, Warszawa, 1985, p.7.

János Kovács

Regulative planning

1. Planned economy or market economy

I must begin with raising the question as to how these two notions explain the essence of the actual world.

Can the world economy of our days be characterised by the absolute domination of the market or by the sole existence of planning? The answer is evidently negative. However, we can establish that in the western countries the market plays a more dominant role in regulating the economic development, while in East Europe planning has tried to influence development forcefully. But all these phenomena are only rough simplifications, because market and planning have coexisted for a long time both in capitalist and socialist countries.

The second question which we have to make clear when we speak about market is how do we define it? Does the market mean a 'free' self-regulating market, or a market regulated by means of central economic policy? Is this market steered only by an interior mechanism, or is it influenced by the whole (social, natural and political) environment? Similarly, does planning mean an overall regulation of the different elements of an economy and of a whole society? Or does it leave space for the market even if it may be influenced by some elements of a market mechanism?

2. Failure of the self-regulating market

The self-regulating market died at the beginning of the century. The infallible sign of its mortal illness was the First World War and the coup de grace was the economic crisis of 1929-1933. The fundamental cause of the disease was that the self-regulating market contained too many utopian elements. An essential condition of its existence was the gold base, the preservation of which was subject to further political and economic conditions. Among these conditions the termination of the balance of power first appeared during the Second World War.

All these are, however, only symptoms. The fundamental problem was the fact that the self-regulating market crushed and destroyed the physical and social environment of human beings. The function of the self-regulating market did not tolerate intervention in any of the elements of competition regulated by demand and supply, neither in the defence of society nor of the human environment.

At the same time unrestrained market laws began to separate human beings from the earth, combined with the ever-stronger gradual erosion of the ecological environment. Society had to defend itself against this process. After that, when the crisis made it perfectly clear that efforts to restore the free market following the Second World War were unable to protect workers against unemployment and mass poverty, nor could they protect capital against devaluation, and hence protect society against instability, economists started to seek possibilities of defense.

The search for a way out took practically two main directions. One of them was the New Deal policy based on Keynes' doctrines, the other was the planned socialist economy based on Marxian principles. (There also existed an attempt of a third type: the fascist-corporative system, but this is of no importance here.)

3. The Keynesian economy

Attempts of a New Deal type – not limited in the least to the USA, since their French and English equivalents existed as well – proved capable of progress. In other forms the New Deal continued after the Second World War and finally involved most of the developed capitalist countries in 'welfare economy' policies. The main point of these policies: efforts to ensure the security of existence to the highest degree, first of all through an asymptotic approach to full employment and thus the maintenance of socio-political stability. Its means was the regulation of the market by decisive fiscal methods, using of course the possibilities offered by monetary means as well, and not shrinking in the last resort from direct state intervention.

It is very interesting to observe that after the Second World War there appeared a sort of paternalism, in the form of the welfare state or welfare economy. This form shows clearly that the state assumed responsibility for compensating for the differentiation generated by market mechanisms by means of the public budget which influenced the function of tertiary sector. The impact of this activity mainly concerned those elements of this sector which were interested in manpower reproduction, consequently affecting the mode and standard of life.

A great many people are of the opinion that the end of this policy was marked by the oil crisis of 1973 and the recession that followed it. In fact since the second half of the seventies the new liberal economic policy resting essentially on a neoclassical theoretical background moved ahead and many people speak about the victory of the neoclassical school.

The neoclassical school accepts monetary regulation in the first place – the wing representing the most radical version of this theory is called the monetary school – but can by no means reach the degree of liberalism of a liberal state resting on the classical school of the 19th century. Naturally this way of regulation will work too. It seeks to do so essentially by monetary means, but it does not omit fiscal regulation from its resources and should the occasion arise, if the interests of the nation require it, the practice of direct state intervention will be applied without hesitation.

4. Evolution of the planned economy

The socialist planned economy constitutes the other main tendency in surmounting the risks arising from the spontaneity of the self-regulating market. In its first outward shape in the Soviet Union from the nineteen-twenties it appeared as an economy following direct plan instructions. Its main point is the fulfilment of the plan by any means, the result of planning work. The fulfilment of the plan is to be achieved by putting centrally conceived instructions into effect.

Paternalism also appears in this type of economy. It seems that here paternalism takes the form of an enterprise's paternalism, while in fact it is a state paternalism as well. But these are enterprises which assume the obligation to maintain full employment even at the price of low efficiency. They are also enterprises which undertake the responsibility to provide the commodities needed by the population. But they accept all these obligations because they are forced to by the central power.

In its first period this system proved to be very effective, since the plan included only a few priorities: establishment of the industry of an industrially backward agricultural economy under a growing autarky isolated from the outside world. That meant that disregarding a few priorities was of minor importance; it was even in the worst case a negligible, disturbing factor. These conditions were, however, historically supportable only for a very short time, just up to the end of the Second World War or at best up to the end of the restoration period. By the end of this comparatively short period it soon turned out that risks are involved in the directive planned economy and the self-regulating market as well.

The most important of these dangers were the following:

a) the inclination to totalitarianism stemming from an effort to regulate everything (this supposition is utopian in itself);
b) release of the economy from the control of effectiveness;
c) getting entangled in momentary acute problems and losing sight of the perspective;
d) extension of bureaucracy.

5. Non traditional regulators

Rgulation has some elements which cannot be traditionally considered as regulators. Nevertheless we come to think of them in practice as a decisive function in the development of economy and of the whole society as well. In the first place I mean here some branches of activity which are comprised in the terminology of socialist economy under the concept 'infrastructure'; the literature in the West includes it often in the expression social overhead capital (SOC). These two concepts mostly overlap each other, however the determination of both expressions is rather vague and varies in the use of several authors. In the Hungarian literature the concept of infrastructure includes generally the following:

- education
- public health

- telecommunications
- traffic and transport
- management of water supplies
- protection of the environment
- research and development.

On the other hand – according to Hirschmann – the concept SOC comprises the following:

- jurisdiction
- policing
- education
- public health
- transport
- traffic
- telecommunications
- energy
- management of water supplies
- irrigation and pipe laying.

It is clear the two kinds of concepts rather overlap each other and also have another common feature:

In the socialist countries there is nearly perfect understanding that the establishment of the infra-structure is a direct duty of the state. The adherents of the market economy also mean generally that the state can support best the function of the market economy by bringing into existence a satisfactory infrastructure and furthermore by keeping as far as possible out of economic activity.

On the other side – although consent is far from really uniform – many experts are of the opinion that the activities relating to the SOC are to be put under the orbit of social control and at the same time they want to accord a greater function to the state in the establishment and operation of the infrastructure. This becomes quite clear with Hirschmann, quoted above, listing the criteria required on the basis of which activities are to be included under the concept SOC.

These are activities which

a) cannot be imported;
b) are necessarily large scale enterprises, being technically more or less indivisible; therefore they cannot work in small sizes;
c) encourage economic activity;
d) are under common proprietorship or under public control.

The lawfulness of these criteria will be mentioned later, at least relating to the social control.

I would point out two items on this list of activities, the role of which – in my opinion – is definitive in socio-economic development, namely education and research-development.

6. Education as a regulator

It is quite obvious for experts working in economic policy that the education system has a decisive function in the forming of the labour structure, in the regulation of the market of labour power and in the formation of structural adaptability of the whole economy. The regulating function of this system is relatively rarely negotiated in the formation of the social structure, in the development of the society. But it is obvious for the expert that education is decisive in the approach to the theory of equality, in the realisation of the theory of equal chances. A democratic education system of high level is able to ensure that the young generations start their active life with roughly equal chances.

This requirement is closely related to the role played by the education system in the realization of the right to work. In international experience it is well known that in the case of unemployment or of increasing difficulties of finding employment the qualified labour-force has much more chance to get a convenient job or any job at all than unskilled labour. It is also well-known that a person with convertible knowledge has much better chances than another whose experience is too unidirectional, specialized. Consequently the school system is crucially important in the approach to full employment and also in the realization of full and effective employment, respectively.

Perhaps no particular explanation is required for the function of the education system in the formation of the social stratification. Sociologists well know the growing role of educational level and learnedness among the criteria of strata building.

Finally, international comparisons are proving the connection between education and demographic processes.

7. The regulator function of the research and development

Another important regulator of the market in industrial societies is research and development, which has grown into an independent economic branch. Without satisfactory research work no economic or social development exists at all. The problem cannot be solved by simply taking over the research and development work and results of other countries, as the adoption of foreign developments also requires the existence of home research and development bases with qualified experts.

In the third place the strengthening of some inland research and development directions and the weakening of others obviously has a great direct influence on the structure of production. That economy will strengthen which has an adequate background of development, and that economy will regress which is unable to apply new technology, lacking satisfactory research and development background.

Research and development affects, however, not only the economy but also the society. These influences do not appear in the indirect effects coming into being through the transformation of the economic structure in societies, although these are more visible and more spectacular. Research and development influences the social structure partly through the education system by increasing the level of knowledge, partly through public health by increasing the average age, and – last but not least – through reorganizing and extending the connections within and between societies. As a result of technical development not only has distance but also time shrunk to an unbelievable degree.

Direct state support to research and development may appear in the form of dotation, but more often we meet its indirect form in the order of the state. Support – whether direct or indirect – cannot be disregarded even in the industrially most developed countries on account of a very simple cause: The financial demands of research and development are constantly growing, and at the same time risk in this activity is very great. (According to statistics of research and development for the seventies, only about 50 per cent of the research work commenced in research institutes has been successful, but it is not easy to define the result on account of the character of these activities.) For this reason the state undertakes the risk or a part of it and the result achieved will be sold or transferred to the branch applying the new technology.

8. Regulating role of the structure of property

In any more or less developed country the state sector is present on one side and the private sector on the other, and in addition a multicoloured population of collective property is arranged between the two sectors. We are inclined to think that the private sector has not or cannot have a role in the socialist world. Others mean that in the so-called market economies the governmental sector has actually no room, as it is contrary to the system. The facts, however, show different. Everywhere in the socialist countries a certain kind of private activity is present. Sometimes, especially earlier, the presence was hidden but now it occurs more and more often and openly. Due to different historical reasons the governmental sector is present everywhere, even in the capitalist countries. What is the reason for this?

In all probability the private sector is not always ready to incur a great risk in the long run, and the state is forced to take this risk upon itself in some form or other. On the other hand the state companies – usually big enterprises – generally show less adaptability. Private enterprise is much quicker its response to the sudden changes of the market, especially if these changes are not too enormous. At the same time the large state enterprise can be very effective, partly in the utilization of the advantage of returns to scale, partly in assertion of the targets of the central economic policy. Hence the capitalist economy is able to assert effectively its common national interests by means of the state sector through the state itself. On the other hand, the socialist economy may render – by means of the private sector – the whole economic sphere more flexible and it may incite competition.

The whole complex can be compared to a car the steering properties of which are jointly determined by the proportion of the three spheres. If the state sector is too ponderous, the economy gets 'oversteered'; conversely if the private sector overtakes the government sector, 'understeering' is characteristic of the whole vehicle. One vehicle easily negotiates the path, the other suddenly skids, even on the best path. Presumably the ideal distribution is reached by the adequate weight of the medium sector, i.e. of collective property, similarly to the excellent stability on the road of cars with their engine in the centre.

9. Structure according to size

According to our knowledge the problem of the above three sectors of property is very often mixed with another structural problem. This is a question of the structure according to size of the set of economic units. It is not the same as the distribution of the economy according to the size of work: large scale, small and medium scale work organizations placed between them e.g. cooperatives. In this half of the world this mixture also appears in a way that large scale work means *per definitionem* a state enterprise, small work means private sector, while co-operative activity appears mostly in the sphere of medium work organizations.

It is obvious enough that the subject mentioned in respect of the state and private sector can be applied more or less also to the structure according to size. The economy where the large scale work is in preponderance is liable to be 'understeered', while an economy in which small work is predominant can become 'oversteered'.

Practice obviously makes the mutual one-to-one mapping of the two kinds of structures unambiguously impossible. It goes without saying that in the capitalist world the state sector exists mostly in the form of large enterprise but the private sector is no less important. It is all the more true that in the existing socialist economies private sector means expressly small work. The situation is, however, less unambiguous in respect of tendencies.

10. Social control

Regulation of the market has its risks, as we have seen. The risk, however, is not only of financial character. Since Chernobil nobody disputes the risks inherent in atomic energy. (If the example of Hiroshima was not enough to take cognizance.) It seems, however, that atomic energy is necessary in any case to satisfy the hunger for energy of human kind. Nobody disputes the fact that an activity involving such huge risk is to be submitted to social control, at most the question can be taken into consideration whether the government control is the only form of control. The best proof of the insufficiency of national control is that in the domain of nuclear power international control, more or less effective, has come into existence and does not hesitate to cross the borders of countries, and those of social systems as well.

The other well known research and development tendency with a huge future before it is biotechnical, biological research. The results of this activity will lead within reasonable time not only to the end of previously incurable diseases, but also to the solution to feending mankind and to the appearance of activities not really known but affecting the existence of humanity. But this is not without any danger. Its abuse, human irresponsibility, can turn on its wrong side as in the case of atomic energy and consequently it can carry the danger of the destruction of humanity itself. Sooner or later it will become unavoidable to place it under social control, first in national, later in an international framework just as the case of nuclear research.

But we can continue the list. In the eyes of ordinary people the so called electronic revolution takes place. The result of this is the appearance of new mass media systems in the workplace, in automation, robotization, in the growing use of computers. World-wide one experiences implications, due partly to growing productivity partly to leisure extension, and at the same time to the utilization of leisure.

Beside the advantageous effect the disadvantageous ones are also to be reckoned with in this case. That means not only the danger of unemployment, pointed out many times by closing the workplaces of labourers who cannot easily find new jobs suited to their knowledge and ability. The thoughtless use of electronics goes together with other social dangers; it opens the risk of interference in human rights, of control of individual life, and through it electronic delinquency appears in certain countries. Social control is indispensable here, too, although it seems that the shaping of its satisfactory form is not quite clear as yet.

I may continue the line with space exploration, space pollution and generally the pollution of the environment, with the remark that not only the natural environment but also the social environment can be polluted. Their prevention requires social control again.

It is generally known that social control does not mean government control under any circumstances: its scale is multicoloured. It runs from the small community to the international control.

May I point out, however, that I am not quite sure of the most effective, the most progressive form of the social control embodied in government control. At most, this form may be the most obvious: many momentary kinds of different collective controls can be conceived, and probably their development will influence, eventually decisively influence, the formation of the whole structure of societies, including the political structure.

11. The path can also be planned

Let us stay with the analogy of the car, the movement of a vehicle is influenced by several facts: the steering mechanism, weight distribution and many other things; but of no less importance are the properties of the path to proceed on. The theory of the path of growth is substantially elaborated. It seems that this practice of pointing out the path of growth operates more or less successfully in a number of countries all over the world. This path is outlined by economic policy. I mean we can speak about planning in cases where the shaping of the economic policy takes place in a professional institutional system. If there is an institutional system possessing satisfactory scientific and technical training in the elaboration of analyses and prognoses needed for the forming of the economic policy, in this case we can speak about institutionalized planning, whether it is called by this name or not. The task of this planning work is to outline social and economic goals in a consistent system that the policy is endeavouring to achieve, irrespective of the denomination of this system of goals by the words 'planning' or 'economic policy'.

The essence of planning is not subject to the denomination and does not depend on the existence of an organization in the institutional system of planning called Planning Office or Planning Ministry. It is possible that a country possesses a Planning Office without planning on merits (the actual situation in some socialist countries); and possibly in another country we find a Planning Bureau but important decisions relating to the economic policy are made in other spheres of politics (e.g. in Japan). The third version is a country without a Ministry of Planning but managing a serious planning on merits (e.g. in Great Britain). Let there be no mistake about it, politics decide the acceptance of plans of the economic policy all over the world. It is not the same, however, whether this plan has been picked out from a variety of plans developed in the course of carefully prepared planning work – securing a certain consistence – or the decision occurred peradventure, on basis of arbitrary decisions. I mean, both are equally true of socialist and capitalist economies.

12. Convergence?

Thus there is no difference between socialist and capitalist planning? In respect of methodology the difference is theoretically not noteworthy. Theoretically the same models can be applied in both types of countries. In respect of content, naturally so many countries so many systems. Any modelling – mathematical or logical – necessarily means the enlargement, the accentuation of certain parts of reality implying the negligence of other parts. It follows from the above that the method of planning is different in a country where all the three social sectors are represented by roughly the same weight and in a country where one of the sectors has considerable overweight.

In the course of historical development so far, the overweight of the state sector is characteristic of the socialist countries, and the overwight of the private sector of the capitalist countries. Is there a convergence between these two systems ? I mean yes in a certain sense, but not in the traditional sense. The asymmetry mentioned above concerning the structures is typical of these systems and of the shaping of the role of the ruling sector of the SOC and of the infrastructure, at the same time and -less or more – the similar handling of these sectors in the economic policy or in the planning preparing this policy is characteristic too.

For me it follows that the world is proceeding – as a result of planning work – towards a market regulated by a developing policy of economy, the aim of which is the attempt to unify in itself the advantages of planning and of the self-regulating market as well, keeping a tight hand on the risks of both (with more or less success).

References

Kovács J., 'Regulatív tervezés' (Regulativ planning), *Gazdaság*, no. 3, pp. 127-37.

Kovács, J. and Tarján, T. G., 'Cycle and replacement', *Acta Oeconomica* no. 3-4, vol. 39, pp. 325-40.

Kovács J. and Malatinszky, I., 'Az oktatáspolitika és oktatástervezés autonómiája' (Autonomy of policy and planning of the education), *Közgazdasági Szemle*, vol. 36, pp.1490-97.

Kovács, J. and Malatinszky, I., 'Mitoszok a bérelmélet-ben' (Myths in wage theory), *Magyar Tudomány*, no. 10, 1988.

Kovács J. and Malatinszky, I., 'Bérelméletek és piacgazdaság' (Wage theories and the market economy), *Minôség és Megbízhatóság* no. 1, vol. 23, pp.3-9.

Kovács, J. and Virág, I., Chozjajjstvennaja struktura i strategicheskoje planirovanije (Economic structure and strategic planning), in *Zakonomernosti intensivnogo tipa vosproizvodstv*a, Nauka, Moszkva, 1988, pp. 128-38.

Tarján, T. G., *Economic cycles based of gestation lags: a formal analysis*. Semecon University of Munich pp.13.

Tényi, G., Socio-economic roots of the French planning, *in this volume*.

Tényi, G., *Struktúrapolitikai irányzatok Magyarországon* (Tendencies in structural policy in Hungary), mimeo, Budapest, 1986.

Halpern, L. and Molnár, G. 'Macro features of the Hungarian economy since 1970', *Economic Systems Research*, no. 1, vol. 1, 1989, pp. 111-20.

Péter Á. Bod

The troublesome micro-macro link in an economy with national planning: Hungary

1. Microeconomic functions of central planning

There is no basis for distinguishing between 'micro' and 'macro' under traditional central planning in which any production or distributional decision, i.e. a
micro decision in our familiar terms, forms part of an integral decision procedure
covering the whole economy. Institutionally speaking, organizational subunits
may have particular tasks and motivations of their own, but they cannot claim to
have independence within the nation-wide planning system.

Early concepts of planned economy appear to contain the assumption of organizational homogeneity: see, for example, Barone's all-embracing Ministry of
Production, or Lenin's reference to a mono-firm organizational model for future
socialist economy in which 'All citizens become employees and workers of a
single country-wide state syndicate' [2, 6]. Thus organizational problems would
be reduced, theoretically, to those of a 'micro' – micro' character within such a
system.

Later, the separation of individual enterprises and a higher economic authority
does appear in the literature, e.g. in the Lange-Lerner (L-L) model [5]. It deserves mentioning that the L-L model implicitly postulates full monetization of
the economy. This is an important reason why the quasi-market solution associated with Lange could not, in my view, become an applicable foundation for
real life reforms. Another implicit assumption concerns higher authority which is
supposed to function in a totally coordinated manner or, to state it strongly,
without dimension. Under this model, a Central Planning Board performs the
functions of the market [5] and also determines macroeconomic variables such
as rate of accumulation. Given the enormous socio-political power of Gosplan in
traditional (Stalinist) Soviet type economies, this assumption has only very
recently come to be questioned.

In fact, no real life economy has ever come close to resembling models of the
L-L type. Planned economies have historically evolved from a mega-
bureaucracy to a more structured institutional arrangement with two distinctive
levels: one of central (macroeconomic) management, and one of the enterprises

(trusts, combines, etc). Seen from the Stalinist 'ideal type', the present-day Hungarian National Planning Office (NPO) more resembles a Western-type indicative planning institution than a Gosplan. However, the NPO still carries certain micro-economic functions – a sign, and also a cause, of trouble for economic policy-making in Hungary.

If the relative proportions of the allocation of time by an institution properly indicate the significance of its respective duties, then *planning* (i.e. the text-book sense of activities such as forecasting, and formulating strategic plans concerning the future of the nation) consumes roughly 15 per cent; *coordination* between government agencies consumes about 50 per cent; and *microeconomic activities*, the topic of the present paper, use up the remaining 35 per cent.

2. An impossible task – and its justification

These microeconomic duties comprise a variety of different activities, such as:

- participation in the inter-governmental plan coordination process within the Council of Mutual Economic Assistance (CMEA);
- project selection and evaluation of large scale state investment programmes;
- planning and supervision of non-civilian production, and military hardware procurement;
- preparation of position papers about 'problems enterprises', and elaboration of recommendations for the government concerning 'lame ducks';
- evaluation of the plans of selected state-owned enterprises (SOEs).

The above-mentioned list includes tasks which are alien to the logic of the post-1968 Hungarian 'indirect' planned economy. Plan-coordination with centrally planned socialist countries involves decisions about *par excellence* microeconomic matters: quantities, prices, delivery dates and the like. In reality the NPO is inadequately staffed to take microeconomic decisions which, under the post-reform Hungarian 'mechanism', belong to the realm of autonomous enterprise decisionmaking. Not surprisingly, the NPO serves mainly as a postman between Hungarian producers and wholesale agents, on the one hand, and bureaucrats of central planning agencies of other CMEA countries, on the other. The 'postman' role is primarily a consequence of the dominant non-market nature of CMEA-cooperation, and would probably disappear if and when Comecon trade is marketized.

Another practical, microeconomic task of the NPO is planning, co-ordinating, and managing a non-civilian production of military equipment. This sector of activities remains outside the market and therefore some government agency must organize production and distribution. In our case this is the task of the NPO.

There exists another microeconomic activity which also constitutes a recurrent task for central planners, namely, the manipulation of the investment process. This remains a necessary regulating task for a macroeconomic policy-making institution in any modern economy. It is interesting to note that under reformed Hungarian macroeconomic management, the share of direct state investments has gradually declined over time (see Table 1).

Table 1 – Share of large state investment projects (planned)

	1970-1975	1976-1981	1981-1985	1986-1988
Percentage of socialist sector investment outlays	19,5	16,8	12,0	6,6

Consequently, the bulk of accumulation and investment activity remains outside the control of central planners. What is more, plan fulfilment data indicate that the share of enterprise investment generally turns out to be overfulfilled, while communal investments, controlled by regional authorities and local communities, tend to remain close to their original plan targets. The share of large projects of the state, however, tends to lag behind targets predetermined in national plans. This phenomenon should not be interpreted as a sign of modesty by the Hungarian state. True, the state does cut its projects (technically: slows them down or freezes them) in spite of its excessive appetite for social capital, but the state cannot behave otherwise during recurrent investment booms that endanger macro equilibria with astonishing periodicity. Under conditions of an underdeveloped capital market in conjunction with autonomous SOEs, local councils, and cooperatives, the state is forced to cut the central investment – thus 'crowding out' part of its own projects. In addition, a cut in state expenditures can be done expediently in contrast with, say, monetary measures which tend to function poorly and slowly in a half-monetized economy.

These are the various reasons for central planners' intervention in company-level issues in a reformed economy, such as Hungary. The upshot is that the agency responsible for macroeconomic equilibria (i.e. the NPO) lacks the very instruments that are available in a market economy for controlling business cycles in general, and the accumulation process, in particular. At first, central planners endeavour to influence the business plans of market agents by adjusting monetary regulators, indicative plan signals, moral persuasion or threats and promises; in short, through a mixture of monetary and non-monetary measures. Money does count, but only to a certain extent. The Hungarian economy is certainly not a fully monetized economy as presumed by Lange.

When these measures do not prove to be effective enough, planners resort to cutting public expenditures, protracting large projects, etc. (i.e. going into extremely sub-micro details).

What is important to note is that neither tactic works effectively. The problem is that central planners, when considering microeconomic issues, find themselves on shaky ground because of a certain informational asymmetry between them and enterprises. While the central planners' scope is primarily limited to macroeconomic issues, enterprise managers are much more at home in the world of technical and market details.

Now, this is where *coordination* comes into the picture. The state is certainly not a dimensionless institution. Planners have their own values, aspirations and powers, but other agencies do, too. The NPO does not, unlike in a traditional planned economy, enjoy an above-ministerial status; the most that can be said about its position is *primus inter pares* – the first among equals. Consequently, the NPO has to fight with other agencies, especially with spending (branch) ministries. They not only play an important role in project selection and spending public money but also have a decisive say in personnel management at SOEs. This means that, for example, the Ministry of Industry in coalition with large scale 'political' SOEs may have the upper hand in controlling resource allocation. This situation can be illustrated as follows. Table 2. contains data characterizing the *revealed* industrial policy. For the last decade or so, the *official* industrial policy has aimed at modernizing manufacturing, trade (including tourism) and infrastructure. In reality, a surprisingly large amount of public money has been channelled to basic industries which in Hungary are characteristically poor in natural endowment, but strong in terms of their political position. The bias in favour of basic industries is strongest in the decision-making category in which the state has nearly full discretion, that is in state investments. Though in this case the term 'state' obviously does not imply the NPO; rather the patterns of state spending clearly indicate the extreme powers of the coalition of 'socialist big business' and spending ministerial agencies.

3. Strategic relationship between firms and planners

In a mixed market economy, the relationship of large scale SOEs – especially those in monopoly or overwhelmingly dominant positions – with central planning and policy formulating agencies should not be of an operative nature. Rather, a strategic link may be justified on logical grounds [4], as compatible with principles of 'enterprise autonomy' and 'SOE as a commercial undertaking'. In practice, however, an 'arm's length' attitude to SOEs can, as Hungarian experiences indicate, degenerate into a bargaining process involving attempts of state agencies to intervene on an ad hoc basis, or attempts of SOEs to blackmail the authorities. Therefore the question of how long the length of the arm should be in the arm's length relationship is eminently justified. [7]

Maintaining such a strategic relationship has also proved to be an impossible task for central planners in Hungary. While in their microeconomic job as business cycle controllers, they are expected to substitute a market mechanism – a task they can not effectively accomplish – in their tasks as industrial policy shapers and controllers of corporate planning, central planners are to fulfil the functions of a capital market. What may legitimize a close firm-center interface from the enterprise point of view is a presumed informational advantage which might be gained through a dialogue with state agencies.

In reality, the macro-planning procedure in Hungary does not organically involve the enterprises, although governments ritually pledge strategic cooperation to firms. Joint strategy-making is sporadic at best, and with good reasons. The process of national level medium-term plan elaboration has time schedules and inner logic different from those of corporate planners. Until recently, strategic (medium–term) national planning has closely followed the five-year time horizon determined by CMEA plan coordination cycle. During the close to two-year long preparation of the medium–term national plans, central planners have

54

Table 2: Share of particular branches in investment resources and labour

	total investment		state inv. credit		investment subsidies		state investment		employment	
	1976	1985	1976	1985	1976	1985	1976	1985	1976	1985
/1/ Basic industries	15.6	25.3	6.9	10.9	14.9	49.8	29.2	65.9	6.7	6.5
/2/ Manufacturing	25.6	19.0	38.9	36.5	17.4	5.9	27.5	2.8	29.2	26.9
/3/ Food-economy	25.6	23.0	26.3	36.6	14.1	15.8	7.5	1.0	26.8	27.4
/4/ Construction	7.2	4.0	11.3	3.2	33.0	4.1	5.5	0.2	11.4	10.0
/5/ Communication	14.0	13.4	8.0	2.3	17.1	21.3	23.2	26.8	9.6	10.2
/6/ Trade	6.5	6.0	6.1	9.5	2.6	1.4	4.0	0.1	11.5	12.2
/7/ Services	5.5	9.3	2.5	1.0	0.9	1.7	3.1	3.2	4.8	6.8
Total	100.0	100.0	100.0	100.0	100.0	100.0	100.0	100.0	100.0	100.0

Legend: /1/: mining, eletricity, metallurgy; /2/: machinery, chemistry, light industry; /3/: agriculture, forestry, food-processing; /4/: construction and building materials; /5/: transport, post, telecommunication; /6/: home and foreign trade; /7/: all services incl. water economy.

Source: Bod, 1988

traditionally invited large scale SOEs to participate in plan formation with draft project proposals, but these have generally turned out to be totally useless. The problem remains that enterprise planners, first, do not possess basic macro-information on projected growth, inflation, and structural policy orientation. Second, monetary and other regulators are not known to firms at an early stage of the national planning process. Third, enterprise managers have no incentives to reveal their true aspirations concerning subsidies, soft loans, tax reliefs, etc. Therefore, the draft project proposals submitted to central planners tend to be closer to a shopping list rather than serious inputs of national planning. Corporate planning has characteristically started after the completion and publication of the government's five year plan, making it practically impossible for firms to influence the course of national planning.

In addition, the whole concept of joint strategic planning only makes sense in a predominantly state-owned economy. Cooperatives, privately owned firms, or those with foreign capital participation cannot be expected to share their business plans with state agencies. This is why the position paper of the present planning reform committee talks about abolishing the 'obligation of economic units such as enterprises (public or others), cooperatives, councils to conduct calculations and elaborate proposals necessary for laying the foundation to the National Economic Plan'. [1] This is a break with the present regulation promulgated in the Act on the National Economic Planning, No II/1985. Therefore, the on-going planning reform initiative acknowledges the multisectoral nature of the present Hungarian economy. The ad hoc task group, of which the present author is a member, recommends the final separation of firms, whether public or private or mixed, from any government institution, including central planning. Thus, the concept of 'economy-wide' planning is to cease to exist, and Hungary is to become an economy *with* national planning.

However, Hungary will not become immediately a monetized economy under the reign of the 'invisible hand' of commodity and factor markets. As characteristically in 'late industrialized' economies, the state must assume an pp role, as well as market-building, and even certain temporary and phased market-substituting functions. Therefore, it will probably be a long time before planning is reduced to an exercise in pure information gathering. Public facility planning and public investments programs will remain an integral task of national planning. Externalities, and the weaknesses of the capital market justify selective government intervention. However, it should not take the form of regularly second-guessing the decisions of SOEs at the NPO, nor maintaining an extensive reporting relationship between firms and national agencies. Firms will, no doubt, initiate two-way binding, commercial commitments in their search for opportunities associated with government induced development programmes. This assumes however, a model which is different from both those envisaged by Barone, Lange, or representatives of the 'cybernetic control' concept, and also the logic of Soviet type central planning and distribution.

4. General Conclusions

In the process of marketization, central planning must undergo a profound change. Bureaucratic, market-substituting coordination will gradually yield its functions to market coordination. The latter also requires planning, although one of a different type. Therefore, planners should not worry about their jobs, unless they mistakenly identify 'planning' with microeconomic market-substitution. On the other hand, it is also clear that in an economy with underdeveloped factor markets, certain micro-macro cooperation is not only permissible but also necessary, even if PLANNING in capital letters mixes badly with microeconomic activities of a market surrogate character.

References

[1] Act on the National Economic Planning, No II/1985 *Public Finance in Hungary*, Ministry of Finance, Budapest, 1986.

[2] Barone, E., 'The Ministry of Production in the Collectivist State', in F.A. Hayek (ed.), *Collectivist Economic Planning*, Routledge and Kegan Paul, London, 1935.

[3] Bod P.A., 'Van-e jó állami strukturapolitika' ('Is there any good state structural policy'), *Társadalmi Szemle*, no.11. 1988.

[4] Dietrich, M., 'Organisational requirements of a socialist economy: theoretical and practical suggestions', *Cambridge Journal of Economics*, no. 10, 1986.

[5] Lange, O. and Taylor F.M., *On the Economic Theory of Socialism*, McGraw-Hill, New York, 1976.

[6] Lenin, V.I., *State and Revolution*, Collected Works, vol. 25, Progress Publishers, Moscow, 1964.

[7] Liukas S.K.: 'Investment Planning and Arm's Length Control in a Nationalized Industry', *Management Science*, vol. 31. no 8. August 1985.

PART II
THE TRADITIONAL WAY
OF PLANNING

Pavel Belousov

Perestroika in socio-economic planning in the Soviet Union

Socio-economic planning – as the only method to regulate human activities and consciousness – can be characterized by a colorful manifold of quality, form and efficiency. It has however some general features as well. A plan is nothing more than:
- an appropriate program of coordinated processes, events and acts, the result of which is the solution of certain contradictions and the birth of new contradictions;
- balance of needs and resources;
- dialectical unity of interests, conscience, intentions and voluntarism; community of science, professionalism, dilettantism and art. Among the designers of plans can always be found the representatives of these groups.

1 Therefore the place, the role and the real significance of plans in the historic situation of different countries has always been ambiguous. These are determined by many factors with influences in many directions.

1. The first steps

Economic planning originated in the Soviet Union and it has developed there. Just a couple of months after the October Revolution, in spring 1918, the general directorates of the Supreme Economic Council (of the rubber industry, of coalmining, of the sugar industry, of the milling industry, and so on) started to elaborate plans for the production and allocation of the most important products of the nationalized enterprises. These plans were basically simple balance calculations in physical units.

In 1920 a small group of specialists – altogether 18 people – under the leadership of G.M. Krzizanowski and in close collaboration with Lenin, rapidly prepared the first economic plan of Russia which went into history as the GOELRO plan. This was the first program for the electrification of the country, which aimed at setting up 30 power plants in the already liberated parts of the country.

The electrification plan was supported by calculations concerning the development of heavy industry, agriculture and transportation. This plan was a big step forward in development of the methodology of economic planning, first of all in the area of the analysis of social needs, under conditions of very limited resources. Therefore the balance calculations were completed with efficiency calculations in many variants and in accordance with a system of economization.

In 1921 the GOSPLAN (State Planning Committee) was set up, which in a couple of months had elaborated the foodplan – more precisely, the balance of bread of the country in accordance with the provision of the population with basic foodstuffs. After another year the plan of production and allocation of metals, rubber and sugar was elaborated. At the same time documents were prepared concerning perspectives of development for the entire industry and the necessary investments.

In 1922-23 the plan for reorganization of agriculture was drawn up. At the same time work had started in GOSPLAN on elaborating a plan for the entire economy, concerning product movements among the most important branches of economy. This made it possible to elaborate the control figures for 1925-1926. At the same time the first five year plan was drawn up. This originated in an atmosphere of very sharp political and ideological struggles and therefore its final elaboration was delayed.

2. The era of five-year plans

Between the Twenties and Thirties the switch to five-year plans was a major change in the development of the methodology and practice of economic planning in the Soviet Union. This undoubtedly entailed a qualitatively higher plane, and such newer steps led to a new economic mechanism which assured the realization of wide-ranging structural changes in the production mode in a very short period of time. On the other hand, this was also a step toward an administrative-directive system, within the framework of which voluntarism and bureaucratism would burst into flower very quickly. The conception of the first five-year plan (1929-1933) was based on many assumptions, some of which, although very important, were not corroborated by reality.

One of these assumptions was a significant growth of efficiency and a decrease of industrial production costs. This was supposed to be the basis for the growing profits of industry,which should have served as a resource for financing the industrialization investment program. In reality at the end of the first five-year plan heavy industry became unprofitable and instead of bringing profit it needed subsidies.

Another unrealized assumption was the linking of the plan with developed forms of commodity and money relations. In accordance with this, the following was taken into account:

a) investments would be financed by long-term bank credits;
b) the wholesale trade of means of production would survive;
c) the general level of prices would not only be stabilized but even reduced to a small extent. In reality, investments were financed from the state budget. Because of the deficit, there was a return to centralized material-technical supply. As far as the costs of production were concerned, prices started to

rise.

These and various faulty calculations and unrealistic aspirations logically led to a situation where plans were in harmony, not with economic methods, but with administrative directive methods. ('Plan; it's a law'). The result of these methods was to gain time for the technical reconstruction of the economy and the accelerated development of production (regarding the volume of industrial production the Soviet Union moved foreward to first place from fourth place in Europe) and this served as the material basis for victory in the Second World War. The price, however, was high: slow growth rate, the decline in the well-being of the population in certain periods of time, although there was some success in broadening the knowledge of workers employed in mass production, and in establishing wide strata of the technical, scientific and creative intelligentsia. And neither the question of exaggerations nor the distortions in political structure could be avoided, and this caused no little sacrifice both in material and moral senses.

During and after the war the system of economic plans and the administrative and directive methods of their realization survived without any essential change, although there were some attempts to reform them. Two reasons can be mentioned: over-strenuous competition with the leading country of the capitalist world in military areas, and the permanent shortages of the most important raw materials, energy carriers, machines and consumer goods.

The balance of this period is ambiguous: on the one hand the approximate parity was reached in the military area with the USA, and peace and security were saved and assured not only for the Soviet Union, but for the entire socialist community. But on the other hand the Soviet Union could not engage to the necessary extent in the revolutionary changes in the world's production processes, which started in the first half of the seventies. This had a bad impact on the quality of national product and, as a consequence, on the efficiency of production. It was also inevitable that there would be serious difficulties in solving social problems. The introduction of radical reforms became more and more necessary and urgent, including the deep perestroika in planning.

3. Attempts at reforms

The radical change in economic planning in this period is not simply part of economic reform but the necessary precondition for its successful realization. The global interests of state will be connected in a new way with local interests. At the same time two closely related problems must be solved both theoretically and practically: first, central economic planning should be linked with an extension of the rights of enterprise, so that they can elaborate and approve their own five and one year plans; second an efficient economic mechanism should be developed which includes central planning, commodity production and the socialist market.

Sometimes very categorical statements can be heard that combining central planning with the self-reliance of enterprises, or making the plan consistent with the market, means mixing fire with water. From the point of view of formal logic such statements seem to be correct. It is another thing, however, if we look at them from the viewpoint of dialectics; that is, if we set out from the favourable features and weak sides of the plan and the market.

The advantages of the plan prevail in the possibilities of harmonization, which means that a permanent proportionality can be reached in the economy. The advantage of the market is that it evaluates the quality of a commodity in a normative way: it evaluates the efficiency of the work of every single producer. The problem of quality and the problem of economization with resources should be solved both with the help of the plan and of the market.

The plenary meeting of the Central Committee of CPSU examined the question of the most reasonable connection of the plan with the market. Generalizing the most important historic experiences, the plenary meeting composed Lenin's well-known thesis in a new way: '...the centralized planned control of the economy should be connected with the independency of the single links of the economy'. [1]

Real progress in connecting the state plan with local self-management and market took on a special significance. As M.S. Gorbatsev said: 'A new conception of centralism is concerned, the basis of which is the activities of employees and the independence of enterprises, i.e. the really democratic centralism in its leninist sense, which has an invaluable strength compared to a centralism plunging into attempts to regulate everything'. [2]

The question is not whether the general economic plan should be linked to the self-reliance of enterprises, to the 'khozraschot' of republics, regions, towns and counties. The answer to that is unambiguous: it is needed and necessary! The problem is how it should be achieved, with what methods and in what forms. The planning system has four basic levels: the levels of the entire economy, of republic, of branch and of enterprise. Perestroika should cover all the four levels.

The All-Union planning organs should give up the planning nomenclature, should give up their attempts to regulate production processes on the primary levels in detail. The new conditions of the economy, the enterprise law and other legal regulatory measures have put a stop to this practice and it should be given up independently of this fact – whether certain employees of the central highest authorities like it or not.

It is assumed that economic plan would assure progressive structural changes, first of all through the accelerated development of advanced electronics, automation, biotechnology and other science-intensive productions, and it would assure a rapid increase in quality and a decrease in that the resource need of final product.

In addition to this, GOSPLAN, the Ministry of Finance and the central banks should set the fields of finance and credit system in order; the purchasing power of the rouble should be strengthened, because without this commodity and money relations cannot develop, and the material incentive system and economic mechanism cannot function effectively.

In planning on republic level, social problems moved to the forefront: these relate to the supply of the population with foodstuffs and durable goods, to the accelerated development of social infra-structure where problems of housing, health care, transport and communication, and culture are serious.

On the Ministerial level planning concentrates on the question that demands of the population and economy should be satisfied by those products which are produced by the branches belonging to the given ministry. These problems link with the problems of quality, technology, the application of the latest results of science, and of specialization and cooperation. Regarding quality, technology and efficiency, it is impossible to achieve results without increasing the professional knowledge and culture of leaders, specialists, and employees of mass industry and without solving grave social problems. The new task of middle level planning is to use rationally the financial resources of the ministry, including subsidies to enterprises showing deficits or low profit during the transitional period, while they are switching to new conditions of economy.

Especially radical changes have take place in planning at the level of those enterprises which were granted the right to set up and approve their own five and single year plans in the framework of independent 'khozraschot' and self-financing.

4. An outline of the future planning system

The theoretical model of future Soviet society is being built in a more complex way, as a consequence of the mutual relationship between two kinds of factor: technological and socio-economic. The first word should be spoken by science. Science investigates past and present, foreign experiences, shows the tendencies of consumer demand, the changes in final product, in technology of production, in raw materials and energy resources and elaborates the long term project for technical scientific, economic and social development of the country.

In parallel with this, the ministries, the higher authorities, the soviet republics and the regions elaborate technical-scientific and socio-economic programs. They lay down the basic tendencies of international and economic integration in contracts and other documents of the CMEA countries.

All this work and other information manifest themselves in general form in the 15-year conception of the economic and social development of the Soviet Union. This is a strategic document which contains all the social priorities and purposes of economic development. It determines the most important features of investment policy, technical and scientific progress, limits of social development and all the tasks concerning the increase of the level of education and culture, and the defensive capability of economic and social development of the Soviet Union.

This work is conducted by GOSPLAN jointly with the Academy of Science, involving leading scientific research institutes, scientists and specialists. Following this, the project is discussed and approved by the Central Committee of CPSU and the government of the Soviet Union.

The third step is to establish and elaborate the plan document for the main trends of 15-year socio-economic development in the Soviet Union. This contains the figures and tasks underlying the Party's economic and social strategy. In this there are already numeric parameters which determine the dynamics of economic development and structural changes, the main resources of intensification, the most important tasks of technical and scientific development and large scale social duties.

The main trends are broken down into three five-year plan periods. Out of them, the first five-year plan is elaborated in a more detailed form. The indicators are determined for every single year, and there are numeric parameters for the most important branches of national economy (machine industry, fuel and energy, metallurgy, chemical industry, construction, agriculture, consumer goods and services, and so on) and for federal republics. The conception and the main trends are elaborated for every five-year period. These outline the future movements of Soviet society for the next 15 years. GOSPLAN, after having received the approved main trends, starts to elaborate the control figures for the next five-year development of the country.

At the same time, unlike previous years, the enterprises do not wait for directives from above, but start to prepare their own conceptions of development, which involve scientists and specialists of scientific research institutes. They investigate and evaluate possible changes in demand for the production of a given enterprise, market prognoses, the main tendencies of tecnological development, the necessary modernization and change of production equipments, the unsolved problems of the communities' social development. They contract with their permanent partners – that is, the outlines of production as a future plan of the firm, are shaped independently.

The control figures of the Planning Office are broken down to enterprises through ministries. This represents the dialectical unity of central direction and self management, of the central plan and the plan coming from below. The enterprises have previously prepared alternative plans too, but the directive tasks of the GOSPLAN were so different that hardly anything remained of the enterprise plans.

Control figures are not obligatory for enterprises. This is one of the novelties the economic reform has brought. It should be mentioned that sharp and long debate went on over this while elaborating the conception of the perestroika. Many planners simply could not imagine that these control data – which are the most important link in fulfilling the economic plan – might lose their obligatory character. The whole process seemed to be jammed, but finally the logic of the qualitative restructuring of direction won, and the obligatory administrative methods were given up.

The Soviet economy already has abundant experience from the time when the obligatory indicators enforced on enterprises from above were followed by indicators of 'khozraschot', which were hardly different from the former. The new Law of Enterprise however states that the 'enterprise independently elaborates and approves its own plan and contracts with partners' (2. parag. 1.section). The control figures are not obligatory for the enterprise; they are not directives but form an important basis of support to elaborate its own five year plan. The analytic and informative character of the plan becomes stronger. The control figures express the needs of society for production and the minimal output of the economy – that is, these figures are suggestions for enterprises as to directions for development in the next five-year period. At the same time the enterprises receive normatives for profit distribution, new prices, conditions of credit, development and incentives. All these serve for optimal use of the available resources of production. In such circumstances, if the control figures are well-founded and realistic and if the material incentives, normatives are quite efficient, then the enterprise plan would not be lower, perhaps even higher, than the control figures.

Planning from above and from below is well connected by state orders, which are guarantees of structural correspondence of production and consumption, and are supported by central resources and investments.

The enterprises are given state orders for products which are necessary to solve the production and social problems of state, for the accomplishment of technical-scientific programs, for the assurance of defence capability, for the transportation of agricultural products to the federal and republic funds and for the installation of production equipment for social purposes from central investment funds. The plan should involve the state orders, so their completion is compulsory.

Unlike earlier central plan tasks, the state orders do not necessarily cover the entire production program of the enterprise. In practice, however, for example in the plan of 1988 and 1989, in many enterprises state orders covered 100 per cent of the production program, so the earlier practice has changed little. But this is a transitional phenomenon, an infantile disease of the new economic mechanism. In certain cases this is connected with the transitory character of the recent planning and directive system: some elements are old; the others are new. The lack of harmony was again dealt with by a special directive. For example, a couple of chemical factories were unwilling to make contracts for some synthetic products with machine factories, because their production was not profitable. In this case, harmony between demand and supply was reached by pressure – that is, through state orders. It looks as though the present way of connecting five-year plans between GOSPLAN and enterprises is temporary. The main emphasis is still on state orders and centrally distributed resources – that is, essentially on the elements of the old system. To these are added some modified elements, like the somewhat new 'khozraschot', material incentives and self-financing. For the time being, price formation is completely absent from this connection, and long and short term crediting is very weak. Therefore the linking should be accomplished in the old way, by 'manual control' and administrative methods. In the future this will function automatically, with the help of such economic methods and regulators as affect the interests of working collectives. As a consequence, the share of state orders and central sources will decrease radically. We think that the 'state order' means a contract which contains the minimum between the two partners, and determines clearly the rights and duties of both sides. The adjective 'state' refers to the special significance of the contract, but does not change its character. The Planning Board could not undertake the duties originating from the state orders. Therefore, in the future, the government, or the Planning Board in the name of the goverment, assigns the ministries and enterprises which accomplish specially important programs and enjoy priorities against other ministries and enterprises. Although the state orders are justified for the country by specially important tasks, these should be stipulated in adequate contracts, in which prices, the form of bank crediting, tax allowances and other stimulating conditions are laid down. Resources necessary for fulfilling state orders are obtained by enterprises from wholesale trade through direct contracts.

When the designated changes in the economic mechanism and in the planning of national economy take place, enterprises will have strong motivation to perform their state orders and to broaden the circle of their buyers to the maximum extent. In this way socialism potentially becomes a higher order and more complex form of a purposeful labour organization. But this requires a longer period of time, and the process will be gradual because it is complicated and dynamic. "Millions of years were needed for nature", F. Engels wrote, "to produce intelligent beings, and now thousands of years are needed for these intelligent beings to consciously organize their common activity in order to recognize not only their individual acts, but their acts in mass as well, to act together and to reach their jointly designated common purpose". In the acceleration of this process, an active role is played by the science of economics, which is destined to provide theoretical foundations through the analysis and generalization of international experience in order to improve the methods and forms of purposeful activity by millions participating in socialist production.

References

[1] Proceedings of the Plenary Meeting of the Central Committee, CPSU, June 25-26 1987, Moscow. Politisdat, 1987. p. 90 (in Russian).
[2] Ibid, p. 52.

Martin Kornek

How to use Commodity-Money Relations in the Socialist Planned Economy of the GDR

The national economy of the GDR is faced with the task of continuing its dynamic growth during the years to come. Annual growth rates of about four percent are considered necessary to maintain in the future the approved policy of translating economic progress into social improvements. This aim is within reach if the national economy succeeds in developing in accordance with the laws particularly required to utilize scientific-technical progress steadily as a source of growth. Thus the GDR must develop modern key technologies with new dimensions and employ them with high economic efficiency and on a very broad scale based on already existing results (1-megabit-memory switching circuit, CAD/CAM technology, industrial robots).

From these targets new questions result as to how to develop further the system of management, planning and economic accountancy in the GDR, an important part of which is the development of the relations between the central governmental management, the self-responsibility of the economic units and, within this framework, the relation between plan and market.

I consider central management, however, and planning to be an important advantage of socialist society. It must actively reflect the structure of social interests, i.e. it has to organize the interests on a total society scale to bring them in line with those of industrial combines and enterprises and of the working teams, as well applying the principle of democratic centralism on an continually improving level.

In this process we take it for granted that socialist production is commodity production and thus that the economic units are commodity producers striving after their adequate interests. In the GDR commodity production has always been looked at upon a phenomenon immanent to socialism with a nature of its own determined by socialist property relations.

Two basic elements are considered here to be indispensable to efficient operation of the planned economy:

1. Elaborating and targeting obligatory governmental planning indicators in terms of use-values and values for the production and utilization of funds as governmental tasks or targets, respectively, for the activities of the enterprises.

Governmental planning indicators express interests on a total society scale towards economic units, especially concerning issues of national economic proportionality, efficiency and structural development. An increasing number of indicators will autonomously be planned with full responsibility of the economic units, with the further growing self-responsibility of combines and enterprises for their reproduction processes aspired to, and comprehensively implementing the principle of self-financing. Simultaneously, centrally-planned indicators will progressively take the nature of long term, stable normatives, within the framework of which the combines will be increasing responsible for an accurate and flexible response to new tendencies of sciences and techniques, of domestic economic demands and of foreign trading relations.

2. Implementing these governmental plan targets through economic relations.

This means that nationally-owned enterprises must regulate their relations amongst themselves and with other partners by means of money, price, credit and interest based on the plan.

1. The leadership of the planning

The planned economy in the GDR has always been based on the dialectic between national planning by the state and economic relations among socialist commodity producers. Each economic process has been and will be implemented through commodity-money relations. The reproduction cycle in the whole national economy cannot be thought of without the existence of such commodity-money relations. At the same time, central planning concentrating on decisions concerning fundamental problems has always been considered to be the superordinate momentum. Our experience refers to the requirements of the scientific-technical revolution and to the growing social character of the productive forces in improvement of the positional rank of central governmental planning; the necessity of long term decisions for the sake of the whole society increases.

In our opinion the market meets by its limits because of its tendency to a short-term evaluation of processes and its striving for states of equilibrium which render it incapable of contributing to the development of new technologies and to the restructuring of the national economy by itself alone. It is here we see the advantage of qualified governmental planning in accelerating the scientific-technical revolution and improving the competitiveness of our national economy as a whole.

Thus the increasing significance of the categories of value, their measuring, controlling and stimulating functions, does not mean that regulation by the market is replacing the plan. By means of the plan we concretely develop social relations and adjust the market into the socialist planned economy as a necessary condition. We consider it to be a fixed and objectively proven fact that a self-regulating market mechanism instead of the plan would finally mean that social conditions are determined by the market, which leads to negative social differentiation. As a consequence the synthesis of economic and social policies would have to be abandoned.

Full employment, the realization of our housing programme, the modification of the national economic structure, along with ensuring social security and solving ecological problems would not have been possible if we had left the regulation of these problems to the laws of the market.

2. The growing role of commodity-money relationships

The reproduction cycle of the national economy as a whole includes commodity circulation. The realization of commodities to meet demand is, above all, done in the markets. Hence, in our opinion, the market is part of the effecting and utilization mechanisms of the economic laws of socialism. Especially, interrelations between supply and demand and the transformation of economic work performance into a collective and individual satisfaction of needs are mediated via the market.

Concerning the relation between plan and market, planning is thus required to respond better and more flexibly to the demands of the market. Furthermore, the acknowledgement and information functions of the market gain an essentially greater significance for qualification of the planning.

Since the 1970s various steps have been taken in the GDR's national economy to improve the system of management, planning and economic accountancy. These have created the conditions for the combines and enterprises to meet their responsibility as commodity producers in a better way.

Stress is to be laid here on measures to improve industrial, building and construction, and agricultural prices and forwarding rates:

- The modifications of industrial and building and construction prices and a reform of agricultural prices have been carried through in several stages so that prices correspond to the necessary expenditure of social labour.
- The introduction of a contribution to the social funds (which reflects – together with wages – the actual social input to reproduce living labour within the prime cost) and the revaluation of fixed assets aimed at showing the actual amount of inputs of labour, working media and subjects of labour and at integrating them into the cost-profit accounting of combines and enterprises.
- By introducing standard rates of profits into the price calculation, an important condition was created for the function of prices. Since these standard rates of profit are normatives, in fact, they ensure that long-term sectoral financial requirements are satisfied and stimulate the combines and their enterprises to fulfil and to overfulfil planned profits.

These measures have laid the basis for regulations aiming at an improved management of the reproduction process by the comprehensive use of the principle of self-financing. These regulations will be gradually introduced into our national economy. These decisions touch on the question of how to remove or alleviate the contradiction between the combines' claim for resources and their offered output performance for the sake of social development. Thus the point is to find a better harmony between performance for society and the supply of funds by society. These regulations provide the funds of the combines and enterprises to be formed on the basis of long term, fixed percentage of amortisation and of net profit. This will have a beneficial influence on the increase of labour productivity, the reduction of prime cost, a high level of utilization of

71

fixed assets and an acceleration of the reproduction cycle.

With these measures we are taking a line which combines structural development, a margin for decisions and the disposal of resources. This results in higher requirements of the heads of combines and enterprises. Through economic relations they are increasingly urged by self-financing to concentrate their activities on the reduction of inputs and on the further development of the principle of performance evaluation.

The new structures of social interest that thus develop obtain a clear picture, especially through the example of financing sciences and techniques, of the base of the productive effectiveness, on which the reproduction process of combines will increasingly depend. Our combines today decide on the utilization of more than 80 per cent of the means for research and development. The decrees on comprehensive self-financing stipulate the funding of research and development, no any longer from prime cost but from profits.

A new standard in the planning process will result from implementing the principle of self-financing. This is especially true of the commodity-money relations actively retroacting to planning. Profit as a performance standard of combines and enterprises will gain increasing importance in their extended reproduction. The new aspect is the replacement of the method of mainly planning the absolute volume of financial funds with the method of planning them relatively with the aid of long-term stable normatives. The normatives act as a medium between the profits earned and the formation of the funds. Thus the definition of these normatives, promoting work performance and corresponding to the plan, is given a decisive importance. First steps have been taken in practice, but we have also to state that additional theoretical and practice-related work needs to be done in order to manage these questions.

With these decrees on self-financing the active part of the money in our national economy will grow; therefore a short remark on this category of value will be added. Money possesses a decisive importance in the functioning of the reproduction process and shows, at the same time, how this process comes about. It is up to normal economic conditions that first delivery is checked, afterwards it is paid for. A financing automatism cannot be accepted, the principle is to be applied: first the goods, then the money. Our experience as to currency stability teaches us that it is necessary:

- to apply such prices in the economy which meet the necessary expenses in social labour and stimulate the most economizing use of resources;
- to secure a state budget balanced by the development of work performance; and
- to warrant an economically founded issue of money and to grant credits in relation to efficiency.

The best way to meet these requirements is considered to be the dynamic and proportional growth of the national economy aimed at the satisfaction of demand and based on scientific-technical progress.

Veselin Nikiforov

The development
of society and planning

Planning is defined by various authors, schools, organizations, organs, and by groups of countries in various ways. From this viewpoint it can be said that planning does not have a generally accepted definition.

Any conscious activity of a human being entails a certain kind of planning. Although this is essentially an accurate statement, it is still not sufficiently defined. When it is asserted about planning, one thinks about a strictly determined planning. Conseqently, complementary definiteness has to be introduced into the above statement in the form of the complementary characteristics of planning by virtue of which it is not simply a conscious activity of a human being, but his peculiar, special conscious activity.

Among these characteristics the first is the circumstance that planning is a conscious activity of man which generally refers to objects which is very complicated and important to him.

The second characteristic of planning has to do with ensuring the maximum of conciousness. For this reason it becomes necessary to apply special procedures – quantitative and qualitative analytical methods, computing systems, technical means, etc.

The third characteristic is the constant coordination and control which has to be realized continuously for aims, means and activities in order to be always in the required unity and harmony.

Planning, therefore, is the choice and determination of aims, means and activities by means of which aims can be attained. Secondly it requires coordination and control for the constant maintenance of harmony among the aims, means and activities, and thirdly the realization of all these through elaboration and fulfilment of plans in order to attain the estimates by optimal economic, social and other effectiveness. Consequently, foresight does not yet mean planning. Neither is coordination in itself, nor compilation of written or unwritten plans, planning. One might talk about planning only if the organic unity of foresight, coordination and the use of plans for the realization of aims is evident.

This definition gives us an opportunity to mark off planning from the usual elementary, conscious activity of man, which although in its most general feature also has a character of planning, strictly speaking does not require planning. It is not so important to realize and organize this kind of activity by the

73

the aid of plans. This determination enables us to delimit planning from prognostication. Prognostication contains foresight elements, but unlike planning, does not contain the elements of coordination and action plan. Planning can also be delimited from scientific activity also by means of this determination. In the latter, foresight is equally and frequently evident. However, unlike planning, this foresight in most cases does not constitute an immediate task for scientific activity; it appears as a indirect result of efforts to clarify the essence, character and regularities of changes and development of real phenomena. On the other hand, which is even more important in this case, in scientific activity, even when this foresight manifests itself (be it indirectly), the coordination and the plans for its realization are lacking, since it is not the business and object of science. Figuratively speaking, if men are not only authors of their drama, but also its performers, then planning comprises both the writing of the drama and its performance, i.e. in the form of a previously determined scenario (foresight, coordination and their blending in the plan).

From the point of the above determination it is evident that even in individual human activity there is also planning – if the point under discussion concerns an important field and if it becomes necessary to exercise systematic and important efforts and provision in order to realize the forecast (to select the aims, determine the means for their attainment, to accurately outline the mode of realization of the activity), to realize the coordination and to elaborate and implement the written and unwritten plans.

These provisions and efforts aimed at the forecasting, coordination, and at the elaboration and performance of the plans might be called *individual planning*. All fairly self-standing economic organizations – enterprises, associations, companies – have their plans. In big sectoral and intersectoral agglomerations – ministries, associations, bodies, transnational companies, etc. – there is also executed planning. However, our question is confined to whether in reality and where planning is realized in the dimensions of *the whole national economy*.

Private ownership constitutes a serious hindrance to such planning. It also hinders foresight, as a component of planning. But it especially hinders general economic coordination. Holy and intangible private ownership is completely incompatible with general economic coordination realized through the elaboration and fulfilment of the respective plans and which in like degree and form does not leave untouched the intangibility.

However, the interpenetration of industrial capital with bank and finance capital on one hand, and the interpenetration of capital with the capitalistic state on the other, provide not a few possibilities for the appearance of some elements of planning (such as foresight and coordination in a national economic dimension). Let us think, for instance, of the role of the bourgeoise state and great monopolist capital in the preparation and realization of one or another strategic breakthrough – e.g. the realization of fifth generation computers, artificial intelligence, biotechnologies, arms systems etc. Let us also think of those economic coordination measures, the aim of which is the prevention of such economic dangers as the imbalance of foreign trade and the lack of means in the bourgeois state for the realization of certain national programmes. In this context one might point to the U.S. foreign trade law passed in 1988 in a full 1000 pages, containing an enormous system of general national coordination provisions, and also the continuous coordination of provisions in connection with this law. One

74

might also point to the general coordination measures implemented in the USA at the end of the Seventies and the first part of the Eighties. In order to accumulate means for the financing of the armament programme in the USA, special measures were introduced with respect to state loans, credit interests, taxes, the dollar rate etc. As a result of such and similar measures truly enormous amount of means were accumulated, but balance of payment problems also became complicated. This produced the requirement to implement coordination measures of an almost opposite character in the form of the above-mentioned foreign trade of in 1988.

In spite of this, the real realm of general economic planning remains the economy based on collective property. Collective property, by its essence, requires and enables general economic foresight and general coordination, as well as the elaboration of general economic plans and their fulfilment by the utilization of means of professional character.

Unfortunately however, these requirements and possibilities were used inefficiently so that general economic planning degenerated into an imperative centralism on the part of the central planning organs, and the subjects of labour became mass executioners of the centre's instructions, with minimal personal initiative and entrepreneurial vigour. On this basis, both the people and the working collectives and the interests of the central organs were distorted. All this caused serious damage to the effectiveness of general economic planning, to its reputation and attractiveness. The mass of people distanced and delimited themselves from the general economic planning under the conditions of collective property.

However, one should not forget that there is a marked difference between degenerated and distorted planning and national economic planning originating from and adequate to collective property. Collective property requires and enables the realization of planning based on interests of the people and the working collectives with respect to those of the centrum and its organs and, thirdly, based on a mainly new, mutual relation between the centralism and the self-management.

In order to create new socio-economic development planning corresponding to social property, even on a purely theoretical basis, certain important, decisive conditions have to be fulfilled.

First: it is necessary that individuals and working collectives as economic organizations should formulate their concrete interests related to work on the basis of such new criteria as arise out of collective property. Such a criterion could be an increase in the combined (i.e. international and domestic) competitiveness of products and services produced by economic organizations. This combined competitiveness can be maintained without difficulty, on the basis of self accountancy and planning, and with the aid of data on the international market received from the official state information organs. The increase in combined competitiveness could be taken into account and planned by the aid of the growth index of the share in the total turnover of corresponding product groups on the international socialist and non-socialist market. On the other hand, this competitiveness should be taken into account and planned, parallel with the first index, by the growth index of the returns from export in both fields of the international market; and as far as the non-export products are concerned, by the price reduction index of products and services which are not new for the respective economic organization. Regarding the prices of new products for the company, they have to be determined initially according to the following guideline: the prices of new products should be raised more slowly – for instance twice as slow – than the improvement of the use features of consumer goods or that of the production features of capital goods. After a certain time these new products cease to be new and henceforth the price reduction requirements of internal competitiveness will be valid.

In this way, the two indices – the growth index of sales share vis-à-vis the suitable combination of the export returns index and the reduction index of domestic prices – properly indicate the fulfilment of the mission of economic organizations: that they should achieve a rapid increase in the overall complex satisfaction of human demands on the basis of their competition, according to international criteria.

The payroll and investment funds of companies should be composed on the basis of these indexes. For this purpose the centrum must approve normative tables which regulate the sums accruing to these funds.

The wage fund will be also composed on the basis of suitable normatives. Thus economic organizations, by elaboration, approval and application of their internal statutes, will divide the fund themselves and will fix individual wages. The same must also be done to the contribution of individual workers. If competitiveness increases, the wage-fund will accordingly be increased, and the respective individual wage as well. If there is no increase, then the funds will not increase either.

Second, an important precondition for the increase and operation of competitiveness is that the economic organizations operating on the basis of collective property should have significant scope for economic liberty and self-management. They should be able to solve by themselves all problems of current operation and a significant proportion of problems connected with the medium-range development of the company. The centrum naturally has to solve much of the strategic development of these organizations and some problems of their medium-range development, through dialogue with the economic organizations. As a consequence, market mechanisms will regulate what they can regulate – the whole of current development and a great part of medium-range development. With a strategic perspective there is usually no market. Above all, one needs strategic coordination.

Third, an important condition for the shaping of a new type of social-economic development is the introduction of concrete rules for the forming of proper interests corresponding to the essence and character of collective property both at the centrum and in its organs. One of these rules should be the introduction of the requirement that the centrum should be responsible for the rate of the combined competitiveness. In this way a special division of labour will evolve. Each individual economic organization will be responsible for its combined competitiveness, and the centrum will be responsible for the combined competitiveness of the whole economy. This will be for the centrum its 'own' dynamics of competitiveness. However, for this function of the centrum another rule will be required: that that the centrum should be placed completely under the public control of society. When the centrum is responsible, and its activity assessed on the basis of the dynamics of general combined competitiveness, and when the centrum functions under the public control of society, such concrete interests will inevitably develop to stimulate the centrum to ensure the optimal growth of the general combined economic competitiveness within the framework of its activity, bringing about maximally competent decisions, ensuring against voluntarism and enabling the self-management of the economic organizations.

Fourth, in order to organize new planning based upon collective property, at least one more condition is required – also at the level of pure basic principles. And this is the accomplishment of a new consumer statute by which a maximal increase in the consumers' role will be ensured in economic and social life.

In point of fact, the introduction of the growth index of combined competitiveness, as an optimalization criterion, increases by itself the role of the consumer, since it stimulates and urges producers to influence the consumer and win his confidence. However, this is still not enough. It is also necessary to increase the role of the customer independently. Under the conditions of the economic mechanism, and according to certain laws, the customer has to be empowered to shape prices in a decentralized contract system as a direct contracting party. He must be guaranteed, should he be a producing or non-producing consumer, real alternatives in choosing the supplier or the product, in the assessment of its quality through the establishment and utilization of independent laboratories carrying out objective tests of product characteristics, in returning unsuitable products, in obtaining guarantees on purchased products, in the refund of losses caused by the producer, etc. The forming of a consumer with real powers, who is interested in the purchase of more, better quality, diversified, demanded, new and cheaper products is the absolutely indispensable condition and requirement for bringing producer behaviour into line with the demands of the consumer.

At best, only the most important requirements can be outlined here with respect to the new interests of the producers, the centrum and consumers, and to developing new relations between them. As regards the new interests, the point under discussion concerns the creation of such conditions as can guarantee general competition among producers, and which is aimed at winning over the customer by producing better and better, more up-to-date, varied and – what is especially important – relatively or absolutely cheaper products and better service. From this viewpoint, a new economic mechanism, new planning, self-management and direction are the most important factors in the whole complex of transformation for creating such interest. However unusual it may seem, the main condition lies neither in greater economic liberty and self-management for the economic organizations, nor in the limiting and modification of the centrum's functions. These are necessary, but not only insufficient but not even the most important, conditions. The most important condition is the introduction of new optimalization criteria for economic organizations and the activity of the centrum in the form of a growth index of combined international competitiveness, an increase in the customer's role and the development of real, new interests. Economic liberty, self-management, the limiting and modification of the centrum's function might begin to operate and provide a major contribution, but only after the materialization of this latter condition. Because there is a danger that without the previous shaping of new interests in extensive creation and competition, economic liberty and the limitation of the centrum's functions offer great scope to the assertion of other interests which produce inflation, increase incomes without an increase in quality and quantity of production, and lead to a price reduction of products without the required increase of creative work. Further, they produce a constant lack of export resources and balance of payment problems relative to the capitalist countries.

Naturally, this does not mean the undervaluation of economic liberty and self-management of the economic organizations and enterprises, nor limiting and modifying the centrum's functions and placing them under full democratic control. On the contrary, after development of the new interests of creation has been ensured through competition, the said conditions and requirements will have a decisive importance from the point of the appearance and self-assertion of the new interests. The role of the conditions and requirements will attain even greater importance if their new combination is taken into consideration. On the basis of the new interests, the limiting and modification of the centrum's functions under democratic control will not damage the interests of the whole society, nor constrain the liberty and self-management of the economic organizations and enterprises. And this is true in the opposite sense. This is how the matter stands; economic liberty and self-management widens and propagates in one dimension, while the modification of the centrum functions in another. As a consequence, they will not enter into conflict with each other, but will agree. The central control management will harmoniously associate itself with self-management.

All these statements provide an answer to the question: What is role of planning in the socio-economic development? Planning, as a means of increasing the effectiveness of individual labour and of working collectives, unions, associations, branches and the whole national economy, is an enormous tool for enriching the socio-economic environment and for the accelerating its growth. And the more planning is based on the interests of creation through competition and development, and the more it contributes to the optimalization of these interests and their balance, the better it will be in harmony with socio-economic development, the better it will organize and make it more effective. It will contribute to the greatest degree to the enrichment of society, people and individuals in economic, social and spiritual matters compared with the dynamics of the most advanced capitalistic countries. It will help to shape and develop people, first of all as a creator.

PART III
RADICAL CRITICS – REFORM

Józsefné Huszár

On macroeconomic planning – an alternative approach

Macroeconomic planning [1] has so far been aimed at defining the comprehensive programme of economic development, postulating that different economic activities would lend themselves to concerted development control in a sectoral system. It was thus assumed to be possible and even necessary that a political-administrative centre should successfully control business activities in mutual division of labour as well as develop of these activities.

The main basis for this assumption was provided by the conviction that in a system of the almost exclusive state ownership the political-administrative centre is able to integrate the manifold interests of the economy and society into the so called 'general societal interest'.

In this approach the objective of planning was to achieve the best possible aggregate performance through central macroeconomic programming. This would require the central distribution of resources, selecting the privileged spheres of economic goals, as well as specifying the proper conduct of authorities and business management to suit planned and programmed development.

Formally, planning was performed as a task of the administration, while the responsibility of plan approval was assumed by representative political bodies. Thus each plan of the past 20 years reflected the ideas, aspirations and requirements of the actual system of political and social leadership.

1. Planning as a reflection of social and economic leadership

Planification and central control have remained predominant factors of the Hungarian economy since 1968. Because of the almost absolute freedom of intervention enjoyed by central social, political and administrative control, it became a matter of routine to apply central measures and actions in all cases where the actual state of affairs did not conform with planned forecasts. Hence the status of long-range strategic plans was gradually devaluated. Consequently, the five year, the long term and the annual plans were in constant and painful disagreement. This process finally led to a situation in which yearly plans were accepted as authoritative, thus calling into question the importance of strategic planning, i.e. discrediting an eminent function of central planning. Various business and local autonomy organizations underwent similar processes.

Planning was a statutory obligation of companies, cooperatives and local council. However, their activities and development possibilities in plans and especially in practice were based not only on their own results, but also on their bargaining power, which they tried to exploit in order to procure more of the available resources. The actual opportunities of these organizations were exposed to the simultaneous influences of their standing in the social and economic division of labour, the profitability of their business, the decisions of the political and administrative authorities, and their political-social weight. It would be hard to tell to what extent this bargaining power depended on results prior to the given planning period and to what extent it was expressed in the plans themselves or rather in non-plan factors. At any rate it is a fact that long-term plans did not represent decisive values at any level of the economy. This was increased by the administrative interventions aimed at the control of purchasing power, thereby further reducing the investment opportunities envisaged in the plans.

The actual value and limits of macroeconomic planning were practically determined in the last 20 years by the fact that the central plans represented a specific type of political and administrative decision in the intricate decision system of political and state leadership. This specific quality is best described by the historical recurrence and 'ceremoniality' of the central plans through which the political and state authorities issued their comprehensive programmes to the general public.

Thus, while the plans apparently represented (at a given point of time) a summarized and macroecomically coordinated system of decisions, they could not act as proper programs because of the intricate system of repetitive interim redistributions and curtailments of investment funds. Many important decisions surfaced which had not been fully considered, or even ignored, in the plan. All this le to regular disagreements between the 'dreams of the future' laid down in longer-term (five year) plans and real life.

This inconsistency became apparent as 'overdistribution', i.e. as a surplus of purchasing power which was drawn off by the administration, partly by actions elaborated in yearly plans and partly by single out-of-plan measures. Although the methods and optimism of planners were frequently criticised and the criticism is hard to answer, the key problem of planning is rooted in the disagreement outlined above.

As a result of the method of planning developed in the last decades, the important long term programmes of social and economic development (i.e. planning itself) did not become part and parcel of the whole system of administrative control. Although this was a fact already in the early 1970s, it escaped criticism because it was then accompanied by favourable changes (five year plans were overfulfilled). The implications of the situation reversed in the last decade, for the last two five year plans were not fulfilled and the current one is also unlikely to be fulfilled, hence criticism is obviously justified.

2. Planning and plans

According to the classification adopted in planners' vocabulary for several years, *planning* (the activity of planning) and the approved *plans* have different meanings in terms of content and scope. While planning – through its several phases – provided a summary and evaluation of a multitude of facts, opportunities, forecasts and approaches, the plan itself or its deliberations for adaptation gave only a summary of a possible and optimum version based on the assumptions and calculations of planning.

With some simplification, planning work is still similar in content and methodology to the pre-1968 routine, the goal and task being an accurate review of the operation of the economy as a whole, as well as all facets of its development opportunities, preferably in sectoral details.

In the plan, on the other hand, the 'status' of central support was achieved by a few partial objectives which could be considered the outputs of planning. (These have been defined in recent years as 'priorities', stressing once again that objectives are not all equal.) It is even more important that, from the point of view of participants, planning is a multi-actor administrative activity, whereas some key objectives laid down in plans have no governmental agency responsible for their achievement. For example, the most important targets of economic development that were approved in the previous plans, i.e. increase in the national income or improvement of the balance of payments position, do not and actually cannot be addressed or assigned to a specific governmental organ.

It follows that responsibility for the implementation of key plan objectives may be interpreted in a formally global sense only (in terms of macro-economic total) and only for the whole administration as a body. To put it more simply, this means that the administration is the sole assignee, the only body responsible for implementation or performance of the plan, whether the plan was passed by the government or by Parliament.

The hazards of the planning approach outlined above surfaced mainly when the key objectives of the economic policy were not met (and the actual reasons were to be found) and when the adoption of selected objectives had to be justified and correlated with the key economic political objectives.

The general authorities and ministries have dual roles in planning. On the one hand they support the planning process as providers of proposals and information. This implies that their ideas, forecasts and studies are integrated in the planning process. At the same time, as members of the administration, they participate in approving the plan and in responsibility for its fulfilment. This double function is important, especially because, so far, the different ministries have had to commit themselves to plans and take responsibility for the implementation of plans in the drafting of which sometimes only a part of their original suggestions were adopted.

The methods used by planners in selection and evaluation of the alternative proposals, and the method of arriving from numerous ideas to the version promoted to the rank of draft plan, are essential features from the point of view of plans. It may be stated at this point that no predetermined and uniform parameters were used in the acceptance or rejection of concepts in the course of planning. The worst gap was the lack of a methodology in prioritizing centrally-accepted sectoral plans (such as investment projects) in the context of the key plan objectives. (Naturally this has never prevented elaborating individual justifications for any given objective approved earlier.)

The opportunity or right to formulate various concepts has so far followed from the structure of the administration, i.e. from the assigned heads or supervisors of the different sectors of the economy. These organizations have supposedly covered the entire economy with respect to planning. This was legitimate, considering the dominance of the state sector in the previous system of ownership, since the planners were thinking in terms of the state sector. It is well known that until the early 80s, recognition of the private sector was limited at most to home and holiday cottage building. From the point of view of management technique, though not formally or legally, the co-operative sector was given the same treatment as the state sector. So in this approach the sectoral principle, and especially the hierarchical structure of control, were suitable for formulating the concepts of central intents to be enforced in the economy and then for asserting these concepts.

As a result of this organizational system, the economic sphere was given priority in the formulation of interests. Advocacy of public interests was the task of 'mass organizations' (e.g. Patriotic Front, Communist Youth Organization, trade unions, and Councils): they could not enjoy genuine and equal rights in the various decision processes like planning aimed at the distribution of goods in society. This state of affairs was left practically unchanged by the so-called 'public discussions' of plans, undeniably a new element in the plan drafting process after 1980.

Top level leadership of these mass organizations might study and comment on the plan drafts in a stage preceding formal approval, and put forward their respective points of view and criticism. However, the final texts of plans themselves prove that the drafts were essentially not revised according to the various comments. Nevertheless these 'societal discussions' gave an opportunity to those concerned to elaborate their objectives and their reasons for objecting. But the most typical 'reception' on the part of the administration of these suggestions was to quote their lack of professionalism or to promise further scrutiny.

Thus planning, up till now, can be considered as a self-assertive administrative process in which the central control authorities have enjoyed priority over the whole people. This concept stemmed from the fact that economic development was directly programmed by the plans as documents of the administration, assuming that economic performances are decisive from the point of view of development standards where what has been produced is available for distribution or export. It followed from this approach that we cannot achieve a rapid growth of production unless the greater part of available resources is spent on the expansion of sectors of direct production.

Naturally the inclusion of the public interest [2] as an objective following the economic targets of the plan, was not precluded from above; on the contrary, it was occasionally postulated. Therefore plans also contained development objectives which it was hoped would gain the confidence of the people.

3. On the methodology of planning

After the experience of the past decades it may be stated that the selection and use of planning methods were dominated by traditions. Convincing evidence of this can be found in the function and treatment of the balance and analysis methods. With some simplification, the balance method can be considered as a tool for taking central account of each process of the economy by simultaneously diverting their transactions into the desirable channels.

The balance sheets of the national economy are certainly a convenient instrument for a static aggregate representation of the consumption of resources and of the mutual relations between different sectors and activities. Thus the balance method can be useful for recording value flows at an aggregated level. However, it cannot be used for harmonizing demand and supply, which change permanently and autonomously, despite some expected fulfilment of this task on the basis of the mistaken role of the plan. That is, instead of information, impact analysis, forecasting etc., the balance system has been used in planning for the purpose of minute elaboration [3] of most of the plan objectives. Thus its main role was identified with income distribution expressed partly in regulations, partly in the direct distribution of state revenues.

In turn, overdistribution justified subsequent interventions to restore the equilibrium already elaborated by means of the balances. Individual measures could divert from the five year plans enacted by Parliament as well as from long term targets without any risk of enquiry about the implications of the given intervention. Thus the methods themselves deprived planning of its strategic programming function.

In the meantime it was also realized that the balance system (due to its comprehensive and static nature) was not suitable for dealing with several sets of problems. Balances are not usually the instruments to set priorities or to handle urgent situations. This gap in planning has been filled so far by analyses and recommendations which deserve a brief review in the context of planning methodology.

The objective of analysis applied to planning was to evaluate the fulfilment of plan forecasts and calculations, assuming that this would be evidence of successful economic development and a reference basis for compiling subsequent plans. That is, the objective of analysis was to qualify the simultaneous relationships: partly by stating the degree of progress over past years and partly by measuring the fulfilment of the plan. [4] However, reality, in its complexity and with its corresponding methods of approach, asks for more types of methods, modelling techniques, etc. The methodology of analysis has also failed to handle the total of and the interactions between economic and social processes.

Quantitative indicators based on sectoral frameworks cannot tackle such interactions, not to mention the projection of past changes to the future. Once this is admitted, the correct way of studying the dynamic structure of economic and social changes is to understand the salient characteristics of processes, to get acquainted with interactions, and to try to qualify and forecast them.

4. Time horizon of planning

According to the accepted classification there are operative (yearly), medium (five-year) and long-range (10-15 year) plans. Ideas of the future as prognosticated in plans of different time horizons are similar in nature but different in terms of accuracy. It is consequently therefore that the shorter-range plans operate as tools for implementing the objectives detailed in the longer-range plans, for example, in comparison with a long-range plan, a medium-range plan operates as a programme of action and control.

The reform ideas adopted in 1968 assumed that favourable social and economic changes could be achieved by means of plans drafted with competence and on democratic grounds. On this basis, medium and long-range planning was reformed in Hungary by the early '70s in both approach and practice. Despite the correct assumption, the past two decades have shown that the system of central planning was intrinsically incapable of operating in any but its original role. [5] The demonstrable reasons are manifold. Apart from the attitude of political-administrative control, i.e. its permanent readiness for intervention, it is also a fact that up until now strategic planning could not achieve more than, at best, a temporary concertation of different interests and, what is still more important, planning itself, with its methods and interpretation of functions, took charge of discrediting longer-range plans.

From the point of view of yearly and longer-range plans the previous decade and the 1980s differed only insofar as 15-20 years ago the yearly plans usually uprated the objectives of the five-year or long-range plans (since the five-year plans were regularly overfulfilled by the yearly plans) while in the last ten years the yearly plans have assumed a downrating quality (i.e. falling behind the five year plan). This can be proven by contrasting the five-year and the annual plans. (Objectives related to the balance of payments and to external trade relations differ from the general trend because these had to be repeatedly reduced in the yearly plans on basis of the actual situtation, as from the early seventies.)

According to the formal standpoint concerning national economic planning as laid down in the Acts of 1972 and 1985, the five-year plan is to be considered the standard type of macroeconomic planning. The ritual ceremonies of plan approval provided distinguished occasions for our social and economic leadership to display its commitment to planning and plans. Five-year plans were enacted by Parliament [6] while the yearly plans were simply passed by the Government. (On the other hand the long-range plans were no more than references for Parliament because such plans did not have the privilege of being approved.)

For this reason, when party and state leaders were to shape their political-economic targets, they could not ignore the need of also proving the success of their social and economic system through the plans. The success indicators of economic development mainly included the growth of the national income, of investments, of the standard of living and of foreign trading performance, considered key success factors for a long time. This assumption implied the belief that the population would be identified with these objectives, i.e. with the plans, and committed to implementation, since higher economic performance would mean higher consumption. What is more, some selected development projects (such as housing) would directly contribute to meeting society's requirements.

Failures occurred at several points with respect to the above assumptions. It was found that the growth of national income lost its old dynamism and did not qualify for the status of success factor. Planning could provide only temporary harmony of interests in resource distribution. The people, on the other hand, had to 'understand' that the original values of objectives set in their favour gradually decayed in the course of implementation of medium-range plans. [7]

Thus the plans were downrated not only because of inescapable facts, but also because of the method of planning itself, in which neither the interfaces

86

between different plans nor responsibility for implementation were given real content. An alternative could have been, for example, the Planning Office reporting to Parliament in yearly plans about the progress of the actual five-year plan or about the departures of yearly plans from the enacted five-year plan. [8] However, this approach was absent from the operative planning routine, once again acknowledging the priority of yearly plans (planning). (If this was true in the case of five-year plans imagine how much a real role was missing from the long-range plans!)

I have tried to show that the state of affairs where five-year plans could not discharge their role in the control of economic processes, and in which consequently planning was deprived of its very potential, advantages were actually created by the approach of central control and planning. This recognition has been a fact for at least a decade. Up till now, however, all the 'experiments' trying to change this state of affairs have sought compromise solutions tailored to reinforce the accepted approach. This type of solution included, for example, proposals that the five-year plans 'should be open' or that they should lay down itemic decisions only for the first half of the plan period. In my opinion, the present suggestion of using three-year plans instead of five-year plans falls in the same category. While these ideas propose new names but nothing new in content, and no consideration is given to the new planning function, it must be noted that the principles claimed to be new after 1980 already existed 10/15 years ago and even as early as about 1970. [10]

References

Csikós-Nagy, B., 'Overall renewal of socialist planned economy', *Tervgazdasági Fórum*, no. 2, 1987.

Balassa, A., 'Planning in difficulty', *Tervgazdasági Fórum*, no. 3, 1987.

Báger, G., 'Public discussion of the new medium range draft plan', *Tervgazdasági Fórum*, no. 1, 1985.

Berend T., I., 'Economic solutions sought and found in the Hungarian practice of socialist construction', in *Actual problems of the development of socialism in Hungary*, Kossuth Könyvkiadó, Budapest, 1987.

Faluvégi, L., 'Bridge between science and planning', *Tervgazdasági Fórum*, no. 2, 1986.

Hetényi, I., 'On planning and versions', *Tervgazdasági Fórum*, no. 3, 1987

Hoós, J., 'Key areas in planning', *Tervgazdasági Fórum*, no. 1, 1985.

Huszár, J., 'Planning and democracy', *Tervgazdasági Fórum*, no. 3, 1987.

Kulcsár, K., 'Shaping of society, planning, science', *Tervgazdasági Fórum*, no. 2, 1988.

Notes

[1]   The term national economic plan is used for central plans. The term is derived from the notion of a homogeneous economy where the only acknowledged category is the state sector. Considering the increasingly realistic content of alternative forms of ownership and the changing scope of

central planning the term is becoming less and less appropriate.

[2]   In this logic of distribution, 'the public', i.e., the people, were included as a double category. This also implied that the active population (as a basic factor of production) was a subject of planning in the form of employment, job creation, real wages, training, etc. At the same time it could not be forgotten that declared welfare tasks (communal supplies, social policy goals, etc.) were not to be omitted.

[3]   Thus the desirable – and attainable – increment of the national income, the balance of payments and foreign trade, the level of consumption and stockpiling, the degree of price level raise, the possible volume of investments, etc. were to be derived from the plan.

[4]   Planning methodology has been developed in recent years by giving more accurate definition of some indicators and by increasing the number of organizations in charge of analysis.

[5]   It is an about a decade-long issue whether the plans should be made for five or three years. This point is given more consideration in the present discussions about planning than it would actually merit. I am convinced that the basic problem of planning is that of interpretation of planning functions and of time horizon.

[6]   The significance of 5-year plans was emphasized by political decisions as well as by the understanding that they were the basic documents of coordination and development of CMEA relations. While the 5-year drafts were repeatedly discussed by the top bodies of the HSW Party, the key targets of 5-year plans constituted a issue on the agenda and were set by the Party congress.

[7]   This is easy to demonstrate by considering e.g. the housing programme, always a 'state financed' priority project, on the basis of plans of different time horizons vs. facts.

[8]   Poland in its practice of the past several years did not fail to do so.

[9]   As it can be shown on basis of documents, the 4th and 5th 5-year plans were actually passed as 2-3-year plans. However, the '5-year task' maintained its dominance with respect to the key objectives (e.g. national income growth, investment volume set in Forints, the corresponding main proportions of distribution, etc.)

Karel Dyba and Tomas Jezek

Czechoslovak experience with central planning

1. Introduction

At the beginning of the 1950s, central planning (administrative, command planning) was introduced in Czechoslovakia. It was based on a rather comprehensive nationalisation of the means of production, except land. It was conceived as a complex hierarchical system and its ambition was to coordinate practically all economic activities in production, trade and services.

This system, in which crucial economic processes were coordinated to a prevailing extent by central planning apparatus, seemed to be well suited to implementing a limited number of goals during the period of profound political, social and economic transformation in a rather short period of time.

Yet it was certainly not conceived as a temporary set-up, but as a rather permanent feature of a really socialist society. In fact it proved to be so deeply implanted by the 'founding fathers' that, no matter what profound changes in the external world, domestic economy and society at large have taken place, the basis of the system of mandatory central planning in Czechoslovakia still survives.

This is not to say that there were no attempts at changes in the system established in the early 1950s, all of them in the direction of its decentralisation, i.e. of shifting some decision-making power from the centre to the firms. Thus, various operational shortcomings of a rigid and overwhelming system of mandatory central planning were quite early diagnosed [1], and towards the late 1950s there was a first attempt at a kind of significant rearrangement in the system. Because of various reasons described elsewhere, see Dyba, K., Kouba, K. (1988), this, however, did not bring any lasting results, only a deepening of general mistrust in central planning.

From this experience there emerged in the 1960s, a genuine attempt at market-oriented reform, i.e., substituting market coordination of economic activities for their bureaucratic central control. Yet this reform experiment did not last long, and by the early 1970s Czechoslovakia returned to the traditional system of central planning. This system successfully survived another attempt at its 'perfecting' at the beginning of the 1980s, and only now (in the late 1980s) after several years of stagnating economic performance and under outside influence has its comprehensive restructuring been contemplated.

In fact there is a draft reform, and the first steps have already been taken to implement it. It is obviously too early to say if it will develop into a really market-oriented reform which will finally do away with administrative and overwhelming central planning, or if it will end with the 'normality' of central planning gaining the upper hand again. (The 'no planning, no market' in-between solution is, as experience tells us, obviously unstable.)

Let us hasten to say that we believe that for administrative (mandatory) central planning – put into practice at the beginning of the 1950s and more or less practised since then – there is no more future in Czechoslovakia. This kind of central planning might have produced some results only in the early 1950s when it inherited a solid, industrially well-developed economy with a reliable network of diversified market relations, monetary institutions, management experience and skill, labour discipline and performance, a high level of education, an infrastructure of very good schools and 'invisible' morals of the market. All this well functioning machinery could be given goals. It existed by mere inertia. These potentialities were gradually eroded by the system, which proved not to be conducive to adequate human capital development. By means of central planning, the Czechoslovak economy was transformed into an energy-steel-machinery producing complex. However, seen dynamically, this proved to be of dubious value, since in long run Czechoslovakia has lagged in its economic and social performance behind once comparable Western industrial economies.

By implication, we must attribute this relative decline to a great extent to traditional central planning as practised in Czechoslovakia. Perhaps the most negative Czechoslovakian experience with planning has been the ultimate loss of an alternative, more efficient and welfare-oriented development path which the country might have taken had it been able to get rid of mandatory planning in time or not institutionalised it at all.

2. Strategic versus short-term thinking under central planning

Czechoslovakian experience with nation-wide planning started with the Two-year Plan for 1946-1947, the main goal of which was to reconstruct the Czechoslovakian economy; more concretely to increase the level of output in most fields up to or above the pre-war level. This plan was worked out in a co-operative spirit, though occasionally in an atmosphere of sharp conflicts of interest, since professional people as well as politicians were engaged in its elaboration [2] The two-year plan was not an overwhelming plan and specified only certain concrete goals in verbal terms (such as the reconstruction of railway bridges and automobile transportation according to their importance, the reconstruction and restarting of production in enterprises according to a specific timetable and in a particular order etc.) Most of these tasks were implemented by means of budgetary allocations and preferential credits supplied by banks, and by obliging ministries to perform particular policies. This meant that the two-year plan was conceived as an economic program of the government (and a political document) for a mixed economy system in which market forces had an important part to play.

A traditional type of administrative central planning was gradually introduced in Czechoslovakia at the beginning of the 1950s. Instead of a complex and cumbersome system of selective planning (programming) based on bargaining between state organs, enterprises and social interest groups within the context of a mixed economy, as exemplified by the two-year plan for 1946-1947 period, a 'simple' system of 'physical' central planning with an explicit breakdown of mandatory input and output quotas from the centre to enterprises was taken as the genuine model of really socialist central planning. (There were 100 explicitly stated production quotas in 1949, 400 in 1950 and 1100 in 1951. By 1951 two thirds of the volume of industrial production was explicitly planned from the centre by means of physical indicators).

This kind of central planning was seen as a necessary tool to achieve extremely ambitious goals of the 1950s: profoundly restructure the whole economy (the socialist reindustrialisation), improve defence potential, serve the needs of other socialist countries, and (later in the 1950s) somewhat improve the standard of living of the average consumer in a relatively very short time. In fact the restructuring of the economy and society at large in the 1950s [3] predetermined patterns of Czechoslovakian economic and social developments and, henceforth, the substance of central plans – i.e. their basic priorities as well as the means of their achievement – for decades ahead. During the 1950s, therefore, truly strategic decisions were taken which created new economic as well as organisational structures; and these, because of strong forces of inertia, tended more or less to reproduce themselves. Under these conditions central planning was less and less concerned with evaluating basic alternatives of development or with assessment of main development priorities – since these, as well as the means of their achievement, seemed to be predetermined forever. Hence central planning was increasingly preoccupied with short-term stability problems (solving bottlenecks, controlling permanent tension related to overfull employment, and rigidity of price structure confused with price, stability, etc.). There was no scope, no time and no will really to assess dynamic efficiency problems in the planning process – i.e. to pay attention to longer-term strategic issues. In fact, so pervasive was preoccupation with short-term stability, with all kinds of detail, with excessive balancing etc., that it greatly influenced approaches towards medium as well as long-term planning. Though, in words, a difference of principle between the content and methods of short, medium and long-term planning was recognized, in practice the real content of long-term plans (or, better, outlooks) was a less detailed copy of the short-term (i.e. annual) central plans, very much under the influence of the prevailing short-term situation or simply projecting past trends into the future.

For example, at the beginning of the 1960s, a long-term outlook for the economy (15 to 20 years) was elaborated which again strongly emphasised the energy-steel-heavy engineering core of the economy. This conceptual thinking was transformed into the more concrete tasks of the third five-year plan, which were strongly heavy industry-oriented, as in the 1950s. Yet attempts to implement them under different domestic conditions, as well as under unexpected changes in the international economy, led to increased tensions in the internal economy which spilled over into external imbalance. There was a rather irrational reaction to this by the controlling authorities, and the economy slid into a deep unplanned slump in 1962-1964 which was unique among socialist as well as Western developed economies at that time. [4] Hence the third five-year plan disintegrated and for some time the economy only drifted.

Another example of the inability to think and handle in strategic terms is provided by analysing developments in the 1970s and the 1980s. After experimenting with a market-oriented economic reform towards the end of the 1960s, Czechoslovakia returned to traditional central planning at the beginning of the 1970s. The fourth five-year plan for the 1971-1975 period, which was conceived entirely in the centralist spirit, is considered to be rather successful in the history of planning in that planned, rather high, rates of growth of output, personal consumption etc. were achieved [5], while internal and external equilibrium or 'normal' state (in J. Kornai's terminology) prevailed in the economy. Yet in view of subsequent developments we have to question the extent to which this may be attributed to a return to traditional central planning as claimed by its adherents. In fact, attempts to pursue the same ambitious domestic growth targets in the 5th five-year plan for 1976-1980, as in the 1971-1975 period, brought about unsustainable successive trade deficits with the West, and towards the end of the 1970s this finally compelled the authorities to revise the original planned targets substantially downwards.

There was also a revision of the 6th five-year plan goals for the 1981-1985 period as international developments caught central decision-makers by complete surprise. With the benefit of hindsight (and comparing across countries) over the last twenty years or so one can see that the Czechoslovakian economy was performing relatively well when the international economy was in a good order. When this latter was disturbed there was relatively good short-term economic performance only if the planners (cum politicians) were willing or able to buy time by borrowing abroad. Once they were unable or unwilling to do so, they were forced to accept a trade-off between a considerable reduction in growth rates and a temporary improvement in external balance.

Looking at secular declining growth rate of the economy in the past 20 years or so and gradually increasing external indebtedness in convertible currencies over the same period, on the one hand, and comparing it with persistently relatively high energy, material and 'ecology' intensities of the economy and its declining international competitivness on the other, one has to conclude that there has not been any structural adjustment of Czechoslovakian economy to changes in the international economy. This, of course, means that there was no significant move towards an efficient economic development path, which over the years has been a constantly reiterated long-term (i.e. strategic) aim of all plans. Basically, strategic growth patterns and social priorities as established in the 1950s are still very strongly imbedded in any short or medium-term central plan, and it is these patterns that must be changed in order to achieve long-term efficiency objectives. In fact, as past experience proves, these patterns and priorities can hardly be changed unless mandatory central planning itself is abandoned. In other words, such goals as flexibility, adaptability and efficiency of the economy are not compatible with the practice of mandatory central planning, with its excessive stress on short-term stability priorities.

3. Social planning

Central planning in Czechoslovakia has always aimed at broad, ultimately non-economic goals. Yet, over time, when conditions within domestic economy as well as abroad have changed without adequate response in terms of a change in the system of central planning, there have been increasingly evident tensions and conflicts. Narrowly defined economic goals were less and less in harmony with broadly conceived, ultimate (and evolving) social goals. These tendencies gave birth in the 1970s to a extensive campaign for the institutionalisation of what was called comprehensive 'social' planning at macroeconomic level.

However, no new solutions were achieved which would significantly change the prevalent practice of central planning; no doubt partly because it has never been clear what is the content of social planning at a macro-level, even among the proponents of such ideas. In fact, the emphasis on social planning at macro-level (at least in words), especially as regards achieving certain goals in living conditions and standards, was no doubt one of many attempts at reaction to the declining efficiency of the economy. The loss of efficiency was evidenced by a strong long-term relative decline in the share of personal consumption in the global social product, by deterioration in qualitative social indicators and environment, etc. The stress on social planning also reflects a way of thinking which considers the increasing inability of the economy to meet ultimate social goals mainly to be a consequence of wrong planning (wrong goals) and much less a consequence of the inherent logic of the operation of central planning.

4. Money and finance under traditional central planning

Traditional central planning relies on direct administrative coordination of the economic activities of enterprises by issuing them with mainly input and output commands. Therefore it limits the functions of money as far as possible.

This salient feature of the central planning is reflected in a factual as well as formal ranking of the respective financial and monetary institutions into a hierarchy of planning institutions. In fact a passive role of money under central planning means that these institutions do not participate significantly in making the most important decisions in the economy. That is, they play a only secondary role when plans are put together. This has been a sort of constant or definitional feature of central planning, despite numerous attempts to upgrade the role of money and monetary institutions in the planning hierarchy.

In traditional central planning, the state budget and banking sector (also restructured) are assigned a passive role, in the sense that they only finance the tasks handed down to all enterprises by the Central Planning Board (CPB). In other words, the function of the state budget in centralising and reallocating resources (created by enterprises) according to central preferences and goals formulated in central plans and to 'socialize' any enterpreneurial risks, is very much pronounced. There is practically no other active and independent role assigned to budgetary or monetary policies in influencing economic activities in order to achieve other targets but those fixed by the central plan.

The introduction of central planning was accompanied by basic changes in pricing and income policies. It will be known that freezing of prices and wages was widespread after the Second World War in order to avoid inflation. Yet by 1949 it was felt that price policy should be substantially modified to serve planning entirely needs. Hence CPB, ministries or the government took over pricing policy responsibilities formerly held by the Central Price Office. Wholesale prices became more and more cost-plus prices devoid of any scarcity and demand influence and, hence, any allocational function. They were assigned an accounting function, aggregating physical quantities only. This was a logical step, complementary to demonetisation of the business sector and in fact a necessary prerequisite for the practice of central planning which relies on a rigid relative price structure changed by the centre at discretionary intervals only, and any income effects of these changes (if any) were neutralised as much as possible by corresponding changes in tax policies.

Since 1951 the extensive planning of wages has also become an indispensable part of central planning. The total wage fund of the economy started to be broken down among the ministries, which afterwards allocated it to industrial enterprises. At the macroeconomic level the planned wage fund started to depend on the planned structure of production and especially on the planned share of consumer goods production in total final output. This meant that aggregate balance on the consumer goods market (consumption market aggregate 'equilibrium') was to be assured a priori by planning relevant variables, that is, by equating planned supply (i.e. consumer goods supplies times predetermined prices) with planned demand (mainly planned wage fund after deducting intended savings).

A practical device to accomplish balance in the consumer market as well as to provide some material incentives for plan fulfilment and eventual over-fulfilment was a system of wage regulation in annual plans: planned wage funds were made to depend on a planned average earnings. (The picture is a bit more complicated when we take into account services and incomes other than wages. We would have to work with a balance of incomes and expenditures as a main tool for achieving balances at the consumer market level, yet the essentials as described above for the case of wages only would not be different.)

Income and wage policy for controlling total demand were obviously the main tools planners used to achieve macroeconomic balance on the consumer market over time. In the case of Czechoslovakia, the planners achieved some success in this respect, though there was no doubt some hidden inflation (which planners probably implicitly took for granted and more or less welcomed, though explicitly they were very much against it). Only sparingly was an increase in the level of consumer prices used as a tool to equilibrate consumers' market.

Originally, the volume of wages to be paid out to employees depended on the volume of gross production, i.e. enterprises could have higher wage funds, even due to socially undesirable production (false cooperation, using heavy materials, producing the wrong assortment etc.). Later on, there were several attempts to change it by introducing other indicators on which the volume of wages depended, thus changing the pattern of enterprise behaviour. The primacy of short-term macroeconomic balance on the consumer market persisted, and the wage fund distributed to enterprises according to what they offered in terms of variously measured results has been a prevalent practice over time.

Occasionally, there were discretionary shifts in relative prices, but seldom of basic foodstuffs and utilities, to remove structural imbalances. In the realm of retail prices, however, prices were also manipulated to achieve some distributional goals, i.e. equity purposes. So in Czechoslovakia microeconomic shortages or forced substitution have always been present in the market for consumer goods, and in the official economy there has been no automatic response to this situation either in terms of price movements or supply reactions.

It is important to note that under central planning as practised in Czechoslovakia there has never been a clear distinction between the role of the state budget (Ministry of Finance) and monetary and credit policies (State Bank of Czechoslovakia). There is only a single monetary or financial counterpart of the central plan: the so-called 'aggregate financial plan' which is put together by the Ministry of Finance and the State Bank. Yet it is only the passive counterpart to previously largely independently-formulated central plans for the national economy. What is more, in the aggregate financial plan which includes the state budget and credit plan, the basic functional distinction between credit and the state budget (subsidies from the state budget) is blurred, as if it were not economically important from which sources business activity is financed (either by the budgetary assignments or by bank credits which must be repaid). In fact this practice takes it for granted that what is important is the total amount of financial resources or money to finance passively all the needs of the business sector as envisaged by the central plan, and that it does not matter from which sources financial resources come (i.e. either generated by taxes or banking deposits).

In fact, this practice presupposes a perfect central plan and, hence, a totally passive role of money. Yet is impossible in reality to live in such a world: the central plan is far from being a perfect one: it is not totally comprehensive; there cannot be total neutralisation of money.

This has also been recognized; and there have been attempts over time to take this into account, allow for a more active role of money in the business sector of the economy, and make greater use of monetary tools to achieve planned goals. However, the logic of the comprehensive central planning as established in the 1950's has never been abandoned; i.e., the ambition to determine a quite detailed structure of output of the whole economy and, hence, of output for nearly each enterprise by a state plan has never been abandoned. Therefore monetary categories like prices, finance, wages, credit, etc. had to continue to play a very subservient role in the business sector of the economy; and budgetary, monetary, wage and price policies were not used as the prevalent and most important tools for achieving overall economic goals, but only as supporting tools for the achievement of a set of particular targets.

Another salient feature of administrative central planning is its autarchic character. Import and export quotas have practically always been administratively prescribed to enterprises so as to achieve, in the state plan, desired trade or balance of payments results. Exchange rates as well as tariff policies have never been explicitly used in any significant way to achieve foreign trade targets. (With respect to socialist countries, there are longer-term bilateral agreements and annual protocols derived from them, which may be considered an extension of administrative central planning across borders). When planning foreign trade flows, notably exports to non-socialist countries, central planners have nearly always been over-optimistic and extremely unsuccessful both as regards the planning of revenues in foreign currencies as well as efficiency of exports – i.e. outcomes nearly always differed downwards from the planned targets. What is more, despite planners' intentions over time there has been considerable loss of competitivness of Czechoslovakian exports in western markets.

5. The real mechanics of traditional central planning

Formally, the process of formulating central (state) plans starts with party congresses, which formulate general political and economic guidelines for the next five-year plan. Behind this is extensive preparatory and analytical work in the various research institutes and administrative organs; work in which the CPB always has a strong voice.

In the first stage, party guidelines are concretized by macroeconomic departments at the CPB into a first draft of a comprehensive state plan. After that, respective sectoral departments at the CPB and ministries, associations and enterprises engage in a mutual exchange of information and bargaining, and this process of mutual communication hopefully brings a consistent and 'satisfactory' formulation of a particular five-year plan.

After a central plan is put together (for which the CPB is responsible) it is submitted by the government to the Federal Assembly, approved by it and promulgated as a binding law. Plans of individual enterprises are approved by particular ministers. The same planning machine oversees plan implementation and plan fulfilment as well; under traditional central planning it is therefore useless to try to separate plan formation from plan implementation.

Obviously, this is just a sketchy and idealized picture of what in reality is an extremely complex, cumbersome and demanding process in which many participants with differing interests take part. It frequently gets stuck; therefore there are various informational delays, and the whole economy or enterprises in fact work more or less without their plans being approved in time, etc. When one tries to see the real world of planning, one sees a hierarchical system which is full of opposing pressures between participants in the planning game. Moreover, participants frequently change their behaviour at different stages of the planning process (plan formation, implementation and control). [6]

In the real world of planning there are vertical hierarchical structures with respective relations, and horizontal relations among enterprises as well. As to vertical relations there are mutually interconnected informal coalition structures which comprise people working in enterprises, associations, ministries as well as in the so-called sectoral departments of the CPO and respective political structures. Given this complex institutional structure, the process of planning is similar to playing cooperative games, yet with temporary unions, informal coalition structures, lobbies etc. This in fact makes managing of the economy along a vertical structure impossible as there is no relatively clear line separating the 'business sector' from the centre. Obviously this bargaining over resources and targets is for enterprises the gist of the game, not searching for optimal solutions under given external parameters.

Another consequence of this state of affairs is of course the extremely weak capability of the centre in steering the economy over time. At first glance we may still see an extreme directivity prevailing in the economy because each enterprise is given a plan with a number of indicators as well as lots of other operational tasks by superior economic and political organs. It would, however, be misleading to take this as proof of directivity and thus implicitly assume the institutional independence of central organs from the business sector with clearly defined and independent interests, as if the centre were a nonpersonal entity following only social interests. In fact, each of the various central organs looks after its special interests. Above all, however, some organs of the centre find common interests with especially large-scale and powerful enterprise and this of course predetermines 'social goals and tasks'. So what seems to be directive tasks imposed from above may in fact often be enterprises' interests embodied in planned tasks and goals, as their formulation is significantly influenced by big business in cooperation with regional and sectoral administrative and political bodies.

This, however, also means that the behaviour of enterprises is significantly influenced by the mere existence of planning hierarchy, as this set-up allows enterprises to externalise entrepreneurial risks and costs of production. It is understandable that under such conditions the economy largely drifts along a predetermined longer-term course, since it is hardly possible for the centre to attain any strategic tasks involving significant innovation and a deep structural change.

6. Use of mathematical methods in central planning

There is widespread modelling activity in research institutes, ministries, as well as in the planning organs. [7] The models are used for analysis and sometimes for forecasts (econometric and input-output models or their combinations) or for decision-making purposes (mathematical programming models, optimization models). However, in fact, the real value of mathematical models in the framework of the traditional central planning has been negligible because the reality of the traditional planning is extremely hard to formalise. Perhaps an exception is the preparatory phase of long-term planning, when either econometric or input-output models, eventually their combination, are used to make analyses or explorations of future development possibilities of the economy. Yet, very often even these exercises, which obviously suffer from a certain kind of rigidity (which is by necessity embodied in a structure of the model, while real planning is always 'fluid'), remain within research institutes; and there is hardly any meaningful communication between 'modellers' establishment' and staff in the institutions of traditional planning.

Moreover, there are other reasons which hamper modelling efforts in Czechoslovakia and the use of models in planning practice in general. Above all, there is no relevant, generally accepted theory of centrally planned economies, either macro or microeconomic. [8] Therefore econometric studies sometimes suffer from theoretical vagueness. In particular, to make greater use of modelling in the traditional planning process, one should introduce elements of game theory and theory of management to form the behaviour of the business sector and of planners when constructing plans, and this should somehow be also respected in econometric modelling efforts.

As to optimization or decision-making models, there have been attempts to make use of them in the field of investment and foreign trade. Yet (in particular in the field of investment) models are more often than not used to provide only a sort of scientific cover-up – that is, to prove post factum that an investment project satisfies formal criteria for inclusion the central investment plan. So the use of optimality calculus is rather meaningless in this respect.

Another example of the misuse of models within the framework of the traditional planning is obviously an attempt to recalculate prices in the economy by means of an input-output model, and to use the calculated prices in the planning process as more 'rational' ones than the old price structure. This practice shows major theoretical misunderstandings as far as the formation and role of prices in the economy are concerned, and an overestimation of model possibilities. It also assumes that the information or data on which models are based are adequate and accurate, which, for of obvious reasons, is simply not true. Yet this attempt at an administrative recalculation of prices in the economy by means of models is repeated again and again, though there is enough experience to prove that it simply cannot work.

On the basis of experience with mathematical modelling and its use in planning process in Czechoslovakia, including our own experience with econometric modelling, we strongly believe that traditional central planning can do without any mathematical modelling efforts, and the only indisputable contribution of modelling is a label of 'scientificness' affixed to traditional approaches after they they also passed through the computer.

7. Planning, politics and democracy

The organisational hierarchy of central planning (from the Federal Assembly to enterprises) which is more or less responsible for formation and implementation of the state economic plans is paralleled by political, labor/union, and other hierarchies which enter the planning process at its various stages. In fact, in a sort of amalgamation of respective hierarchies one has to search for reasons why attempts to streamline mandatory planning and the increasing independence and decision-making power of enterprises did not lead to any significant changes in the behaviour of enterprises. These attempts tried to make enterprises more independent from the state hierarchy but they never aimed at making them independent from the political hierarchy.

The party hierarchy, influences planning hierarchy in three very important ways:

1. it more or less sets development goals, supervises their decomposition and their fulfilment at all its levels;
2. it controls personnel policy ('nomenclatura'), at all its levels;
3. it controls in a similar way all other hierarchies parallel to it.

The party hierarchy apparently exerts its influence most decisively at the highest level of the central planning when setting the basic goals for the economy. On the other hand, labour unions seem to be most directly influential at the enterprise level when its organs codetermine decisions on labour matters such as wages, overtime work, fringe benefits, labour conditions etc.

Czechoslovakian experience concerning the compatibility of central planning and democracy suggests that, despite a number of proclamations, central plans in Czechoslovakia were hardly ever a result of really meaningful discussions of development alternatives in the representative bodies (the National or Federal Assembly) or in the society at large. Such a procedure was envisaged by some early thinkers, in the days when there was a relatively limited practical experience of central planning, or rather no experience at all. In fact, the possibility of a genuine deliberate social choice from a set of possible states of the economy by means of parliamentary democratic procedures was considered to be a substantial feature of central planning. This is not to say that representative bodies in Czechoslovakia, i.e. the Federal Assembly at the level of federation and the National Councils for both republics, do not engage in discussions of the five-year central plan drafts before they enact them. Yet a central plan, elaborated by the planning hierarchy (mainly the CPO) and put before the representative bodies in one variant only, has never been rejected as such. In fact, after forty years' experience with planning in Czechoslovakia, one can assert that formalism in the work of representative bodies when they discuss central plan may not be attributed to the composition of parliamentary bodies, to the shortcomings in election of the members of parliament, or to the unsatisfactory professional qualities of the parliamentarians, important though these factors no doubt are, but to a fundamental impossibility meaningfully to evaluate a comprehensive central plan by a voting procedure or by a discussion.

Moreover, any true democratic discussion about goals of central plans would tend to require some time, and practically all the necessary information during preparatory stages of work, as well as a more or less full final draft, would have to be accessible to the general public. This has never been so, and an atmosphere of secrecy has always been associated with some vital parts of the formation and implementation of central plans in Czechoslovakia.

A central plan is a complex document, the parts of which are mutually interconnected. So a change of one part calls for a chain of other changes. An expert or a group of experts could study all the consequences of a particular change only after several days of hard work supported by computing techniques. And, moreover, there are no generally accepted standards by which parliamentarians could evaluate either any alternative elements of a central plan, their eventual changes, or a plan as a whole.

8. Current economic reform...?

We mentioned above that Czechoslovakia has recently proclaimed its variant of a 'radical' economic reform. However, it is obviously too early to say to what extent the current economic reform will really substitute prevalently market coordination (with related supporting institutions) of economic activities for administrative central planning; and whether it will establish competitive market discipline under which autonomous economic agents pursue their own entrepreneurial interests and the government looks after macroeconomic targets by an appropriate blending of monetary, fiscal, exchange rate, etc., policies in a democratic set-up.

By looking into the reform concept as well as analysing the first steps to implement it (the reform should be in full swing only by 1.1.1990), one obtains a picture with numerous inconsistencies, which is capable of developing in either direction, i.e. towards central planning – more precisely to what J. Kornai calls 'indirect bureaucratic control' – or forward towards a genuinely market-based economy. In what follows we would like to pick out some of the major controversial points only.

The respective inconsistencies are well reflected in the proposed changes in the system of planning. On the one hand, annual mandatory central plans in the traditional form ought to be abolished [9]; on the other, the 5-year central plans should persist in the form of uniform and stable normatives (such as the ratios for the distribution of after-tax profits etc.), limits (such as on the maximum use of energy input) and obligatory targets (state procurement) handed down to enterprises by the centre. As experience shows, however, an abolition of annual central plans does not mean that market coordination of economic activities emerges spontaneously. Rather, the planning bureaucracy, which has more or less stayed intact to formulate, implement and control 5-year (and longer term) plans, may use the limits, targets and normatives in such a way as to fill any eventual void created by an official renouncement of annual mandatory plans.

Next, instead of gradually enhancing the role of free or contract pricing in the economy, as would be required by the logic of a market-oriented reform, the authorities have again resorted to an administrative price reform to 'rationalise' the structure of prices in the economy, which was considered a precondition for other reform steps. Similarly, as in the past, this is bound to fail because of biased and outdated information supplied by enterprises to price authorities, because of the economic tools available (input-output model and verbal dialogue) and, above all, because of the fundamental impossibility of finding a 'correct' price vector by means of ex ante computation, and not by means of a real market test.

Furthermore, it is important to note that organisational restructuring in the economy in 1989, as part of reform measures did, in fact, preserve a strongly skewed industrial structure in favour of big units artificially (administratively) created in the past so as to facilitate central planning. This is hardly compatible with a competitive market structure. Here, there probably bounced back inconsistencies in the reform project, which has not up to now properly envisaged any legal infrastructure to regulate competition. Needless to say, the crucial question of a proper regulation of free entry and exit (which is related to a clear definition of property rights) has not been properly tackled either in the project up to now.

Last but not least, foreseeable changes, as far as the external opening of the economy are concerned, seem to be too muted to expect from them any significant effects as far as the contestability of domestic markets by foreign economic actors is concerned, which under Czechoslovak conditions is a sine qua non of a competitive market structure.

So in the light of this it remains to be seen how some of the basically sound principles of the current attempt at reform in Czechoslovakia may and will be realised. Here we have in mind:

- the principle of self-financing of enterprises and enhancement of their decision-making power in terms of disposing freely of their products and seeking out commercial partners etc.;

- restructuring of a banking sector with a separation between Central Bank activities and commercial banking; commercial banks should be more independent, motivated by seeking profits etc. (Will the Central Bank be really autonomous and acquire much more economic power at the expense of the CPO?);

- tightening budgetary discipline by more strict control of subsidies provided to enterprises;

- limiting distribution of financial resources via ministries or state budget. (Will the authorities really allow bankruptcies?);

- gradually doing away with a multiple exchange rate system and reactivating exchange rate and tariffs as policy tools, i.e. by starting auctions organised by the banking sector in which enterprises may freely sell and buy foreign exchange at a market-clearing rate etc. (Will this work if a market discipline does not emerge?).

Table 1. Planned and actual increases of national income in each five-year plan (in %)

Years	Plan	Actual
1961-1965	+ 42	+ 10,2
1966-1970	+ 22-24	+ 38,4
1971-1975	+ 28	+ 32
1976-1980	+ 27-29	+ 19,8
1981-1985	+ 14-16	9,1
1986-1990	+ 18-19	9-10 */

*/ Expected.

Source: Compilation from party documents.

References

Brus, W., 'Institutional Change within a Planned Economy', in Kaser, M. C., (ed.), *On the Economic History of Eastern Europe 1919-1975*, vol. III., Clarendon Press, Oxford, 1986.

Dolansky, J., 'Za vyssí efektivnost cs. národního hospodárství'. UV KSC, 27 and 28 February, 1957.

Dyba, K. and Kouba, K., 'Czechoslovak Attempts at Economic Reform: 1958, 1968, 1988'. Paper presented at IWM project 'Plan and/or Market', Vienna, 16-18, December, 1989.

Jezek, T., 'Assumption of Symmetry as a Methodological Problem of Comparative Organizational and Society Analysis'. Paper presented at Fourth Workshop on Capitalist and Socialist Organizations, Budapest, 1986.

Klaus, V.,' Reformen ohne Theorie', *Neue Zürcher Zeitung*, 26.2.1989.

Kupka, V., *Investice a ekonomicky rust v CSSR*, Academia, Praha, 1983.

Mlcoch, L., Mikroekonomické aspekty ekonometrickych modelu. *Ekonomické modelování, CSVTS-SBCS*, Part 1, 1980.

Long-term Planning, United Nations, New York

Wiles, P., *Communist International Economies*. Basil Blackwell, Oxford, 1971.

Notes

[1] See e.g. respective party and government documents in the early 50s. For a more comprehensive contemporary review see Dolansky, J. (1957).

[2] For more on this period, see Brus, B. (1986).

[3] One can use a number of figures to document how deep the transformation of the Czechoslovak economy in the first five-year plan was. One of the most suggestive is a change in the territorial distribution of Czechoslovak foreign trade. Whereas in 1948 40% of Chechoslovak foreign trade was with socialist countries and 60% with non-socialist countries, in 1953 these shares were 70% and 22% respectively.

[4] For more on this see e.g. Wiles, P. (1968), Kupka, V. (1983).

[5] See table 1 for an overview of five-year plans since 1960 up to now, i.e. planned increases in net national income and actual outcomes.

[6] In the Czechoslovak literature there is a very instructive discussion of the real world of central planning, especially of the behaviour of enterprises, in various studies by L.Mlcoch, see e.g. (1980). See also T.Jezek (1986).

[7] For an earlier rather idealised view on the use of various models in the practice of central planning see United Nations (1971).

[8] See V. Klaus, 'Reformen ohne Theorie', Neue Zürcher Zeitung 25. – 26.2.1989.

[9] The law has already been passed in mid-1989.

Pavel Kysilka

Problems and outlooks of the Czechoslovak program for reforming the centralized planning system

After two previous reform programs have been abandoned (in 1962 and 1969), the Czechoslovak economy has now begun its third serious attempt at reform of the economic mechanism, the system of centralized management and the planning of the economy.

It seems evident that the paradoxical fate of both preceding reform attempts is closely reflected in the content, scope and approach of the present reform program. Ironically, the reform programs of 1958 and 1966 were finally abandoned not because of their fundamental shortcomings in content and economic purpose, but as a consequence of external factors. The abandonment of the first reform program in 1962 was caused by extensive disequilibrium in the economy, the outcome of an unrealistic growth and structural strategy implemented by centralized economic policy. The reform program of the 1966-1967 period was abandoned in 1969 for ideological and political reasons. None of the reform attempts ever reached their consolidation stage. Thus for all practical purposes because of the problems, shortcomings, obstacles, domestic as well as foreign barriers to implementation, and the development of both, reform attempts never had a chance to prove their worth.

Before I try to discuss the inclusion of the Czechoslovakian reform program into a classification of reform programs of socialist economies, I think it might be worthwhile to offer some comments concerning the problem of a model description of the pre-reform economy and the problem of classifying system reforms.

It is interesting to note that the problem of a model description of a non-reformed socialist economy is the subject matter of highly polarized discussion among Czechoslovakian economists. To be more precise, there is agreement over an approach which describes the area of consumer goods and labour as fields where models of the market coordination of independent agents are clearly valid (even when the important role of central regulation and interventions in the labour market and consumer goods market, as well as strong influences of the non-market production sector, are generally acknowledged), and at the same time states the non-existence of a money market. On the other hand, differences in opinion exist in the approach to a model which describes the production sector of a non-reformed socialist economy. I am convinced that for a description of the production sector of a non-reformed socialist economy, and in empirical explanation of it, the best is that current of thought which, to put it as briefly as possible, has developed from the work of Barnard to Simon and, finally, to the interesting methodological reinterpretation of this theoretical apparatus by Papandreu. The fact of the matter is that an interpretation and application of the theory of organizations in explaining and describing the production sector in a non-reformed socialist economy is viable and seems to lead to satisfactory results.

I consider a socialist pre-reform economy as a system which is a mixture of the labour market, the market for consumer goods and a single, complicated superorganization of the production sector. This organization (the production sector) of the economy does not include the productive activities of the agents active in the so-called individual or private sector (whose size, however, in Czechoslovakia is negligible), as well as the activities of agents in the 'grey' and 'black' economies.

The problem of reforming socialist economies traditionally and logically concentrates on the production sector of the economy. My further comments will thus be limited to this sector. The approach which considers the production sector of a non-reformed socialist economy as a single complicated organization interprets the basic terms of the theory of organization in the following manner:

1. The production of material goods and services is the external function of this organization.

2. Substantive planning in the organization concerns its external function, i.e. production.

3. The procedural planning of the organization concerns the intentional coordination of activities within the organization. So-called enterprises are actually sub-organizations (plants) within the super-organization. Their plan is a mere component of the super-organization's plan. Intentional coordination within the organization includes both vertical links and strong, intentional horizontal links. Links of the authority and influence type are implemented. Influence and authority are implemented in vertical relations in both directions, upwards and downwards.

4. The central authority in itself is a sub-organization with internal horizontal links, authorities and influences, including external influences.

5. External forces (moral, political, ideological, etc.) have a very strong impact on the activities of the whole super-organization, especially through agents whose activities are part of the organization.

6. A low degree of substantive rationality in the behaviour of members of the

organization leads to the intensive development of motivation and stimulation systems within the framework of procedural planning in the organization. Within this procedural planning some functions of the market are imitated (for instance there exist pseudo-enterprises, pseudo-prices, pseudo-money, pseudo-interest) for this purpose and also for the purpose of records and inspection. In spite of the fact that these are intentionally used instruments within the framework of procedural planning in the organization, their degree of imitation or degree of quasi-real economic content differs. Those elements of economic instruments which are immediately linked to the categories of the labour market and the market for consumer goods are those which come closest to having real economic content.

The constant increase in the complexity of super-organizations, and especially the existence of strong external influences, have led to an erosion of administrative vertical links in super-organizations and, together with low economic performance, also to the ineffectiveness of the stimulation system.

It is interesting to note that not only the first reactions to these phenomena, but also some present reactions are based on attempts again to forge vertical links in the organization. But this has proved to be very difficult. This paradoxical situation seems to have led to the opposite reaction: to attempts to weaken vertical links and strengthen horizontal coordination links. This strengthening of horizontal coordination links in the production sector, and the strengthening of the subjectivity of participants in economic life, have since then become two mutually connected directions of systemic reform changes in socialist economies. It is in these directions that it is meaningful to discuss a classification of reform strivings.

The most basic and rough classification of reform programs assumes the existence of three basic categories:

1. The first class includes such programs that represent only a change in the content of substantive planning in the super-organization. Thus this change is limited only to a re-assessment of central growth and structural (branch) strategies. The huge scope and detail of substantive planning does not, however, diminish. What is essential is that the whole system of procedural planning remains without change. Hence this is a 'non-reform', or a 'reform without reform'. In Czechoslovakia such a non-reform has occurred several times, for the first time in the period 1953-1955.

2. The second class of reforms includes a decrease in the scope and degree of detail in substantive planning in the super-organization. Part of the functions of substantive planning are transferred to sub-organizations. This change is accompanied by a reform in the system of procedural planning, especially by the intentional weakening of vertical coordination links and the strengthening of horizontal coordination links. But these are still intentional coordination activities within the super-organization. The close imitation of categories and links found in the functioning of the market are still only one item among the instruments in a system of procedural planning within the super-organization.

3. The third class of reforms represents an overcoming of the organizational

pattern in the production sector of the economy. Here the super-organization is replaced by another coordination system, i.e. the market. The super-organization disappears and the production sector is atomized into administratively independent agents-organizations. The whole system of substantive planning by the super-organization is broken up into the substantive planning of individual subjects-organizations. The system of procedural planning in the super-organization is replaced by the market. The central authority is changed from the central authority of the super-organization into an independent organization with its own substantive planning.

The economic mechanism becomes a mechanism for implementing ownership rights of economic agents.

Official reform programs in Czechoslovakia, including the present program, have not overstepped the boundaries of the second class of systemic reform. It is worth mentioning that in 1969 some drafts were developed for reform programs which aimed beyond the limits of the second class of reforms. Their aim was to overcome the organizational patterns found in the production sector of the economy, their replacement by the market and the process of subjectivization of economic activities connected with it. During the 1970s these drafts became the object of sharp ideological criticism.

The basic problem of the second class of reform programs is their lack of stability. The erosion of vertical links in super-organizations is replaced by a weak and ineffective imitation of market links and categories, without their real economic substance. Thus the coordination system is eroded and this is connected with increased disequilibrium, inflation and crisis. Regularly, a return to pre-reform systems occurs. Such returns take place either officially, by abandoning the reform program, or unofficially, by the implementation of shadow management systems under conditions where formally the reform measures are still valid. The first Czechoslovakian reform attempt in the period 1958-1962 was from the very beginning accompanied by the operation of a central shadow management system, which copied the pre-reform system. Thus *de jure* the economy was being reformed, but *de facto* it was unreformed. In 1962 the reform program was also abandoned *de jure*. The shadow management system was intensively used also during the reform attempt in the period 1967-1969 and during the validity of the so-called Set of Measures in the 1980s.

It is interesting to note that a weakening of vertical links in the present Czechoslovakian reform program is not achieved even as much as the weakening achieved in the reform program in 1958, not to mention the year 1966. In spite of the present negligible weakening, it will still probably lead to the intensive operation of a central shadow management system.

At the beginning of 1989 it is already beginning to become evident that even a minimum reduction in the administrative breakdown of the plan and the liberalization of some rules of horizontal coordination will lead to the disintegration of links between enterprises and to serious disorders in the economy. Under such conditions a return to the pre-reform system is very probable. In view of the fact that the official approach to the self-government of enterprises takes the form of a halfway measure, is formal and hence no barrier to the implementation of a central shadow management system, it is only to be expected that a return to the pre-reform system will occur, at least in the first stage, precisely in non-official, shadow centralized management structures.

Even if a return to the pre-reform system can overcome the most marked disorders in the coordination of production activities, it cannot lead to a reverse in the long-term trend of decreasing economic efficiency in Czechoslovakia. It thus appears that the more than thirty-year long pendulum movement of the Czechoslovakian economy between a reform objective and back again will continue also in the future.

The only viable solution to the problem of this pulsation of the economy towards reform and back to pre-reform, as well as the problem of the loss of performance of the Czechoslovakian economy, would be the drafting of a program aimed at 'reforming the present reform', i.e. the implementation of a third type of program.

Such a reform program, which would include the replacement of organizational forms of intentional coordination with a market structure and the creation of a structure of economic agents in the production sector of the economy on the basis of the diversification of ownership forms and the consistent introduction of self-government in state enterprises, has not, however, so far been the subject of official discussions in Czechoslovakia or of official program drafts.

Moreover, since 1987 Czechoslovakia has been rapidly losing its relatively advantageous conditions for the implementation of a reform program of the third type:

- there is a tendency towards deficits in the production and investment sectors, which are rapidly increasing;
- the debt in freely convertible currencies is again growing, while at the same time its potential positive effects (i.e. a decrease of existing deficits in the economy) are negated by an increase in the creditor status (in outstanding credits) of Czechoslovakia in relation to some developing and socialist countries; however, this creditor status cannot be solved in the short or intermediate term on the basis of suitable imports from the countries in question or by obtaining repayment in freely convertible currencies;
- after 18 years we are for the first time seeing global deficits on the consumer goods market;
- the organizational reform which has been carried out has increased the organizational concentration of Czechoslovakian industry and strengthened the totally monopolistic structure of the economy.

Jakov Sirotkovic

Planning of socio-economic development in socialist Yugoslavia

1987 marks the completion of the fortieth year of planning in socialist Yugoslavia. The first five-year plan was brought out in April 1947 for the period 1947-1951. It became the basic document of economic policy and played an extremely important role in mobilizing the available manpower and material resources of society to attain its ambitious goals of development.

The fundamental objectives of the first five-year plan were faster development for dealing with prevailing underdevelopment, strengthening the material basis of the country's independence and creating conditions for a constant raising of consumption and living standards of the people.

The basic tasks were formulated so as to eliminate economic and technical underdevelopment, to strengthen the economic and defence power of the country, to strengthen and develop the socialist sector of the national economy and new production relations which result, and to raise the general wealth of producers in all three sectors.

At this stage of development planning in Yugoslavia, because of the country's federal constitution, the role of the republics was already very important, both in making the federal plan and then in the simultaneous adoption of all six republic plans and their connection with federal plan.

In the first five-year plan of Yugoslavia the special task was to eliminate inequalities in the economic development of the republics. Connected and quantified with these were the tasks of industrial growth and investments, which were set higher than the Yugoslav average in case of the less developed republics (Bosnia-Herzegovina, Montenegro and Macedonia), and lower than average for the more developed republics (Croatia, Slovenia and Serbia).

In order to bring out and realise such a development plan, it was necessary to implement certain material and social prerequisites. Thus, the plan follows a successfully completed period of renovation in 1945-1946 and the creation of competent planning institutions.

We must also add that the basis of socialist production in Yugoslavia was already formed during the national liberation war, i.e. a well-organised socialist state with a strong state-owned sector, which soon became a crucial factor of development.

In 1946 the first law of planning institutions and planning was adopted, and on the basis of this the federal planning commission, planning commissions of national republics and planning institutions of other socio-political communities and economic enterprises, were constituted.

At the same time, as early as the beginning of 1947, the state-owned sector of the economy was strengthened rapidly, so that it became dominant in all parts of the economy (with the exception of agriculture only).

Such an organisational and material strengthening of the State on the one hand enabled a successful realisation of the five year plan; but on the other, it also started showing some major bureaucratic deformations, which sharpened the inner contradictions and posed a danger for the young socialist state. The idea of socialist self-management was thus born as a result of the quest for solutions.

Reliable support in this search came from the Marxist theory of economic development, the experiences of the Paris Commune, and from a critical analysis of development of socialism in the Soviet Union. Moreover, the most important cognition came from our own experiences during the revolution and at the beginning of the postwar development, where the key for success was the wider participation of the people in democratic national authorities, in developing various forms of self-help and self-organisation of the working people, as well as in different forms of self-management practices and control.

The first step toward implementing self-management as the basis of socio-economic system of socialist Yugoslavia, was the adoption of the 'Basic Law of Managing State-owned Economic Firms and Higher Economic Associations by Working Collectives' in the National Assembly of SFRY on 26, VI. 1950. Josip Broz Tito called it as a historical act, and while explaining said: 'Someone can think that this Law will be premature, that workers will not be able to surmount complicated techniques of managing enterprises and other firms. One who think so, is not right, and such an attitude would mean not to have trust in our workers, that would mean not to see the big creative force that this very management would develop among our workers, because this Law will open up the perspectives for the future of our workers, the future of our entire community.'

How deliberate the entrance was into the process of self-management transformation of society is obvious from the fact that already in 1949, on the basis of special decisions, worker's councils in a number of big firms were formed. This served as a reappraisal for the future solutions adopted by the general Law of 1950, on the basis of which were founded the worker's institutions of self-management in the entire country in 1950 and 1951.

About the theoretical basis, the clarity of objectives and firmness to make such a historical turn in the development of society the words of Boris Kidric are very clear:

'Standing firm on the positions of state (bureaucratic) socialism longer than necessary, as the 'first step' of the revolution, is inevitably connected with the growth, strengthening and privileging of the bureaucracy as society's parasite; with suppressing rather than with developing socialist democracy and with a general degeneration of the system, which at first stagnates, and then falls into degeneration of a special kind: the state socialism is assuming the character of the state capitalism of 'pure' type (without its own middle class, but with the almighty parasitic bureaucracy of a capitalistic nature). 'New' economic laws are now being discovered as a simple monopoly of the State's capitalist character. Building of a real socialist society requires development of a socialist democracy and a far reaching trans-formation of the state socialism into a free association of producers.'

At that time Boris Kidric was a leading theoretician and practician of Yugoslav planning. Therefore his views on the course of action are to be taken as fairly relevant in this context:

'In the beginning of transformation of state ownership into a national property under the management of direct producers, general planning is still in the competence of the state, while operational planning, due to its nature, passes into the competence of the direct producers, and the state keeps control only in the terms of maintaining plan proportions. However, this situation (of general planning almost completely within the hold of the state) cannot last too long, because it will, in this case, retain and strengthen the dangers of, on one side, the tendency of direct producers, contrary to planned proportions, to return entirely to the involuntary laws of commodity production, and on the other side, the tendency of the state apparatus to monopolize general planning.'

In that context Kidric was talking about the need for de-statization of general planning and gradual transformation of the planning institutions of general planning by the state institutions into mixed institutions with direct participation of delegates from direct production.

In the complex process of Yugoslavian socialist social development under the influence of the changing social relations on the basis of self-management, the system of planning was also changing. When we look at planning in the wider sense, i.e. as the sum of the social impact on economic development, then we can talk of the adaptation of planning to self-management as being continuous; but if we look at it as organisation and methods of such influence, then it was certainly lagging behind to the same extent as which the state functions in the economic field were behind self-management and were becoming a hurdle to its development.

The most important changes in the self-management transformation of Yugoslavian socialist society, which were both profound and revolutionary, took place in the first ten years 1951-1960, and manifested themselves in the constitution of an entirely new political and economic system, system of planning and of economic and development policies, which were all a logical consequence of the introduction of worker's management in economic enterprises, on the basis of the mentioned Law of 1950.

In 1953 the 'Constitutional Law About Elements of Social and Political System of FPRY and the Federal Institutions of the Government' was enacted, and so were the corresponding laws in the republics, which represented the qualitative changes in the constitutional system of 1946. The same year, on that basis, the representatives were elected to both councils of the Assembly, one of them being the 'Council of Producers'. The idea of constituting these councils was linked with the idea of transforming government institutions into self-management institutions at republican and federal levels.

That same year (1958) the 'General Law of National Boards', was adopted and was supposed to mark the beginning of the new communal system based on self-management. This moment was very important for the further development of the self-management system and for development planning, because it was the way to change the organisational forms of the higher associations of producers, as anticipated under the 'Basic Law' of 1950. Thus, the 'commune' was now supposed to take over this function. This problem was not solved satisfactorily neither then, nor later.

By 1954 the new economic system was established both in terms of organisation and of ways of managing the economy. The state's institutions and its apparatus were sharply reduced, and new forms of self-organisation were instituted both in the basic organisations and in business and professional associations. The Banks, Chambers of Commerce and the Product Exchanges were founded.

Instead of an all-powerful ministry, the Federal Planning Commission, Federal Institute for Planning – with sharply reduced functions and apparatus, subordinate to the Economic Council and entrusted with analytical and advisory work – was founded. 'Social plans' were introduced, which could be adopted separately or as part of the five-year plan.

Introduced were the new accounting system, distribution system, tax system, social insurance system, system of financing the budget – which was reduced significantly due to the switch to the system of investment credits. There was a change to market criteria of price formation, in association with the planned impact on the global relations between product and purchasing funds. A new system of foreign exchange and import-export trade was under way, which was also intended to bring them in line with market criteria.

Worker's councils as the basic self-management institutions in economic organisations thus gained a high degree of independence in business policy, and soon pressed for major changes in the global economic and development policy of the society. In this context, in 1956, the one-sided policy of capital formation was abandoned and a policy of balanced development was adopted during the five-year plan period of 1957-1961; and in 1958, the concept was incorporated into the entire ideological platform of the Programme of the League of Communists of Yugoslavia.

It is at this stage that one can speak of the establishment of the essential elements of socialist self-management as a new system of productive relationships, and say that some far-reaching results have been achieved in the democratisation of the society, in utilising its creative potential, in economic development and work productivity, in raising the standards of living of the people. These achievements have undoubtedly proved the superiority of socialist self-management compared to the preceding system. To this has contributed the fact that the five-year plan was fulfilled in four years i.e. by 1960, when such high rates of growth in production and living standards were attained that in international terms they were labelled the 'Yugoslav miracle' in history.

However, not everything was as satisfactory as it appeared at first. Greater difficulties appeared in the functioning of the market – inflation at home and external deficit – which were not envisaged by the plan. There was, especially at the end of the plan period, an explicit tendency towards a stronger central state regulatory role of the government once again, particularly in the fields of extended reproduction and of prices, i.e. in fields vital to the creation of the conditions for independent and rational behaviour of subjects in domestic and external markets.

A first attempt to revise the system and economic policy was made in the 1961-65 five-year plan period. It was soon clear that the plan was drawn up poorly in the professional and political sense. Once again, the willingness of socio-political forces to continue the process of self-management transformation of society was strengthened, which required a deep and critical examination of the past and new changes to follow. In the meantime, the five-year plan was already abandoned in 1962, and thus the policy now became yearly social plans.

It turned out that changes made in the political system, like the creation of producers' councils and the proclamation that the commune was a higher association of producers, did not in themselves secure progress in self-management simply by converting the functions of the state into self-management functions – until they were tied to an enlargement of the self-management rights of economic organisations to decide on the entire income and to act independently in the market.

The warning by Boris Kidric that the exclusive competence of the state should not continue too long, because of the danger of monopolisation of functions, turned out to be very realistic: it became clear that the above mentioned solutions in the political system were not very effective.

Such lessons were the starting point for drawing up the new SFRY Constitution, which was adopted in 1963. It contained a number of important innovations for the political system which laid the basis for the changes in economic system which took place in 1965 – the so-called reforms. These were the starting point for the new five-year plan of 1966-1970. This reform was introduced with the aim of transmitting the decision-making right of extended reproduction to working collectives, along with the strengthening of credit and market mechanisms. Connected with this, the material base of self-management was considerably strengthened in the intention to continue in the same way. Price relations in the domestic market were significantly changed, so too was the relationship between domestic and foreign market prices, with an overt orientation toward liberalization, i.e. free price determination according to market conditions.

Reform was not long-lasting: it failed its first serious test in 1967, the year of major world recession (as a matter of fact, the beginning of the crisis in the sense that it has lasted until today). It soon became evident that the changes introduced in the political and economic system were based on very unstable foundations, at least as far as self-management was concerned, and therefore the functions of state (planning included) were protected. Thus, planning in organisational and methodological terms was constantly adapted to the changing economic functions of the state, which meant that it was losing in its comprehensiveness along with the process of diminishing state functions. Since organisation and methods of planning of self-managing institutions in the society were not developing simultaneously, the directional and analytical basis of planning of socio-economic development, as a whole, was narrowed.

Once again, important changes in the political and economic system came with the Constitutional Amendments of 1971 and with the new Constitution of 1974. On this basis, a new Planning Law was enacted in 1976, which was supposed to enable a real incorporation of associated labour in the process of adoption and realization of the plan, on the assumption that self-managing decision-makers would attain their constitutionally established rights of decision by making over the whole process of reproduction.

The basic postulate of the 1974 Yugoslav Constitution states:

'The basis of our socialist society consists of social ownership of the means of production, which excludes the return to any system of human exploitation, and which, abolishing the alienation of the working class and working people from the means of production and other work conditions, assures workers' self-management in production and distribution of goods, and direction of society on the self-management basis.'

The essential novelty of the 1974 Constitution was the delegate system, which in our assembly system means the introduction of the 'Council of Associated Labour' in communes, republics and autonomous provinces. On the federal level, besides the 'Federal Council', the 'Council of Republics and Autonomous Provinces' was founded. The assumption was that such a mechanism would enable self-management decision-making at all social levels.

The Constitution also gave rise to changes in the planning system, the sense of which derives from the following formulation:

'Workers in basic and other organisations of associated labour, and working people in self-managing interest communities, local communities and other self-managing organisations and communities where they manage business and means of social production, have rights and duties that are based on scientific knowledge, on which are based judgements of possibilities, and by observing economic laws independently bring out their plans and programmes of work and also the programmes for the development of their organisations and communities, and that they adapt these to the social plans adopted by the socio-political communities and on that ground ensure coordination of relationships in overall social reproduction, in managing global material and social development in consonance with the common and self-management interests and aims.'

In further articles the Constitution sets out in detail the planning system in special sections containing articles on systems of general information, social accounting, records and statistics, which serve social planning directly:

'The socio-information system ensures the recording, collecting, processing and presenting of data and facts important for the follow-up, planning and directing of social development, and also is the diffusion and accessibility of these data and facts is assured.'

These articles of the 1974 Constitution were the basis for appropriate legislation, of which of particular importance is that relating to planning, i.e. the already mentioned planning law drawn up in 1976 together with the corresponding laws of the republics; and so is the Law of Associated Labour of 1976.

Although operational systemic legislation was not yet enacted during work on social plans for period 1976-1980, attempts were made to rely on this new approach, which in some cases gave very good results. This time too, it turned out that the carriers of self-management decisions were far more realistic planners then socio-political communities.

But since the changes in favour of associated labour were not made simultaneously, nor were the dominant positions of central governmental institutions abandoned in the sphere of extended reproduction and the price system, the interests of the state proved to be more powerful and aligned with bank capital.

Major transformations on the world economic scene at that time, accompanied by an inadequate domestic economic policy, reflected very unfavourably on the

Yugoslavian economic situation and also on its economic development. In such a situation the balance of power in the country enabled a further strengthening of central state regulations and a weakening of basic economic subjects. The rights of associated labour were essentially restricted, and its financial position deteriorated, particularly in the field of extended reproduction. With a high degree of debts and liabilities to procure the means for simple reproduction, this led organisations to sacrifice some of their traditional rights for the sake of free decision-making in the field of the distribution of income, and the administrative regulations were introduced again.

In the approach to the five-year plan 1981-1985 self-management was completely neglected, although this was in contradiction of the Constitution; and by some totally irrational logic of decision-making centres, a very unreal plan projection was made (the same as happened during the plans of 1961-1965), which collapsed in its second year of operation. Later, the plan was abandoned, and economic policy was guided by annual plans until the plan for the period 1986-1990 was adopted, the realisation of which is in progress, but with much worse results than anticipated.

This situation has imposed the need for reexamination of the political and economic system, so that adequate changes are now taking place (on the basis of constitutional amendments), which should be completed during 1988.

Marjan Senjur

The role of planning in the process of structural adjustment in Yugoslavia 1988-1989

During the 1980s Yugoslavia has sunk into deep economic and social crisis which requires economic and political reform and a new look at the economy, economic development and the role of planning. The aim of this paper is to point out some approaches to the problem of structural adjustment in a reforming socialist country under the pressure of overall crisis.

1. Stabilization (anti-inflation) programme: Yugoslavia, May 1988

As can be seen from Table 1, Yugoslavia has a rather high rate of inflation. Inflation is a consequence of deep-rooted economic problems and also aggravates existing and new economic problems. Inflation is problem number one to be solved: no other economic problem can be solved without the prior solving of inflation.

The Yugoslavian anti-inflationary programme which the country accepted with the collaboration of IMF in May 1988, was directed toward three goals:

1. reduction of inflation,
2. improvement of balance of payments, and
3. revival of economic growth.

These three different goals were to be achieved by a combination of different measures.

1. The temporary control of prices and permanent control of wages in order to create antiinflationary expectations.
2. Restriction of all kinds of demand. This should be achieved by setting nominal anchors.

117

Table 1. Movements of prices (yearly rates of growth)

Year	Yearly rates of growth			Interest rates
	prices of consumer goods (1)	exchange rates (2)	wages (3)	(4)
1976	-	-	-	
1977	14.5	1.2	16.7	6.0
1978	13.6	0.9	21.4	6.0
1979	21.3	3.0	20.6	6.0
1980	29.9	52.9	22.0	6.0
1981	39.8	66.1	37.0	6.0
1982	31.5	41.6	27.7	14.0
1983	40.2	90.9	27.4	30.0
1984	54.7	57.8	45.3	47.0
1985	72.3	65.5	77.2	61.0
1986	89.8	62.8	104.9	56.0
1987	215.6			

(1) Yearly rates of growth of prices of consumer goods, based on consumer price indexes, year 1980 = 100.
(2) Yearly rates of growth of exchange rate in YUD per 1 USD.
(3) Yearly rates of growth of personal incomes.
(4) Nominal discount interest rate.

Source: IMF, International Financial Statistics, 4/1988, 4/1984.

The need for a significant reduction in aggregate demand stems from two reasons.

The stagnation of production, the transition from deficit to surplus in the balance of payments, and servicing foreign debt caused a curtailment of disposable aggregate supply, which required an appropriate reduction in aggregate demand.

The second reason for curtailing aggregate demand is much more important, and essential for the type of the economy Yugoslavia has had in the past. Throughout the last 40 years, a policy of excess demand has caused a sense of shortage in the economy. A shortage economy protected producers; they did not have to worry about market, buyers, quality of products, efficiency of production. Because of excess demand they were able to sell everything and cover all costs, regardless of efficiency. On the other hand, a shortage economy enabled and justified the administrative regulation of the economy. Since prices were not allowed to adjust to the situation of excess demand, administrative rationing and regulation of the state was required – the so called fixprice mechanism.

Yugoslavia has abandoned to a great extent administrative, fixprice, regulation and freed prices. Because of the prevailing conditions of excess demand, the transition from the fixprice to the flexprice mechanism of economic regulation manifested itself in higher prices and inflation. It was necessary to cut excess demand in order to equilibrate aggregate supply and demand and thus stabilize prices in order to enable the operation of the flexible-price economic mechanism.

The elimination of excess demand in Yugoslavia is not just an act of short term economic policy as in other market economies. It is a major economic reform which must essentially change the economic conditions of producers.

3. Other measures could be labelled as measures of supply-side economics and which should stimulate the rate of economic growth.

The liberalization of product prices should improve the allocation of resources and enable the adjustment of relative prices to new conditions of newly readjusted macro-aggregates.

A market influenced rate of foreign exchange was expected to play an important role.

Table 2. Growth rates of export and import; balance of trade and current accounts

(original data in USD)

Year	Export (1)	Import (2)	Balance of payment (3)	Balance of trade (4)
1976	-	-	-	-1 963
1977	6.1	32.9	-1 346	-3 786
1978	11.9	6.6	-1 284	-3 764
1979	17.0	34.3	-3 665	-6 061
1980	32.1	7.5	-2 216	-4 836
1981	15.4	-2.1	-958	-3 165
1982	0.9	-7.7	-475	-2 024
1983	-5.2	-10.7	275	-1 231
1984	2.2	-2.0	478	-789
1985	4.8	2.6	833	-588
1986	4.3	5.1	1 100	-702

(1)   Rates of growth of export of goods.
(2)   Rates of growth of import of goods.
(3)   Balance of current accounts in millions of USD.
(4)   Balance of trade in millions of USD.

Source: IMF, International Financial Statistics, 4/1988, 12/1984.

So-called real valuation of factors of production: labour and capital. The rate of interest should be on the level of real positive rate. Wages should be controlled, but ought to reflect the situations on the labour market.

The liberalization of economic activities should contribute to higher rate of growth. The May 1988 programme was in this respect restricted to the liberalization of imports. Other fields of liberalization, which were considered as measures for structural adjustment, were not touched at all. A change in the Yugoslavian constitution and the prevailing economic system is required in order for it to be possible to execute all measures of structural adjustment.

4. In this latest approach the IMF supports the thesis that anti-inflationary programmes which predominantly reduce aggregate demand, and therefore restrict economic growth, should be accompanied by structural adjustment (SA) programmes aimed at reviving the rate of economic growth.

In this regard, two measures were accepted in the Yugoslavian May 1988 programme.

Imports should be more liberalized. There are many arguments for this measure; the most important, however, is the one which stresses the need for increased imports of raw materials in investment goods in order to enable higher production. The restriction of imports in the past was a major factor in the restricted growth of production.

The second measure, also in support of increased imports, was the decision by the IMF that Yugoslavia be allowed to reprogram her foreign loans in order to reduce the burden of servicing foreign loans (lowering the debt service ratio). Yugoslavia was also allowed to raise additional foreign loans in order to enable domestic production to be increased.

It is a very frequently expressed opinion in Yugoslavia that inflation should be reduced by greater aggregate supply and not by lower aggregate demand. That is wishful thinking. Growth of production has, in the Yugoslavian circumstances of over 200 per cent inflation, very little impact on the reduction of inflation. It has another impact. Economic growth enables improvement of living standards, reduces pessimism in the economy and improves positive expectations. In such circumstances it is easier to accept austerity measures required to reduce inflation.

The dilemma is not anti-inflation or growth; the question is whether it is possible to stimulate economic growth without inducing additional inflation.

The measures for improving the flexibility and motivation of the economy are meant to be such. They stimulate economic activity without inducing inflation with additional increases of aggregate demand.

That is the reason why Yugoslavia needs to combine measures for the stabilization of prices with measures for structural adjustment. An additional problem in Yugoslavia lies in the fact that effective measures of SA require a previous, rather radical economic reform.

2. The evolution in the concept of structural change

The policy of restructuring of the economy based on the priority sectors

The development strategy of Yugoslavia in the period 1971-1985 was to give priority treatment to the production of raw materials, energy and food. Priority treatment was also given to some manufacturing sectors.

These development priorities turned out to be too numerous and mistaken.

On the basis of the data provided by the Federal Bureau for Social Planning I have grouped industrial sectors into two groups. [1]

The first group includes the five biggest industrial sectors which in 1985 had a higher share of industrial investment that their respective share of industrial production. The second group includes the six biggest industrial sectors with had a higher share of industrial production than their respective share of industrial investment. These were priority sectors.

The five sectors of the first group take 61.1% of all industrial investment and contribute only 25.4% of all industrial production. The average capital output ratio for the first group is extremely high: 7.7.

It is the opposite case with the second group of sectors. Six industrial sectors take only 25.6% of all industrial investment and contribute 43.9% of all industrial production. These sectors, which are underinvested, have a considerably lower capital output ratio: on the level of 1.55.

Table 3. The structure of industrial production and investment in Yugoslavia, year 1985, in percentages

(prices 1972)

Sector	structure		average capital output ratio
	investment	production	
Industry and mining	100	100	3.1
I. group			
Energy production	22.3	7.3	13.4
Coal production	10.1	2.6	3.7
Iron metallurgy	10.4	5.3	5.3
Production of chemicals	11.0	4.5	5.1
Production of foodproducts	7.3	6.9	3.2
Altogether I.group	61.1	25.4	7.7
II.group			
Metal manufacturing	4.6	8.4	1.1
Machine manufacturing	3.4	6.7	1.5
Production of electric engines and equipment	3.5	6.4	1.2
Chemical manufacturing	3.5	5.5	1.8
Woodworking industry	3.5	5.7	2.2
Textile industry	7.1	11.2	1.6
Altogether II.group	25.6	43.9	1.55

The structure of Yugoslavian investment is an obvious problem. It seems to be a conscious strategy to overinvest in capital intensive and low investment efficiency sectors. This seems to be the result of the strategy of priority sectors.

Table 4. The growth of social product: in constant and current prices

Year	Social product prices 1980 (1)	Social product current prices (1)
1976	-	-
1977	7.9	22.2
1978	7.1	24.2
1979	6.9	29.2
1980	2.4	33.2
1981	1.3	42.2
1982	0.6	32.4
1983	1.0	39.6
1984	1.9	62.9
1985	0.5	79.6
1986	3.6	109.9

(1) Yearly rates of growth of social product in constant prices.
(2) Yearly rates of growth of social product in current prices.

Source : IMF, International Financial Statistics, 4/1988, 12/1984.

The facts as illustrated by the figures in Tables 3 and 4, and severe economic stagnation in the 1980s, led Yugoslavia to the point of reconsidering existing development strategy. The strategy of priority sectors is about to be abandoned.

The policy of changing economic structure based on the priority projects

The new idea on the federal Yugoslavian level, presented by the Federal Bureau of Social Planning, is to switch from the sectoral approach to the project approach.[2] The major concept behind the new development strategy is "project", contrary to the previous concept of "sector". One is looking after priority sectors.

The content of the new policy of structural change in Yugoslavia is a reorientation toward development-export oriented concepts: exports are considered to be a major factor in accelerating development.

The programmes and projects are offered and then should be evaluated through investment criteria in order to ensure social and entrepreneurial economic efficiency for the projects. The best projects would be chosen.

One has to admit that project approach is an improvement compared with the sectoral approach of development strategy. However, one should be aware of the fact that even a project approach is already a little outdated. It is not aimed at the major problem of development of less developed countries and of Yugoslavia.

The project approach assumes that projects are available in sufficient number and quality. One needs only to select the best ones – with the criteria at hand – and put them to realization. However, it seems to me that an even more important problem in LDCs, including Yugoslavia, is the lack of projects, both in quantity and in quality. There are simply not enough projects available. There is no point in stressing sophisticated procedures for selection of projects when projects are not available.

Bearing this in mind, a development strategy should reorient its attention and endeavour to uncover projects, to stimulate and support activities which create and produce projects. Such a new approach is a task for the policy of structural adjustment.

The need for new approaches is also illustrated by Table 5. In the year 1989 we can simply state that planned or projected indicators by the end of the present planning period 1986-90 will not be achieved. Planning in the old way is simply useless. New approaches and new ways have to be applied.

Table 5. Performance indicators of the projection of development of Yugoslavia

(yearly rates of growth in per cent, 1985 prices)

	Actual 1981-85 (1)	Plan 1986-90 (2)
Social product, total economy	1.1	4.0
- Industry	2.9	4.5
- Agriculture	2.6	5.0
Disposable product	1.5	3.7
Employment	2.4	2.0
Productivity of labour	-1.5	2.0
Personal incomes per worker, real terms	-5.5	2.0
Export of goods and services	0.6	6.0
Import of goods and services	-6.2	5.0
Gross investment in fixed assets	-6.6	3.6
Standard of living	-4.2	3.2

(1) Actual indicators in the period 1981-1989.

(2) Planned indicators for the period 1986-1990.

Source: Druzbeni plan Jugoslavije za obdoje 1986-1990, *Uradni list SFRJ*, 75/1985.

3. The policy of structural adjustment

The policy of structural adjustment is a concept which encompasses and binds together short-run economic policy and longer-run developmental policy. Experience has shown that it is not enough to build only new capacities; the problem of equal, if not even of greater, magnitude is the use of disposable capacities. For this reason it is necessary to use simultaneously the instruments of economic policy (which are instruments affecting aggregate demand), the instruments of supply side economics (which centre on strengthening economic motivation), and also the instruments of development policy –which are predominantly instruments of investment policy and changes in economic structure, both from the point of view of structure of production as the structure of economic institutions.

We shall elaborate ideas of policy of SA for the case of Yugoslavia. We shall discuss what new orientations are needed in the field of development policy, and the stabilization programme of Yugoslavia in 1988-1989 in a broader framework of policy of structural adjustment.

1. The policy of SA should enhance flexibility and adaptability of the economy and its structure. The policy of SA should increase the motivation of all economic subjects for economic achievements. And the policy of SA should directly and indirectly stimulate economic growth, both in terms of the rate of growth and in terms of its structure.

One of the first preconditions for the economy to be become more adaptable and able to adjust, is the requirement of being freed from the limitations of many laws and other regulations. Liberalization and deregulation of economic activity is one of the preconditions for greater flexibility of the economy.

Flexibility of the economy requires a diversity of producers, by which is meant diversity of producers in terms of various sizes of producer unit. There should be a complementary structure of enterprises in term of size: small enterprises and bigger ones. Yugoslavia needs more small enterprises. By diversity is also meant the diversity of producer activities. In a small economy a high degree of specialization is neither possible nor desirable. What is important is to be active in various businesses, in different fields. This enables the economy to create, to preserve and to enrich different skills and capabilities with learning by doing.

Table 6. Small scale economy in Yugoslavia
(year 1986)

	Workers	*Social product*	*Workers per production unit*
Share of small scale economy in total economy (per cent)	8	6	
Structure of small scale economy:			
Total small scale economy	100	100	2.4
Social sector of SSE	34	46	86.2
Private sector of SSE	66	54	1.5

Source: Statisticni godisnjak Jugoslavije, 1988.

The diversity of production activities also means and requires changes in such diversity. Ideas and products and processes originate, they either establish themselves or not, and they then all either die away (wither away) or not. This process is under way in existing enterprises. However, it is not enough: it is necessary to stimulate and to open opportunities for the creation of new enterprises. New enterprises spring up (come into being) through new products, or new technology, or not: they come into being as competition against old enterprises by providing more efficient work.

This changing diversity requires the founding of new enterprises, but also the withering away of old, less efficient and less successful ones. The dying off of inefficient enterprises is an important part of structural adjustment.

In the socialist sector of the economy there has been practically no entry and exit of firms, and the growth of the firms has been mainly achieved through the expansion of existing firms. New firms, if created, are invariably of medium and large size. This industrial structure is incompatible with the operation of efficient markets. The future development of a market economy will require radical changes in the industrial structure of the economy. Such a process is always painful from the social and political point of view. But the activities of social policy, reeducation of workers, reemployment should be an important part of the policy of SA.

The need for flexibility and adaptability requires innovations in the Schumpeterian sense, and entrepreneurship as a vehicle for innovations in business.

The economy has to be open to the outside: outward-looking. International trade helps to improve the production structure and therefore helps to improve the flexibility and adaptability of the economy. On the other hand, international trade means a presence in the world, it registers the changes in the world; and international trade is a vehicle, a channel, for transferring changes from abroad into the domestic economy and at the same time for conveying domestic achievements into the world.

Table 7. Rates of growth of GDP, export and import

	1953-65	1972-80	1980-88
GDP growth	7.9	5.6	0.5
Export growth	12.7	3.6	1.9
Import growth	8.6	4.8	-5.3

Yugoslavian economic strategy was outward looking in the period 1953-65 and inward looking in period after 1972. An outward looking-strategy has to be promoted. However, this should not mean that such strategy only means export promotion. A strategy of an open economy means higher export and import shares.

Export promotion and import substitution are two complementary strategies, each with its own function: they are not two substitutable, competitive strategies. The basic strategy has to be one of an open economy; the strategy of export promotion is a too narrow concept. The reason for import substitution is that in LDSs there is a lack of projects. The most natural way to find a project for production is to raise production of imported goods which already have a market and a known technology. Import substitution should be regarded as a program of possible projects; it is a program of developing projects by imitation.

2. The idea of increasing motivation for economic achievements in Yugoslav circumstances means that economic subjects should to be enterprises working in a market environment, and which are self-dependent and striving for maximization of profit.

Increasing economic motivation also requires a wise state or government policy which does not overburden enterprises with taxes. Any reform of the tax system should explicitly strive for a goal of not impairing, but improving, motivation for economic success.

Competitiveness among producers, products, ideas and production and marketing methods is an important aspect of increasing motivation. The creation or maintenance of a competitive environment is especially important for a small country. In this sense openness toward outside is important, because a small-scale economy is too small to provide the necessary competitiveness within the national economy alone.

Privatisation is an important aspect of SA. The problem is of course a socio-political and economic one. From the point of view of economic rationality it is advantageous that the same subject should be responsible for decision making, benefit from economic decisions and also bears the cost of those decisions.

The society looks for such organizational and property right forms which enable the integration of decision making, the bearing of benefits and decision cost by the same economic subject. The whole world is looking for the best institutions in this regard.

Private property is one such property right which enables fulfilment of the requirements that we have defined. The present-day process of privatisation throughout the world therefore has the economic function of increasing economic efficiency by strengthening the motivation for economic success. The process of privatisation is also needed in Yugoslavia, in which context we could talk about two aspects of privatisation.

Direct privatisation means that a greater role and share in the economy should be given to private property relation, to private capital, and to private initiative on that basis. The expansion of small-scale economic activities is the process in this framework.

The share of workers employed in social sector in the total active population increased in Yugoslavia from 23% in year 1953 to 59% in 1981. Paid employment (outside agriculture) was almost negligible. In the period 1974-86, only a few years ago, such a result would have been praised; nowadays it is a matter for concern. There is now much talk of the strengthening of the private sector in order to increase the efficiency of the economy and to stimulate economic development.

However, this is not enough. Since the majority of so-called means of production (capital) is social property and there is no intention to denationalize (privatize) them, some kind of implicit privatisation of social property is required. That would mean that the formal owner of the capital is still society, but that the economic owner is the enterprise. The enterprise economically owns the capital and independently takes all relevant economic decisions, and it bears the benefits and costs of its decisions and activities.

3. The traditional approach to structural and development policy *was based on investment policy* by supporting investment and its guidance (orientation). Austria, for example, had a very well-developed system of investment support (Investionsfoerderung, e.g. Top Investment Action). Although Yugoslavia always wanted to achieve such a system properly and actively, she was unsuccessful, as we have already seen.

This kind of approach to development policy is now being questioned. The Government should not intervene in investment decisions of market oriented economic subjects, but help to create a economically stimulating environment for investment activity.

The Government should, however, actively pursue a process of disinvestment when the production factors are to be moved out of present, and inefficient, economic activity. A lot of economic, social and political problems are involved in disinvestment, and the Government should help this process to proceed more smoothly and less painfully.

Development policy should stimulate savings and the inflow of foreign direct investment in various forms. Of importance here are the policy of interest rates, the development of institutions and instruments of financial intermediation, and financial markets.

The Government should not explicitly determine guidelines for structural adjustment in terms of economic sectors. It should take care, however, over the development of the economic and social infrastructure. In spite of our position against the Government's sectoral approach to the policy of structural change, we do agree that certain sectors need special care and support. The energy sector and agriculture are two sectors which should not be left entirely to market forces, although their products are market products.

The government should be sufficiently well organized and capable to be able to follow and analyze the developmental changes in the world and in the domestic economy and give well-founded opinions, forecasts and analyses about trends in development. Such analyses and forecasts would be then available to the economic subjects for their entrepreneurial decisions.

References

[1] *Savezni zavod za drustveno planiranje: Analiza i ocena stanja privredne strukture Jugoslavije,* Beograd, February 1988.
[2] *Savezni zavod za drustveno planiranje, Osnove politike promena privredne strukture Jugoslavije,* Beograd, March 1988.

PART IV
PLANNING IN CAPITALIST AND MIXED ECONOMIES

György Tényi

Socio-economic roots of the French planning

It seems that interest has focused particularly on French-style planning on two occasions: in the 1960s as a result of the success (and renewal) of such planning, and in the early 1980s, when signs of its decline became undeniable.

The notion of planning first emerged in France in the 1930s under the pressure of the Great Depression. Unemployment and recession convinced politicians, union leaders and enterprise heads of the necessity for planning to remedy the anomalies caused by the free market.

Several tendencies may be distinguished among the forces striving for reform of the market economy:

- Left-wing socialists backed planning as a means to achieve a peaceful transition to socialism;
- There were some who accepted the idea of planning as a technical support for increasing productivity;
- The economic government of the Vichy Regime combined corporatist and technocratic-planning tendencies in a controversial manner. Although institutions of the Regime primarily served the war economy, they also included the possibility of long-term planning.

The Government's traditional role and the planning

The traditional interventionism of the French state might be thought of as a straightforward explanation for the emergence of planning (cf. Shonfield, 1965). Indeed, French history abounds with episodes of governmental intervention. However, this reasoning does not discriminate among various sorts of governmental intervention in the economic sphere, from price control to nationalization. Moreover, it ignores the fact that several periods of liberalism can be found, and also that state intervention has often lacked inner coherence, indeed has often failed.

Traditionally, the great importance of the Finance Ministry has hindered rather than helped the breakthrough to planning. Being responsible for financial orthodoxy, the Ministry draws up the yearly estimates, which more or less coincide with the priorities formulated in the long-range plan.

One cannot find front-line fighters of planning in other bodies of the traditional French state apparatus. It is significant that J. de Monnet, one of the founding fathers of planning and first Commissioner, insisted on reporting directly to the Prime Minister, bypassing intermediate levels of the hierarchy.

In the traditional forms of state intervention, therefore, it is very difficult to recognize the source of an obligation and commitment to planning. Paradoxically it would be possible to reverse this reasoning, and to state that the French planning came into existence in spite of earlier state interventions. More generally: the creation of a separate planning authority is a sign of the end of the illusion of an homogeneous, deliberately acting state which creates the inner harmony of its organs (Delorme-André, 1983).

Corporate capital and planning

Industrialists as a group had lost much of their social and political authority. Leading capitalists were compromised by their collaboration with the Vichy Regime, petty capitalists were condemned – sometimes excessively – for Malthusianism and incompetence. There was an attempt to codify retaliation against 'illegal profits' and 'economic sabotage'. Because industrialists' organizations had lost face and (in consequence of nationalization) important supporters, they had no say in it.

Although their loss of influence proved to be only temporary, the industrial capitalists were not able to elaborate any feasible alternative to the development project suggested by the modernists. One of main factors in explanation of the absence of alternatives was the traditional role and situation of the banks in this period. The most important deposit banks were nationalized in 1945, giving the government instruments with which to control the financing of business banks. Moreover, the latter traditionally did not share in industrial risks, but restricted themselves to the role of 'prudent lenders', who made their lending activity dependent on government guarantees and bonification. This situation contrasted sharply with the behaviour of, for example, the German banks, which invested heavily in industrial enterprises and participated in decisions on industrial strategy.

The attitude of enterprise owners to the plan was ambiguous, with mixed approval and criticism. This depended upon whether the advantages of a protected internal market and sharing risk with the state predominated over disadvantages of limitations, or whether they did not (Balassa, 1979).

Manning: a modernist project

A common feature to all analysis of French planning is the link between the implementation of planning and the appearance on the stage of a new generation striving to rationalize the economy. However, this new generation is able to play a significant role only if it can be part of more comprehensive social change.

Obviously, every change is initiated by small groups. Change cannot be implemented without reaching a consensus among planners, representatives of

132

economic policy, managers of great public and private enterprises and union leaders. The numbers of active participants in the planning process can amount to 1,000-1,500 persons. However a great many enterprises are informed about prospectives drafted in the plans through professional organizations. A survey in 1967 (cf. Carre, Dubois and Malinvaud, 1972) made it possible to monitor the spread of this information and to assess its utility from the point of view of enterprises. It was no surprise that the influence of prognoses increases with the size of the enterprise. Nevertheless, two-thirds of small enterprises reported that their production and investment decisions were influenced by plans. This suggests a relatively important role of planning. The explanation may be found in the technical competence of planners, the development of economic statistics and the sophistication of macroeconomic modelling.

Finding a common language entails a scientific rationalism accepted by all actors. Planners, top- and middle-level cadres of the private and public sector share a common professional credo, by which a strong connection is set up between organizing and economic growth. This not only relates to personal political choices. These bodies organize the work of others at different levels. Appreciation of this organizing function is accompanied by an increase in the relative autonomy of top and middle-level cadres. This autonomy in turn is based on the use of newly-developed scientific decision criteria in the production process. Engineering methods of production organizing had been integrated into a global idea of human society. In this sense we can speak of a 'new industrial ideology' (Boltansky, 1980).

Modernism and Keynesianism

A striking symptom of the expansion of the modernist way of thinking can be identified in the profound impact of the American economy on the management of French public and private enterprises in the 1950s. Obviously, French cadres were attracted not only by the high level of productivity in American industry, but by the new type of industrial and, more generally, social relations accompanying it. Participants in the 2,500 'missions of productivity' organized to the United States (50,000 people between 1950 and 1953) were interested in rationalizing social relations as a whole.

An excellent French analysis (Boyer, 1985) points out that, in the ideological synthesis underlying the acceptance of French planning, the influence of two facets of Keynesianism can be recognized – apart from the above mentioned modernism. First, at the core of the most radical Keynesian writings one finds a central theme presented as a matter of fact and as a theoretical conclusion: namely, that pure market mechanisms are unable to maintain full employment and, more generally, growth and stability. To counter these imbalances, in his *General Theory* Keynes proposed a series of reforms in some key areas:
- progressive taxation and social services to reduce the savings of the rich and increase the consumption of the poor;
- centralized control over the monetary system to provide an adequate stimulus to investment;
- if necessary, direct governmental influence on investment through public works or control over private investment;

- public provision and dissemination of data relevant to business decisions. This can be conceived as a kind of socialization in expectation-formation or indicative planning.

At the other end of the Keynesian spectrum stands the so called 'effective demand' version of Keynesianism, which leads to somewhat more restricted conceptions of economic policy. First, state intervention should aim at maintaining full employment, whatever the transitory effects of such a policy upon the balance of public expenditures and receipts and the purchasing power of money may be. Second, fiscal and monetary instruments must be used for demand management, when effective demand is less than enough to support full employment; or restrictive policies, as soon as excessive demand triggers an inflationary process. Through such 'fine-tuning policies', business cycles could be reduced both in duration and amplitude, growth stimulated, and budgets balanced over the course of cycles.

After the war, the main objective in France was the reconstruction and modernization of the productive sector in the face of a huge increase in consumer demand. Of crucial importance in this early period was the direct allocation of credit, equipment goods and raw materials in order to promote balanced growth in the key sectors (coal, steel, cement, electrical energy).

At this stage French technocrats were more fundamentalist than 'effective demand' oriented. Growth as a mercurial process, potentially subject either to cumulative depression or explosive inflation, was the dominant idea during the 1950s. The aim was radical transformation of the institutions inherited from nineteenth-century capitalism in order to promote mass consumption and the socialization of a large part of investment. After the 'liberation' the common objective of various groups allied in power was to avoid a repetition of the catastrophic interwar period, when the diffusion of new technologies and products, scientific management methods, and a more modern way of life had been blocked.

In this situation of excess demand, external imbalances and quasi-full employment, the General Theory had little to say. Effective demand management was the complement, not the core of this strategy. But later on, during the 1960s, economists and civil servants seemed to refer more and more to a restricted Keynesianism, even if the modernist-reformist-Keynesian approach was still present in medium-term strategy expressed by the CGP (Boyer, 1985).

An important factor in understanding the success of modernist Keynesian policy was the wide acceptance in France of a new social-democratic accord. Support – if only tacit – for the objective of modernization came from workers and unions previously strongly opposed to Taylorian methods. Wage earners were content to restrict themselves to bargaining for their share of the 'dividend of growth'; they left the methods of obtaining productivity increases to management.

As a result of these changes, the majority of workers was able to develop new forms of mass consumption. Thus the circuit of investment-production-employment-consumption was closed in a very growth-dynamic mode.

First plans and policies

During the period of the first plans, potential demand was very vigorous, both in final consumption and in productive investment. The main task of economic policy was the reconstruction of the productive apparatus by eliminating bottlenecks, securing a high investment ratio and correspondingly high profits (see e.g. Boyer, 1981). Most macroeconomic analyses considered the inadequacy of the productive apparatus to be the dominant constraint on development. The representative theoretical models reflecting this type of economic conditions and policy are the input-output and the von Neumann models.

But from the second half of the 1950s onwards, new barriers imposed restrictions on growth. First, growth of production had increasingly to be distinguished from that of productive capacities, because after relieving bottlenecks, full utilization of the capacities was no longer guaranteed. Second, instead of a simple increase in productive capacities, productivity gain became of prime importance. Third, the fight for income distribution intensified and influenced inflation and the growth rate in a decisive manner.

Accordingly, analyses laying the foundation of plans were increasingly focussed on the problem of how macroeconomic policy could correct deflationary (overheated) investment decisions, conditions on foreign markets or inadequate income distribution.

Up to the end of 1950s the French economy was a relatively closed one, in the sense that imports were practically restricted to goods which could not be produced – or not in sufficient quantity – by home enterprises, and exports to a quantity sufficient to pay for imports. Because of the structural weakness of the French export sector and a strong dependence on imported investment goods, in periods of expansion imports increased rapidly and export growth slowed down, long before full employment was reached. From the 1950s onwards the French economy tended to behave in a way similar to the British 'stop-go' pattern: periods of rapid expansion were interrupted by cumulative deficit in the balance of payments (e.g. in 1952, 1956 and 1963), and stabilization periods (in the wake of the expansion periods) more or less managed to restore the foreign competitiveness of the French industry.

A second barrier that the expansion of production came up against was an income distribution unsuited to the necessary structural adjustments. If the income distribution shifted excessively in favour of wages, the self-financing capacity of enterprises deteriorated. Hence, in the 2nd and even more in the 3rd plan, subsequent stabilization measures made their appearance.

After the Fifth Republic was established, planning became important once again. De Gaulle came to office in 1959 with firm ideas on foreign policy and national renewal, but he was willing to let the planners influence the details of economic and social priorities in a way that does not seem to have been repeated since (Estrin-Holmes, 1983). Planners were given the widest scope under the 4th plan to formulate a set of national priorities. The Government took on the 'ardent obligation' of increasing expenditure on welfare services and social infrastructure.

The heyday of planning

We have followed the history of French planning up to the mid-1960s. At this point the chronological order is broken in a somewhat arbitrary way. I use the term 'arbitrary', because modifications in the socio-economic conditions leading to a change in the importance of planning cannot be linked to a definite point in time. Our reason is that from this culminating point of planning we can obtain a general overview of the activities and relationships of protagonists in both the previous and following periods.

Even in the early years, when production targets were defined for individual industries, it was never expected that these would be implemented using Soviet-type administrative methods. The original intention was that state intervention should take place whenever important objectives were not being achieved spontaneously as a result of the information dissemination activities of the planners.

The CGP has never had direct executive power – if we disregard its role in the allocation of Marshall aid. Its function has been that of the Walrasian 'auctioneer', acting as an information agent in the course of plan-making. In a subsequent period, however, it may strive to convince at the very most those responsible for implementing planning decisions. The budget funds of the CGP only serve to finance its organizational and research activities. Founded in 1946 as a quasi-autonomous non-ministerial body, its influence has always depended on the personal prestige of its collaborators and, above all, of the Commissioner.

The CGP was always effectively dependent on the Ministry of Finance, with whom it had an uneasy relationship. Some authors suggest that there was fairly close collaboration during the 1950s, although during the 1960s, the Finance Ministry did all it could to clip of wings of the CGP. It is characteristic of the modification of power relations, that by the mid-1960s, while there had been only three Planning Commissaires, there had been twenty-two Finance Ministers. Henceforth, however, the situation pratically reversed: the CGP was under the almost constant control of V. Giscard d'Estaing – first as Finance Minister, then as a President – while after P. Massé's departure in 1966 there was a series of less distinguished individuals as Commissaires in quick succession. As Estrin and Holmes put it: 'Up to time of Massé, the Commissaire's position had retained a certain political neutrality, as well as some autonomy, but later conservative governments sought to turn the Commissaire into a rather minor functionary of government' (Estrin-Holmes, 1983).

First signs of the decline of planning

In the first period (before the mid-1960s) the emphasis was on mid-term development plans, and short-term stabilization programs (1952, 1956, 1963) were only necessary complements used to keep inflation under control. In the second period, on the contrary, equilibrium considerations played the prominent role. For example, the 5th plan concentrated on the battle against inflation (and in this field the CGP could not compete with the Finance Ministry), the reduced developmental and intervention programs were given the task of alleviating the adverse effects of stabilization.

Another factor that pushed the CGP in the background was a gradual shift in the coordination of industrial policy (and financing) from the CGP to the Ministry of Industry. Moreover, so-called 'modernization committees' which contributed to the preparation of plans had ceased to be the main channel for consultation between the government and industry, and this organizational role of the CGP was assigned to the Ministry of Industry.

To counter their loss of importance, the planners tried to extend their activities to the sphere of macroeconomy – since in general the centre of gravity of government had moved to this area. With the growing sophistication of their analytical tools, the planners could forecast not only state investments, but also global government expenditure by disaggregated budgetary categories. But because of the weakened power status of the CGP, these were only forecasts and had no normative status.

Further, what remained of the former activities was the planning of specific governmental programs, which kept some of their former importance although their volume had been curtailed in the course of the time. The 6th plan, for example, contained six 'priority action programs' of this kind, which were small governmental expenditure commitments actually worked out at an operational level. Even these programs, in fact, ultimately depended on the annual budget for funds, but in practice they could not be easily ignored.

Causes of the decline in the planning

Industrialists regained both more diversified and independent financing opportunities and their previous autonomy in decision-making on production and investment matters. Industrial relations were normalized, employers and workers became more willing to settle labour disputes. The internal organization of large-scale enterprises greatly improved.

One wonders if this represents a failure or success for planning.

The underlying aim of certain elements of the planist coalition was the establishment of a healthy capitalist market economy with free trade and with unnecessary or very restricted intervention. In a sense, then, the decline of planning could simply be regarded as the successful completion of the original task of reconstruction.

I have mentioned that the French economy was rather closed up to the early 1960s. From then on, however, the behaviour of France changed, first for political considerations (the government had to accept the idea of a European community, to prevent the rearmament of West Germany and to increase the political weight of Western Europe against the two superpowers) and second, in later years, because of economic considerations as well. It was recognized that French industry should be exposed to foreign competition in order to carry out the adjustments needed to increase its output.

However, French planners had to forego the use of certain policy tools (import bans, export subsidies). The planned concertation of physical inputs and outputs had lost any practical sense. At the same time, since the government was no longer able to fulfil plan targets, enterprises had little interest in tackling production and investment commitments. Under such circumstances, French enterprises tried to get rid of governmental tutelage. Industrial managers blamed 'the illusion of systematic dirigism' and 'the myth of planning', and demanded that planning should be restricted to preparing projections without any coercive force (Balassa, 1979).

Macroeconomic policy in the period of the 5th and 6th plans

Before the Common Market was established it was possible to use selective industrial policies. Later, however, apart from a few exceptions, rather general policy measures should have been applied (deductibles and depreciation allowances, credits, guarantees etc.). The government supported mergers among enterprises in different ways. These measures and the pressure of competition in the EEC promoted industrial concentration.

With the establishment of the EEC, exports had a greater influence on the structure of output; to avoid recurrent devaluations, productivity, prices and costs could not be allowed to diverge from trends in dominant economies. Self-centred growth became untenable, in the sense that the basis for further development should be the existing production structure (as it was in the reconstruction period).

Thus, at the end of the 1960s, models were prepared which mainly stressed a specific feature of an open economy – namely that industrial growth depends not so much on internal demand, as on the profitability of international markets. This is possibly the explanation for the fact that in preparation of the 6th plan a role was given to the so-called FIFI-model. This model focussed on the notion of an economy exposed to foreign competition. The economy was assumed to have a domestic sector which could set prices to cover costs and an exposed sector which was a price taker on the world market. Production of tradeable goods was determined by the capacities that could be built by firms as a function of their cash flow and access to credit. In this way the growth rate was positively linked to productivity and always negatively to wages. This marked a first departure from restricted Keynesianism for the French closed economy. Competitiveness vis-à-vis the rest of the world determined supply capacity and hence employment. From this stemmed a second departure: government stimulatory policies did very little for employment, but certainly worsened the balance of payments. New policies called for tax cuts and subsidies or selective credit for investment, provided they benefited companies facing foreign competition and had a positive impact on growth. Because the model reflected the general opinions of the Pompidou administration, it was the subject of intense political controversy, with leftist economists describing it as a 'reactionary model'.

Policy dilemmas in the 7th-9th plans

We have seen that economic development in France was rapid by international standards until 1973, but that serious difficulties began to emerge in the late 1960s: unemployment and declining profitability, which threatened future investment and growth. Overall, the capital-labour ratio rose sharply, and calculations (cf. Sautter, 1975) suggested that value added per unit of capital significantly decreased and the rate of profit on industrial investment dropped in the 1960s.

These problems were severely compounded by the post-1973 recession. By the mid-1970s France was showing the traditional symptoms of the 'British disease'; unemployment, inflation and a balance of payments problem. The optimism of the 1960s and early 1970s gave way to extreme pessimism.

The replacement of the Chirac administration, which experimented with a mild reflation policy (without much success) by Barre in September 1976, gave a new twist to macro-economic planning. The first act of the new government was to introduce the 'Plan Barre', a program of fairly orthodox antiinflationary measures. The government rejected all proposals by planners to reflate, and restricted their activities to planning only a small fraction of the budget. These high priority programs amounted to 15 per cent of the budget and were intended to alleviate the consequences of the deflationary policy (for example, unemployment) by specific actions. These programs defined goals in natural terms rather than in terms of expenses.

The room for maneouvre of French economic policy was limited in this period. While the budget deficit in itself was not too high, the balance of payments was in a critical state, and every increase in the budget deficit was likely to increase the balance of payments deficit. The devaluation of the franc and a high inflation rate were threatening.

The planners could increase the efficiency of the small amount of state investment by selecting the entry points of intervention in such a way as to maximize its effects. It was likely that the program of expanding the telephone network, or nuclear plants would make a significant contribution to the growth of French capital stock. But even if we accept the pessimistic hypothesis of the relative efficiency of such investments, we must bear in mind that these investments were implemented at a time when the 'opportunity cost' of domestic products and the labour used up in them was very low, near zero.

Debate on the 7th and 8th plans revealed the intense politicization of what may seem to have been rather technical econometric issues. For many, the FIFI-model came to acquire the ideological status accorded in the United Kingdom to the doctrine of Monetarism, rather than being treated as a mere technical instrument. At the beginning of the 1970s, therefore, there was harmony between at least some planners, their models and the Government. This secured the relative success of the 6th plan until 1973. At the end of the 1970s, however, a peculiar development occurred when the planners prepared an econometric model in perfectly Keynesian spirit. This made the gap between planners and top civil servants unbridgeable. It goes without saying that the decision was not taken by the planners, and as a consequence they became more and more isolated in the last years of the Giscard era.

This surprising turn of events can be explained by the radicalization of planners, who as they prepared the 7th plan saw that they had no real influence on Government policy. And because of its liberal convictions the Barre cabinet, rather than insist that the CGP's elaborate should express the government's standpoint, ignored it totally.

Explanations of the further decline of planning

Our discussion suggests that planning had shrunk to a relatively modest role by the beginning of 1980s and that the socialist government was neither able nor willing to change this situation. What were the causes?

a) The instability of the world economy. New developments in the world economy – opening to the world market, expansion of multinational giant enterprises, the shift of some economic decisions to a supranational level – deprived national government of important decision-making opportunities, at the same time making national choices riskier than they had ever been (cf. Bauchet, 1986).

b) The ineffectiveness of the demand-stimulating policy. The Socialist government thought, in May 1981, that an extension of the welfare system was both a social objective and a basis for economic recovery. However, it soon became clear that social expenditures had created more demand but no adequate increase in production. The situation differed from that of the 1950s and 1960s, when the improvement of the welfare state had been financed by rapid economic growth and had fostered industrial modernization.

c) Indecisions in development policy. Paradoxically, while the government wanted to promote new technologies, it had to devote more and more funding to old industries: hence the difficult choice between a socially preferable defensive industrial policy and the economic necessity of a more aggressive strategy.

It is only in a few sectors that the French economy can hope to conquer the world market to such an extent that it can dominate the conjuncture. How should such sectors be chosen? French economists complain that they receive rather meaningless answers: advantageous initial conditions, possibilities for economies of scale etc. The specific suggestions advanced are also rather trivial: information technology, electronics, biotechnology. The methods that worked relatively well when France's problem was modernizing its industry according to a known mode of development are no longer effective in the 1980s.Throughout the world there is a search for new forms of industrial organization; but the development model offered by contemporary success stories (Japan and the newly-industrialized countries) is not nearly so attractive for France as the American example of forty years ago.

References

Balassa, B., (1979), 'L'économie francaise sous la Cinquieme République', *Revue économique*, vol. 30. no. 4.

Bauchet. P., (1986), *Le Plan dans l'économie francaise*, Presses de la Fondation Nationales des Sciences Politiques, Paris.

Boltanksy, L., (1982), *Les cadres*, Édition de Minuit, Paris.

Boyer, R., (1981), *La croissance francaise de l'apres-guerre*, mimeo.

Boyer, R., (1985), *The Influence of Keynes on French Economic Policy*, mimeo.

Carré, J., Dubois, P. and Malinvaud, E., (1972), *La croissance francaise,* Seuil, Paris.

Delorme, R. and André, Ch., (1983), *L'état et l'économie,* Seuil, Paris.

Estrin, S., and Holmes, P., (1983), *French planning in theory and practice,* George Allen and Unwin, London.

Sautter, C., 'L'efficacite et la rentabilite de l'economie francaise 1954-74', *Economie et Statistique,* no. 68.

Shonfield, A., (1965), *Modern Capitalism,* Oxford University Press, London.

András Semjén

Norway: planning in a welfare state

The formation and operation of a Scandinavian-type welfare state require an advanced level of economic and even social planning. Western economic studies often call Sweden, the best known example, a 'planned mixed economy', and this conception is also reflected in the Swedes' own view of their themselves. [1]

The denomination 'planning society' also suits the Norwegian example, where there seems to be no contradiction between the commitment to private ownership and to market economy and macroeconomic planning. It is obvious that an important role is played here by the work of Ragnar Frish, whose decisive influence on Norwegian economic thinking still prevails today. In the 1930s he laid the foundations of future Norwegian macroeconomic planning with his 'ökosirk-system' (eco-cirk system), a statistical accounting system specifically reflecting the circulation of economy. After his retirement, Leif Johansen's work as an economist and as a teacher ensured that the planning-friendly nature of Norwegian economic thinking remained.

Economic and social planning was gradually integrated into the political and institutional system of Norway after World War II. Although the opinions of political parties concerning the role of planning may differ, one can certainly maintain that no significant political force in Norway would today question the need and legitimacy of planning. Ideologically, and traditionally, the party most committed to the idea of planning is the Labour Party, although, as Bjerkholt and Longva remark: 'The principles of national budgeting and the implied scope of government economic policy were never seriously challenged by a strong political opposition; thus the national budget was never contested by later non-Labour governments.' [2]

1. The System of Planning

Forming the backbone of Norwegian planning are two activities: annual and four-year medium-term planning which are partially separate from each other in their content and organization, while basically similar in their technique. It is worth mentioning that medium-term plans are referred to in the Norwegian economic literature as long-term programmes ('langtidsprogrammet'). One important result of annual planning is the fiscal budget for the central administration and the social security system, while its principal document is the much more comprehensive national budget, covering the total national economy as a whole and containing means, i.e. appropriate policy measures, as well as prognoses of the trends of real variables, reflecting the presumed impact of the measures.

The medium-term plan not only covers a longer period – the four-year plan is prepared taking into consideration long-term, twenty year perspectives – but is much more comprehensive in its content than the annual plan. It is a very complex socio-economic programme, a programme for government action. This programme-like nature of planning has been a characteristic feature of Norwegian plans from the very beginning: already in 1947 Erik Brofoss, Minister of Finance, who worked out the first national budget, selected this approach. The national budget presented to the Storting in 1947 mentioned three alternative principles of national budgeting. The first one, called the diagnostic budget, is simply an accumulation of sectoral plans and expectations. Such a plan does not aim at consistency in the framework of the accounting system of the national economy. What is more, its significance lies precisely in its diagnostic power in the exploration of tensions, shortages and inconsistencies. Prognostic budgeting is a more advanced approach than this, as it contains full and consistent balances which are based on assumptions concerning the behaviour of the economic agents as well as the estimates of exogenous influences. Brofoss, however, gave preference over the above two conceptions to the programmatic budget, which means that the annual plan also covers the targets of economic policy. According to this conception the plan outlines the economic policy instruments through which the targets set can be attained, provided that the assumptions concerning exogenous factors are proved correct. Already this early plan document 'argues against what it calls the common misunderstanding that a programmatic budget is of interest only in an economy with extensive direct government control.' [3]

Although the activity of planning in Norway is built on the cooperation of all governmental organs, there is still a need for a single coordinating body to harmonize efforts. Almost throughout its four-decade development this body was the Ministry of Finance, with the exception of 1980-81, when the planning unit became independent and was organized as an independent governmental body.

Nevertheless in the 'heroic age' annual planning was the responsibility of the Ministry of Trade, and medium-term planning became the job of the Ministry of Finance only after 1962 – until that time ad hoc secretariats carried out the work. However, all this cannot question the fact that the chief agent of planning and economic policy-making in Norwegian administration is the Ministry of Finance. This role, of course, is in some sense technical by nature – the economic policy worked out by the Ministry of Finance must be in harmony with the political targets of the ruling party (parties). The Central Bureau of Statistics has a special role in Norwegian planning. It has to secure the data supply of planning and to work out and develop the analytical models.

This scheme of division of labour and responsibilities has its obvious advantages, originating mainly from the closeness of the data sources and the users, and the positive feedback between the statisticians and the model-builders. The fact that those working out the models are organizationally kept apart from daily politics helps to retain model continuity and relative objectivity, and really promotes the situation whereby the models – as useful devices for placing the plans on sound foundations – are accepted by all important political forces, even to the extent that they work out their own alternative plans based on the same models.

The importance of the role of planning can be assessed from the fact that both short and medium-term plans are presented to the Norwegian parliament, the Storting, for discussion and approval. The government must give account of the implementation of these plans to the Storting. The importance of planning is also indicated by the fact that the plan periods and the parliamentary cycles are coordinated – every government draws up its medium-term plan for the following election period before its mandate is over – and the parliamentary discussion of the new plan are practically embedded in the election campaign, although they do not have a decisive impact on its outcome.

2. The Growing Complexity of Planning

Short and medium-term, i.e. annual and four-year, planning were introduced in Norway simultaneously after World War II. In the autumn of 1945 it was obvious that the aftermath of the devastation of the war could be overcome most expeditiously through a centralized policy incorporating direct economic intervention.

The annual plans – usually referred to as national budgets – in the period between 1946 and 1954 [4] were aimed principally at quantitative goals. These goals were primarily attained through direct intervention, control and fiscal policy. In the years after World War II, for the sake of reconstruction, widespread use was made of direct forms of intervention alien to the market, such as import licences, construction permits and rationing. These were also detailed in the annual plans and, accordingly, they also played an important role in the related specific production balances (especially as concerns the most important building materials). The most important task of planning was considered to be the coordination of direct interventions; it was thought that with the help of a rationing system for imports and for the most important goods in short supply both consumption and investments could be controlled effectively. The means of credit policy and tax policy were thereby pushed into the background in influencing the allocation of resources. Other arguments for maintaining direct intervention were excessive liquidity and low interest rates on the credit market in the post-war years.

As reconstruction progressed there was less need for direct intervention. The analysis of the trends of the credit supply (1948) and prices and wages (1951) became incorporated in the plan. However until 1953 this remained prognostic rather than being a programme.

The next stage of development of short-term planning was between 1954 and 1962. This period was characterised by the completion of reconstruction and the normalization of economic life so far burdened by the post-war situation of shortages. There was no longer any need for maintaining direct state intervention, and since the market eliminated this element as alien to the system, it was also discharged by the system of planning. In the new situation monetary and fiscal policy became more and more active.

An important step forward from the point of view of planning took place in 1961, when the budgetary year was synchronized with the calendar year, thereby eliminating the lack of simultaneity between the planning year and budgetary year; this having previously prevented planning from dealing in depth with the fiscal budget. Local authorities also changed over to the calendar year when preparing their budget, and the definitions and classifications of the fiscal budget were also reorganized in accordance with the requirements of the planning system. At the same time an attempt was made to synchronize fiscal policy with credit policy.

The changes in the limits of the budgetary year were accompanied by earlier publication of the national budget, in the autumn months. However, this solution was not free from problems either: publication of the plan, for example, preceded the negotiations forming the basis of credit policy; planning could not help influencing fiscal policy even after the national budget had been published. In order to overcome these problems, the publication of a revised national budget in the spring was introduced. At the same time this represented an important step toward continuous planning and economic management.

The development of medium-term planning shows great similarity to that of annual planning. The first medium-term plan comprising the period between 1949 and 1950 was presented simultaneously with the first annual plan.This plan dealt mainly with problems related to reconstruction. The next plan (with a time perspective somewhat overlapping the previous one) referred to the period between 1949 and 1952. The elaboration of this plan was earmarked by the American aid programme. [5]

The United States demanded that a plan of reconstruction be prepared to ensure that the aid was used effectively. Therefore it can be understood that the second four year plan served mainly as a tool to confirm and justify the receipt of foreign transfers. In this context, the plan also covered industrial policy, employment policy and investment policy.

Even more than the first annual plans, the first two four-year plans were restricted to volumes, i.e. quantitative indicators and to the real sphere of the economy. At that time the main role was played by production balances for goods in shortest supply (in accordance with the needs of economic policy to have frequent recourse to direct forms of intervention such as import licences and rationing).

From the third four-year plan (1951-1957) onwards, the scope of medium-term planning extended to social fields as well, and henceforth medium-term planning increasingly developed in the direction of a medium term socio-economic programme. (In the annual plans, social aspects did not prevail even later.) Since this period the medium-term plan has devoted separate chapters to health care, social policy, education, culture, science, as well as to their state, aspects of their development and the possibilities of increasing the welfare of society besides private consumption. In the next plan period, further social issues were discussed, e.g. the leisure-time vs. work-time issue. Increasingly greater emphasis was laid on issues relating to income redistribution. Although those chapters of the plans where social problems were dealt with did not form a package of measures comparable in terms of complexity and quantity with the measures and means aimed at attaining macroeconomic goals, social policy implications were enforced in the course of macroeconomic calculations. Another novelty of the third four-year plan was the coordination of the plan period with parliamentary elections dates; since then parliamentary discussion of the medium term-plan has preceded the elections.

Therefore, along with the consolidation of economic life and increasing economic and social wealth in the state's paternalistic role, the gradual establishment of the welfare state shifted to the foreground. This tendency required a change in planning as well, owing to a considerable swelling of the budget. As a consequence, the emphasis shifted from real to financial and income processes in preparation of the plan.

The most important new feature of the period 1963 to 1975 was the foregrounding of prices and incomes policy. The breakthrough was achieved by the plan of 1963, which suggested a new type of incomes policy, more active than those which preceded it. This was not, of course, entirely unprecedented: already, from 1951 onwards, the plan contained, albeit very briefly, prognoses of prices and incomes trends; but until 1965, the necessary coordination of price and incomes policy with other elements of economic policy was made outside the framework of planning.

There were similar changes in medium-term planning as well.

The principal novelty of the medium-term plan period for 1962-1965 was the introduction of medium-term fiscal planning. In 1961 a parliamentary report discussed the guidelines for the policy relating to this plan period, the calculations for which more or less corresponded to the criteria of a quantitative fiscal plan. It was the first plan to be accompanied by a four-year budget for central government expenditures: the aim of which was to help set the annual budgets on a sounder footing. Yet the plan did not cover the whole budget: it attempted – although not too successfully – to coordinate the revenues and expenditures of the central government's budget.

Starting from the plan for 1966-1969, the medium term plan was prepared alongside and in coordination with the four-year budget of the central government. At that time it was not as yet part of the plan publication; in this form, however, it already played a major role in financing the projects stipulated in the plan. The plan for 1970-1973, presented in the spring of 1969, already contained a medium-term plan for the central budget. This was followed in the autumn of 1969 by the introduction of a revised four-year budget of the central government. From 1973 onwards, a new, four-year (rolling) budget has been prepared annually for the central government and the social security system. The existence of a medium-term budget provides a basis for the governmental and state institutes to prepare more established budgets and staffing plans, contributing to a more clearcut definition and realization of priorities.

Since the plan of 1966-1969, there has also been evident demand for the medium-term planning of credit policy. This was the first medium-term plan to lay considerable emphasis on analysing issues related to environmental protection. Beginning with the plan for 1974-1977, specific medium-term environmental programmes were worked out and incorporated in the plan (even at the cost of reducing economic growth).

Industrial policy was an integral part of planning as early as the second medium-term plan. In the 1970s, along with the changes in the world economy and the exploitation of Norwegian oil and gas wealth, macrostructural problems

– such as analysis of the impact the Norwegian oil sector had on economy or the development trends in manufacturing industry – moved into the foreground.

Because of the credit needed for investments to boost the oil extraction industry, the trends in the balance of payments – and, relating to this, the balance of trade – became important issues for planning. This also contributed to the increasing importance of the analysis of changes in the market shares of traditional Norwegian exports, i.e. the unfavourable impact of the rising, oil-economy-induced costs of labour on industrial competitiveness. This issue – namely, trends in cost-competitiveness – is crucial to Norwegian economic policy, as the country has an exceedingly open economy. [6] Planning provides analyses and prognoses concerning trends in the country's main trading partners' economic growth, export, import and cost level. These factors, the expected domestic cost level, and prognoses for the world market are also taken into consideration in drawing up forecasts for the external economy. Exchange rate policy is also related to the handling of issues of competitiveness. [7] The struggle against excessive dependence on the oil sector became one of the key issues of economic policy as early as the beginning of the 1980s, still during the 'success period' of the oil countries.

In addition to the growth in the complexity of planning content outlined so far, two tendencies could be discerned in medium-term planning. One started with the substitution of prognoses for initial directives, then shifted from prognoses to assume more the character of an economic policy programme; at the same time, the means (tax, interest, credit, subsidy and exchange rate policies, etc.) were given an increasing role in the plan. From forecasting macroeconomic indicators the emphasis shifted to a coordinated planning of economic policy means aimed at securing desired medium-term macroeconomic development – in other words, social and economic policy targets. Changes corresponding to the above can be observed in annual planning as well. One trait of the period since 1976 is that the annual plan already covers all the means of economic policy. The plan outlines the development tendencies of the past and its consequences; it also outlines the main economic policy targets which, in Norwegian planning, are always transformed into targets related to the means. In other words, planning is principally concerned with the means of economic policy – in this sense with the work of administration itself – as the plan sets attainable, normative values for its means. At the same time it only forecasts the real processes, taking into consideration the planned values of the control variables. Direct interventions ceased to exist long ago, and today's medium-term plans contain only guidelines for the enterprise sector. In this respect there is no difference between state or mixed and private enterprises. (The share of pure state ownership among Norwegian enterprises is very low; more frequent are mixed ownership enterprises, combining state and private shareholders).

Although planning does not deal with the state enterprise sector separately, the state interferes with the management of a state enterprise which is running a deficit: by securing subsidies or preferential credits, the state bank controls the formation of enterprise policy.

From the mid-1970s onwards another tendency became increasingly evident: the growing coordination of medium-term and annual planning. The increasing role of the medium-term fiscal plan and its actual relevance were of particular importance.

Initially, medium-term planning did not prove to be a successful means in re-stricting resource utilization. That is to say, after the importance of planning (its role in resource allocation) was recognized, there was an increasing tendency in the work of the government to set out and have adopted by the parliament sec-toral plans for a perspective longer than the four-year plan period. Given the fact that the implementation of the plans was followed by the parliament, the sectoral plans, which were in fact not covered or coordinated by medium-term planning, laid increasingly heavy burdens on the government and the budget. That is, sec-toral planning increasingly resulted in a drastic reduction of the freedom of the annual budget, while it became more and more difficult, if not impossible, to keep government expenditure within a workable framework, as determined by the revenues or a reasonable deficit, and to control the various development tar-gets according to central priorities. In this situation it was naturally the medium-term plan where adequate priorities had to be worked out and sectoral needs co-ordinated with the possibilities of the national economy. This required the coor-dination of medium-term and annual planning, which was greatly facilitated by the fact that, from the early 1960s, the same mathematical models were used for both types of plan. However, the realization of the potential advantages, which arose from coordination, was impeded by the fact that both government and par-liament were inclined to consider the projects as if they had already been imple-mented, with the consequent temptation to undertake financing of new projects in the annual plans. This was especially true when, after adopting a medium-term plan, the government who had elaborated it was changed.

The resulting pressure on the budget could be alleviated only through rolling the medium-term plan. This rolling planning was first restricted to the govern-ment budget, and was then followed by the updating of the entire medium-term plan every two years from 1968 onwards. Since 1976 the control variables and the predictions of the medium-term plan have been updated annually. All this, however, has not diminished the decisive role of the plan document published every four years. (The updated predictions have not been completely published; only their abstracts are attached to the annual plans, as of 1976). This coordina-tion, on the one hand, ensures more effectively than before that the annual plan promotes the implementation of targets set by the medium term plan: on the other hand, it also helps to reduce public expenditure to a level acceptable to the econ-omy. Both in solving the problems already mentioned in connection with the sectoral plans, and in setting medium-term planning on a sounder footing, con-siderable progress was made as the time span of analysis expanded. The annex of the medium term plan for 1970-1973 was the first to contain perspective out-looks (until 1990). In the course of preparing the subsequent four year plans more alternatives were worked out for the perspective development of the econ-omy. Taking a longer perspective into consideration leads to the theoretical pos-sibility of coordination between the predictions for medium and long term.

3. Progress in the Institutional System and Methods of Planning

The system of planning and its institutional framework are, in their current form, the result of a longer historic development – the growth in the complexity of planning and the changes in its institutional (organizational) framework took place simultaneously, mutually influencing each another over four decades. The first annual plan was worked out in a centralized manner by the Finance Policy Department of the Ministry of Finance. However, from the second plan onwards the work was decentralized and organized into a more comprehensive routine. Henceforth most ministries actively participated in the planning work. In the course of planning the respective ministries prepared their own production and investments plans (coordinated with the trade unions and based on the economic policy guidelines given in advance by the government).

The sectoral plan propositions were coordinated by the Ministry of Finance, which ensured their consistency by using the system of national accounts. In addition to the balances given therein, separate balances were calculated for manpower and, in the post-war situation, for scarce products (mainly for building materials – wood and cement – to coordinate supply and demand). It is quite evident that the first plan propositions of the ministries contained numerous inconsistencies. The predicted demand for different products usually exceeded the foreseeable supply, and consistency was only possible through repeated revisions of the proposal of the ministries, as a result of a successive approximation process.

The above-mentioned administrative method of planning was characteristic of the period 1947 to 1960. The principal advantage of this method (in comparison with the centralized method used for the first plan) is illustrated by the fact that the plan was not only the central programme of action of the government, but also a combination of the sectoral plans. The sectoral ministries thus involved in the process of planning were more likely to consider the plan as their own and were more willing to implement it.

As planning increasingly covered financial processes, the circle of the bodies involved in preliminary interest coordination also widened and, apart from sectoral interests, the plans also reflected the interests of employees, employers, financial circles, etc. as the result of a corporative coordination process. This process was characterized by a strong endeavour for consensus, great flexibility, and considerable willingness to compromise by those participating. All this, on the one hand, can be traced back to the democratic traditions of Norway, while on the other hand uninterrupted economic development and the fact that there has always been an increment in distribution facilitated the mitigation of conflicts of interests. This kind of interest coordination usually created sufficient grounds for the plan to resolve parliamentary disputes. There was no change in this machinery of interest coordination even after the replacement of the administrative methods of planning by more sophisticated techniques.

In the years when the administrative method was applied, moves were already made to improve the statistical foundations of the plans, and to use quantitative, mathematical methods. The use of data concerning interindustry flows, i.e. input-output tables, allowed for consideration of the deeper, indirect system of economic relations. The first attempt to use input-output technique was made in 1952, based on national account data from 1948.

In the course of planning for 1959-1960 the national account data relating to the year 1954 were already used in input-output model computations. After this came the modelling of consumers and demand, with the aim of testing whether planned consumption was in harmony with demand, and all this was complemented by a Keynesian model analysing the impact of investments and exports on the trade balance.

Notwithstanding the gradual prevalence of mathematical methods, the administrative method of planning remained basically unaltered up to 1960. In 1960 the integration of already existing models (intersectoral and consumption model) made it possible to handle the most important relations simultaneously and in a combined manner. Thus the new method (the application of computers and mathematical techniques) came to rival traditional planning, and this competition – the various phases of which are marked by the improved models – gradually transformed the whole system of planning. The most characteristic feature of the period which began in 1960 and ended without a clear-cut break in the late 1970s was the coexistence of traditional, administrative planning and modern computerized planning based on mathematical modelling. [8]

In the second half of the 1970s, although modern and non-computerised planning continued side-by-side, the model results were no longer used to test or verify the plan figures worked out by the experts: on the contrary, the computations prepared by the traditional method were used to test and check the model's results.

The nature of the successive approximation process, alleviating interest coordination and characteristic of the administrative method, was also modified as this process progressed; it has been increasingly based on the model computations, making use of the great extent of disaggregation of the Norwegian planning model.

Today, modern, computer-supported planning models have completely superseded 'traditional' methods of planning. This computerization, however, has not undermined the democracy of planning. The plan models are not monopolized by the Ministry of Finance. Quite the contrary: models are drawn up and developed at the Central Bureau of Statistics, and are at the disposal of organizations participating in the process of corporate interest coordination. An important advantage of this structure is that the organizational detachment between the models and those engaged in day-to-day politics helps to retain the continuity and objectivity of the models. And, in turn, the stability of the models contributes to the models' acceptance by all the important political groups, and helps to prevent a distortion of interest coordination by a power-controlled professional monopolization of information.

4. New Tendencies: the Limits to the Welfare State

In this closing chapter I would like to mention certain tendencies characteristic of the plans of the 1980s – the medium-term plan [9] developed by the Labour Party for 1982-1985 and the subsequent plan made by the coalition government for 1986-1989. [10]

Although in both cases responsibility for the implementation of the plan left the hands of the party (parties) which elaborated them, due to the aforementioned desire to find a broader consensus than majority opinion, the change of the government after the plan was approved could not (cannot) essentially alter the already established guidelines.

The most striking characteristic of the Norwegian plan for 1982-1985 was that considerable weight was placed on social issues. From this point of view, the most important aspect was not the number of chapters dealing with society, but an attitude which penetrated the whole plan. This plan does not, in fact, contain economic or social issues par excellence. Social processes are, on the one hand, the outcome of economic factors; on the other, they influence economic development – that development whose major aim is, according to the plan, to provide the material basis for the realization of the so-called solidarist society conceived by the socialdemocratic government which elaborated the plan. In this sense, economic development is not an end in itself: it can be meaningful and justified only to the extent that it promotes the realization of the social targets of the plan.

In Norway during the 1970s the institutional system of the welfare state was consolidated and expanded. This decade saw the implementation of the environmental protection bill, the new social security system, which provides full payment for the period of sickness, the law on working conditions, etc. However it was already evident that a oversized budget may result in serious economic problems and declining competitiveness. Thus this plan already indicated that the welfare state cannot assume the task of solving all social problems.

The subsequent plan – under the impact of increasing economic problems only somewhat mitigated by oil revenues – continued along this path. And the sudden decline in oil prices in 1986 provided added justification for this shift in direction. [11]

This plan for 1986-1989 sets out some basic social and political values, such as striving to strengthen democracy, confidence in the individual and commitment to mixed economy, including private ownership as well as secure employment and social security for all, working towards a more equitable distribution of benefits, etc.

In analysing the situation, the plan reveals that during the 1970s, under the impact of certain tendencies, society became too rigid and its adaptability weakened. The key-words characterizing this process might be: bureaucratization, overregulation, bargaining society. The plan aims at reversing these processes, and advocates renewal together with removal of the impediments to initiative.

In this struggle the plan anticipates favourable impulses mainly from the supply side of the economy; even the welfare state intends to replace – or at least combine – traditional Keynesian demand management with supply-side economics. The strategy aims at improving the business climate, production and technology.

The most interesting sections of the plan deal with increasing competition, curbing concentration tendencies, and deregulation policies. Considerable changes have already taken place in central regulations to promote the more effective operation of the market (the elimination of the central rent and housing market regulation, a more liberal licensing system, lifting monopolies on transportation, liberalization of currency regulations, simplification of the operational rules in banks, elimination of measures limiting the activities of foreign banks, etc.).

In this context, new emphasis is given to the welfare state and to public expenditure. According to the plan, in the welfare or social sphere there will always be a discrepancy between what is desirable and what is economically possible. Consequently it is quite logical that deregulation should have its impact on the public sector.

This point coincides with the efforts made to decentralize decision-making and increase local autonomy. In practical terms the political target has become the decentralization and democratization of the system of administration – accompanied by a confidence that the state's ever-increasing welfare role and growing public expenditures can thus be curbed.

In the situation described above a cautious process of demolishing the paternalistic welfare system has started. It goes without saying that the strong Scandinavian social democratic tradition does not allow for drastic measures. The plan for 1986-1989 also emphasizes that 'the welfare state has to be sustained and must continue to be developed', and in addition adequate control must be ensured for public organizations over the reorganization of activities in the public sector. The slogans of the new policy declared in the plan are: new division of work between private and public sector (reprivatization where possible) and the deregulation already mentioned.

If, in conclusion, we look back over the history of Norwegian planning, perhaps the most conspicuous features will be its exceptional adaptability and the variety of functions it assumes. This planning has been able to relaunch production, to lay the economic foundations of the welfare state, to command its expansion and then to integrate political endeavours aimed at revitalizing the market and the Norwegian economy, at the cost of braking the expansion of the public sector. This flexibility can be one of the factors that explain the survival of planning in the welfare state – with changing contours perhaps, but permanently.

Notes

[1]   See Semjén, András, Svédország – tegnap, ma, holnap (Sweden – yester-day, today, tomorrow) *Közgazdasági Szemle*, no. 4, 1982.

[2]   Bjerkholt, Olav and Longva, Svein, *MODIS IV. A Model for Economic Analysis and National Planning.* Samfunnokomiske Studier, no. 43, Statistisk Sentralbyra, Oslo, 1980. p. 10.

[3]   Ibid., p.9.

[4]   The phases of planning referred to here see in Petter Jakob Bjerve's study 'Trends in Norwegian Planning 1945-1975', mimeo.

[5]   As is well-known, George Marshall, Foreign Minister of the United States announced in his lecture, given at Harvard University on June 5 1947, a project aimed at supporting the European states who had suffered losses during World War II and at the same time increasing the economic and po-litical influence of the United States. The project was approved in 1948. It played an important role in the reconstruction of European market economies, including Norway.

[6]   Exports amount to some 46 per cent, imports 38 per cent of the GDP (in 1985, but the same rates are characteristic of a longer period retrospec-tively). Illustrative of the Norwegian way of thinking is the fact that usu-ally, instead of the above data, the trends in percentages as compared to the GDP, excluding oil and shipping, are taken into consideration (which results in values higher by about 10 per cent). A separate analysis is made of the situation without the revenues from oil extraction and shipping, for so-called 'mainland Norway', and this is compared with the situation of the countries which provide bases for comparison. (For example the 'mainland' export/GDP rate is only 20 per cent as compared to the 39 per cent import rate).

[7]   Even so, according to the Norwegian view exchange rate policy (devaluation) could solve the problem only if the mechanisms to ensure compensation for revenue holders did not exist. As this is not the case, in the long run only an adequate regulation of real wage increase – sober wage negotiations – can lead to improving competitiveness.

[8]   Inclusive of the 60s, detailed analysis is given of the evolution of Norwe-gian planning and of the administrative and mathematical methods of plan-ning by Gusztáv Báger in the Hungarian economic literature. See Gusztáv Báger : A norvég gazdasági tervezés (Norwegian economic planning) Közgazdasági Szemle, 1969, 1.

[9]   Norwegian Long-Term Programme 1982-1985 Report, No. 79 to the Storting (1980-1981). Government-Secretariat for Long-Term Planning and Coordination, Planning Secretariat, Oslo, 1981.

[10] Norwegian Long-Term Programme 1986-1989, Report, No.83 to the Storting (1984-1985). Royal Norwegian Ministry of Finance, Oslo 1985.

[11] This question and, in relation to it, the economic objectives of the medium term plans of the 80s, are analysed by the author in greater detail in his ar-ticle 'Gazdaságpolitikai útkeresés Norvégiában a 80-as években' (Economic policy reorientation in Norway in the eighties), Külgazdaság, no. 10, 1987.

István Kiglics

Planning in Japan

In the middle of 1980s I went to Japan on a scholarship to study macromanagement, mainly the planning system. I spent most of my time consulting in universities and government offices. As is usual, I was faced with some difficulties partly due to my expectations and knowledge about Japan.

While I stayed in Japan my image gradually changed. The number of differing opinions I had concerning Japanese planning during my talks with experts from various countries and during my research, contributed to this change.

What is more, I found that planning as a separate topic rarely occurs in the work of researchers dealing with Japanese economics, or it occurs as a sub-topic in works about economic development and economic policy.

The aforementioned facts made me seek an explanation. I think a partial cause of the differences in opinion is that different countries have different definitions of the working system of their own country. The advanced capitalist countries, for which the concept of planning is equivalent to the traditional rigid plan-controlled (plan commanded) system in Eastern Europe, call themselves market economies, in a contradiction which excludes the approval of planning. The Eastern European countries following the plan-controlled pattern have a different point of view. Until now they have concentrated on centrally-organized aim selection, followed by the division of tasks and actual planning work. Japanese planning practice with its tendencies towards indicativity (or stimulation) is not considered in the traditional Eastern Europe terms to be planning.

A Hungarian researcher is in a special position because his home situation is in transition between the plan controlled and market economy models. He might even discover similarities between Hungarian and Japanese planning and control practices as long as he stays within macroplanning and macromanagement.

This attitude is reflected in the definition of the character of macromanagement. An American or an English liberal thinker would define the character of Japanese macromanagement as dirigism. An Eastern European specialist with the traditional plan-commanded environment would stress the influence of big business in a market economy. A Japanese expert, partly distinguishing himself from Eastern European planning practice and partly denying the accusations of GATT and Western Europe, would describe Japanese economic management as an unlimited area of free enterprise with plans which at most follows movements on the market, as well as providing limits of movements for the functioning of the economy.

In my opinion these characterisations are rather one-sided, but each contains a part of the truth. I would like to present a factual account of the subject instead of creating categories.

1. Appearance of macroplanning

Although central control has been an important element in Japan's politics since the Middle Ages and has long traditions in this sense, its connection with central planning has only occurred this century. From the Meiji Period to the 1930s, economic policy meant 'top-down' development initiatives, although this was only stimulating or supporting in character. The attempt to extend plan-based total organization over the economy came to prominence in the 1930s with a militarised economy, and enjoyed its heyday during World War II, although this condition is different from the 'normal peaceful planning environment'.

The initial motivation came from Japan's own hierarchical traditions and the useful lessons learned from the German 'organisation' example' as well as from the Soviet planning success propaganda of the early 1930s, the proportions of which is not clear or definable. [1]

After defeat in World War II the base for totalitarian central economic control aimed at satisfying military claims ceased to exist. With the changeover to civil economic control, different needs had to be satisfied.

Under the supervision of the Allied Supreme Command, (1945-51) organic changes were instituted. The financial-economic mammoth combines (*zaibatsu*) were split up. The reason for this was the accusation that they served military needs and the excessive concentration of the economy. [2] To prevent reorganization of the conglomerates, they were purged of their previous owners and their families under Allied control. In order to maintain the status quo they worked out and accepted the Law against Monopolies in 1947. Young managers became the heads of the concerns and their efforts brought new vitality to the Japanese economy. [3] Following this step a new wave of renewal and an increase in market competition with considerable changes in the entrepreneurial environment took place in Japan.

These changes in organization contributed a great deal to increasing competitive spirit. The liquidation of the zaibatsus meant isolation for the companies which had previously belonged to them. Independence was only one of the aims of liquidation, the other being to bring an end to the existence of the previous monopolistic unity of organisation and power. Within the limits of zaibatsu the independence of companies was rather restricted. They worked together in close cooperation under the direct or indirect control of the centre. These connecting links were broken and the law prohibited further cooperation. Parallel with the removal of the experienced and informed elite, the use of the old brand and company names was also banned.

These new conditions meant new organisational frameworks that had to face the difficulties following World War II. One of the motives for expansion during the war was the lack of raw materials and energy resources in a country seeking the position of a superpower, which was to be remedied by the seizure of traditional supply territories. The well organized system of production and supply was destroyed by military defeat, the destruction caused by the war and the masses returning from the occupied territories (mainly demobilized soldiers and the retreating civilian population). All these factors together caused an enormous market vacuum in the economy. As a result of a lack of goods, which hit both production and the population, prices rose sharply but did not improve the supply of goods, provisions or raw materials. Transport suffered from a lack of energy resources and the existing goods supplies were unsatisfactory. The shock of defeat (the first in the history of Japan) combined with war damage and a lack of goods completely paralysed the economy.

Discontent due to a lack of goods and competition supported by law provided an almost natural stimulus for the central reorganisation of economic life and the restoration of the power balance in control as demanded by tradition. The tight central control of the war was quickly replaced by a similarly tight peacetime central control.

Although the occupying powers demanded a total reorganization of state control, it happened in many cases that ministries were only renamed [5] and the new ministries began with the same staff: with the exception of their purged officials. The use of the old staff was guaranted to transfer the traditions of economic organization from military supply to civil production.

As the zaibatsus were destroyed, and the cooperation of companies was stopped by the Antimonopoly Law and some others, the government tried to meet demands for the recentralization of controlling power by drawing up and enforcing new laws to strengthen the position of a controller. From the point of economic development and economic policy, the most important laws were those regarding foreign currency exchange control and foreign investment control, by means of which the government was able to influence directly all desirable trade and economic development processes.

Although programs similar to plans were prepared during and immediately after the occupation period, they were not officially accepted or published. The first official plan was completed only after the occupation, peacemaking and stabilization that followed the Korean War in 1955. The plans followed one another with the eleventh one in force today. The framework for planning has not changed since 1955. The methodology has been formalized, using the experience of the previous ten years as a basis for planning techniques. Of course there have always been small changes in accordance with the extension of the means of planning, with the changing roles of planning in the economy, and finally with the international role of the country and the need for 'internationalization'.

2. Characteristics of the planning processes

The planning process may be viewed from several stand-points in Japan too. It may be considered to be a social process, i.e. the field of connections, cooperation and conflicts of interest between social agents. In this sense a Japanese plan – as Japanese experts like to stress – is a means of creating social consensus. On the other hand, it may be considered to be a scientific technical process (application of the methods of mathematics). This is the area of the establishment of the consistency of the plan.

Plans are made by the Economic Council (EC) in collaboration with the Economic Planning Agency (EPA) which provides the administration, organization and data. The EC is a social organ comprising leading economic experts, journalists, university professors, representatives of social institutions, etc. At the Prime Minister's request they examine the most important questions of the economic policy of a certain period; they then form various sub-committees and work-committees in which they draw up the various parts of the plan.

The EC's involvement in making medium-range plans has become more frequent. Recently it has met once a year to discuss the problems of the present day as well as to put forward proposals for corrections to economic policy. Similar committees work not only alongside the EPA but also with certain ministries (MITI, MOF) both in preparing medium-range plans and developing strategies in certain areas of industry. The latter have a rather ad hoc character, with a mandate to work out a definite line in economic policy or to carry out particular measures. Representatives from the fields concerned usually take part in these committees.

This is why parties safeguarding their interests and representatives of science and administration always take part at particular levels in the drafting stage. In the case of conflict, they apply pressure through press and political channels, through their umbrella organs and through street walkouts.

The communication system is, of course, much more complicated: everyday communication belongs to all companies as well as being one of the (un)written duties of the employees of administrative institutions. [3] Because of this, partners are well-informed about their own possibilities (limits of movements) and opportunities, and this reduces the chances of conflict. Despite all this, when macroplans are drawn up, serious differences arise among the ministries, with each defending its own position. The aim of the whole process, though, is to create a consensus in which accomplishment does not require serious control or attention. Should discrepancies occur the plan is rethought.

Plans are made by EPA for medium-range periods, i.e. 5-10 years, although they mostly last for half that time, i.e. 2-3 years. One of reasons for this short period can be found in Japanese political practice: the Prime Minister is generally in office for two years. A new Prime Minister usually has new plans made after taking office. The other reason is the discrepancy mentioned above: even with a Prime Minister in office for a longer period, plans do not usually last for more than three years. [6]

Economic development has not always taken place in accordance with plans. In such cases no attempt has been made to adjust the economic processes to the plan; instead the EC meets to rework the plan according to the new conditions. During my consultations in government offices it was generally felt important to stress this process.

The plan which was accepted and came into force in 1983 stands out as an example of the 'one prime minister-one plan' pattern, but the importance of yearly correction and openness increased considerably. According to some observers this change (even the term 'plan' is not used) is due to the views on planning of its constructor, Prime Minister Nakasone.

The two factors determining the life-period of a plan are the mix of policy changes introduced by politicians and the effects of economic policy phenomena. The Prime Minister may partly use the divergence between the plan and the economic processes in order to express his ideas in the development of a new plan. The newly-developed plans do not usually follow a completely different line, but only stress different points or correct certain figures. It is rather characteristic that significant correlations occur between the main tendencies of long-range plans and the tendencies of economic processes during the completion of the plan, while there are slight differences in figures. Apart from the line determined by the economic processes, both the unchanged bureaucracy – working out the plan – and the unchanged composition of social organs (the EC) probably contribute to this relative stability.

The technical side of plan making

The technical side is considered to be a background aspect, although in the euphoric mood of certain periods (period of introduction and promotion of mathematical models) it has not been an important factor in planning. Apart from this short interlude, it is more the social side, the attempt to create a consensus, that plays the decisive role in planning.

In the first plans of the 1960s the background calculations necessary for the determination of aims were carried out by studying the system of conditions put together on the basis of a survey conducted by manual data collection and processing methods.

The 1960s was the decade of the 'Japanese Economic Miracle'. The starting point of the plan was a preference for a high growth rate, and economic policy instruments were selected accordingly. A lot of data concerning product groups and sub-branches were used. With the exception of the latter category, all plans contained figures and tables in the supplementary parts. In the Income Doubling Plan however, tables and figures broken down to the product level comprised most of the main content, and also took up proportionally more space than text.

Mathematical models and computer technology appeared in the planning process during the second half of the period of high growth (starting in 1966). The first medium range macromodels which made the change in the planning process possible were used then. It is possible to examine more, mainly qualitative aims with the aid of models, which help to choose the desirable lifespan of growth, and follow up with the appropriate economic policy measures.

What helped the spread of models was the fact that they uncovered the inconsistencies in planning calculations. Ministries saw this as monitoring their activities and as interference in their internal affairs and were against the excessive use of the models. At the same time the head of the EPA, the government institution controlling the planning process, told Parliament in his proposal (considering it a triumph of science): 'I am absolutely sure of this plan, as it was put together by a computer'. [7]

The oil crisis following this event destroyed such optimism by ruining the calculations in the plan. The authority of the computer and the models was destroyed, and since then they have not managed to regain their position. In planning, the modelling committees were pushed out of their advanced positions. This does not mean that they did not use the models again; on the contrary, after the oil crisis the range of means used by planners was increased by a more developed mathematical apparatus. Multisector models were drawn up to cover several alternatives. In the meantime the previously reluctant ministries built their own model and computer apparatus in order to be better prepared for talks on medium range plans. [8]

The multisector models belong to the planning period following the oil crisis. The basic situation at the time was not determined by growth but by the increasing world market crisis, inflation and the threatening pressure of protectionism by western partners. Economic policy had to decide on this basis and strict anti-inflation policy had to be subordinated to it. The role of the central macroplan (and the role of the EPA responsible for it, further strengthened by formal procuration [9]) and consensus creation became preeminent again. In completion, the informal government instrument in the form of 'administrative guidance' [10] was reinforced, although the plan itself was only meant to provide guidelines showing its aims from a long-range point of view.

3. Changes in plan functions

As long ago as the end of the 1950s the government tried to exercise close control over all areas necessary to the rebuilding of the economy. It held the most important areas: coal mining, iron and steel production and electrical energy production and left a limited role for the private sector. [11]

The 'Economic Rehabilitation Plan', which was put together and completed with probably the closest central control, was produced in this period. Despite all this, the plan is not considered to be an official one. The Prime Minister of the time, Mr. Yoshida, did not accept the term 'plan', and went ahead in forming and achieving his own program. Acting almost as a one-man government, he had a hand in everything and forced through his ideas on economic policy. This period may be characterised as one with direct government guidance.

In order to complete the plan, trade in consumer goods, prices, foreign trade and development activities within the previously-mentioned two laws were centrally monitored. The plan was the basis of central control. Owing to these efforts, the economy started to develop by the end of the 1940s and the beginning of the 1950s, and the transition from rehabilitation to self-support got under way. Although central control did not decrease to any great extent (this period is usually cited as the start of transition to 'free market' economy), beyond direct 'manual operation', the central directorate started to use more indirect means as well.

After recovery from the war shock, the plans of the second half of the 1950s were plans of national consensus created to achieve the overriding aim of a prosperous 'rich country'. [12] The characteristic plan of this period was that of Prime Minister Ikeda's 'Income Doubling Plan' (Shotoku Baizo Keikaku), which incorporated alternative growth rates in the macroplan. At the same time, the macroplan served as a basis for partial plans and was intended to provide consistency between them. In economic policy the quantitative limits of the previous periods were lowered and the application of monetary means were extended, i.e. the completion of the plan took a more indirect course.

The direct cause of this was that Japan joined GATT in 1955, making a move towards another line of economic development, the characteristic feature of which was the working out of conditions for a gradual return to the international division of labour. The guidelines of liberalization in trade and foreign currency exchange in the economy were set out in 1960 and later, in 1964, the conditions for joining the IMF and the OECD were accepted. As a result of these steps, those channels enabling direct control over the companies had to be cut.

The Japanese Government started reducing customs and reexamining laws on foreign currency and investment. Although the coordination of duties were formally carried out by joining international organizations, the process has not yet been completed because of to frictions in trade. [13]

It is indicative that a parallel negative list was also drawn up (in the 1960s) with products which could not come off the embargo list. The first half of the period started with traditional means, involving a wide range of expert opinion and different pressure groups. Yet the plan was heavily criticised. The growth rate predicted by the government was considered by some to be too low and pessimistic; others considered it too high. In reality the economy outstripped the optimal rates of both sides.

Japanese economic control made rather extensive use of an indirect means of control, the institution of administrative guidance (GS), in order to counterbalance reduced direct control. [14] The purpose of the plan at that time was to establish a guideline for the private sector, to set out the main lines of the government's economic policy, and to coordinate the different interest groups in the planning process and to help create consensus.

In the first place, the *Income Doubling Plan* separated the state and private sectors during the planning period (reflected by the structure of the EC) as opposed to their previous joint treatment. The approach to the private sector was of a more indirect guideline type. The critical, unstable period of the 1970s placed renewed emphasis on balance re-establishment and structural changes. As a result of the crisis, not only were those supporting the mathematical models heavily criticised, but the whole idea of planning also become questionable. The plan of the 1980s may be the start of a new period. The economic policy program worked out by the Nakasone government avoids mention of quantitative targets and the word 'plan' does not occur either. The plan itself, unlike previous similar documents, hardly contains any figures or charts.

On the other hand it does not forego economic policy program-making but considers it to be a government duty which requires constant attention and criticism. The so-called 'Rolling Plan' program was also introduced. This meant first of all that the committee supervision of plans, which had only been occasional when problems occurred, became regular. The published so-called 'revolving reports' about the plan's implementation aim to keep pace with the rapid change in world market conditions and to react promptly.

This most probably resulted in a change in previous practice, i.e. the abandonment of medium range plans after 2-3 years. Nakasone remained in office for five years and the same plan stayed in force. Because the hands of the government were not tied by numbers, as had been more or less the usual case, there was no significant difference between the figures in the plan and the completed tasks which provided a starting point to work out new plans.

Although economic processes (tensions in balance of payments, a revalued yen, increasing unemployment, etc.) did not follow the original plan, the main reason for developing a new plan was a change in Prime Ministers. The new

Prime Minister, Mr Takeshita had a new plan drawn up when he took office and this had partly to serve continuity, (e.g. a change in the taxation system) and partly to bring the changes in economic policy direction in the spirit of the Maekawa reports. [15]

The medium-range program of the Nakasone government was supposed only to be an 'outlook and guideline'. More importance was given to the working out of the announced program and its completion, privatisation and administrative reform [16], the activities of committees set up to resolve frictions with trading partners, and determining the completion of actual programs and new guidelines. [15]

In the 1980s the 'Rolling Plans' came to the fore, together with regular, annual supervision of plans, providing a basis for the drafting of annual budgets as well as for program modifications similar to the Maekawa reports. Such large-scale modifying suggestions (they contain questions which could lead to substantial about-turns, or even the giving up of Japan's expansion-oriented foreign trade policy: one of the main economic policy lines and followed since World War II) might be considered to be unpredictable changes in direction. Since the framework of the plan is a lot more flexible, these changes might be interpreted as a speeding up of Japanese internationalisation, of financial and administrative reform and of all stated aims.

Besides traditional planning and macromanagement, new means appear as well. The first signs of these appeared in Mr. Nakasone's financial-administrative reform, the gradual opening of the money market starting in the mid-1980s, and the allowing of foreigners into the Japanese financial market. The above-mentioned privatisation and the introduction of the western type Value Added Tax after long hesitation, may be considered similar signs.

Traditional government means like GS are still present, even though they are of less importance. They are used in either car exports or the 'voluntary' restriction of VTR export, or in MITI checks of petroleum import for the domestic market. [17]

4. Some conclusions

The spirit of central direction derives from a long tradition and is an important element in the country's policy. Since World War II this has been connected with Central planning as well. In the methods applied in planning we can distinguish a dual trend. One of these is the traditional functioning of mechanisms based on interest links and their inclusion in the planning process, and the other is the application of mathematical methods, i.e. prediction with the aims of models and consistency examinations. However, the main characteristic is the attempt to achieve consensus, i.e. traditional method-providing continuity. The environment of consensus achievement and the level of government control over the whole process, plan preparation and economic policy realisation have changed.

While the 1940s and 1950s were the golden age of direct central guidance, the 1960s were the beginning of 'an easing off' period in which financial means, considered as indirect guidance, existed alongside the special means of state intervention such as the instruction of 'gyosei sido'. The government uses indirect guidance to exercise direct intervention, in similar fashion to central guidance, when problems occur caused by extensive use of GS (e.g. after the oil crisis).

After restabilization it was possible to return smoothly to more flexible government and management behaviour, without suffering ideological or prestige loss of any kind. So, for example, the Nakasone change in the 1980s did not cause any particular shock by formally abandoning the idea of planning. The government seems to have withdrawn from all planning obligation and by non-interference allows the economy to enforce free market principles. Although changes of such importance have not occurred in government practice, as one would at first expect, internationalization, the modification of financial and tax systems, the reduction of customs and import restrictions as well as the allowing of foreign capital into the Japanese market, might bring considerable long range changes. Foreign penetration may be the Trojan Horse, and the country's increasing openness may undermine macromanagement's strongest feature: the traditional attempt to achieve consensus.

Notes

[1] I have found only a few sources concerning the formation of the planning system of Japan. One of them (Johnson, C., *MITI and the Japanese Miracle*) in referring to Soviet experience, mentions the name of Stalin's planning ideologist of Hungarian origin (Jenô Varga) whose works had an influence on the formation of Japanese planning thought.

[2] The big industrial combines controlled the main part of the Japanese economy within the framework of family enterprise. They were the zaibatsus: Mitsubishi, Mitsui, Sumitomo, Yasuda, etc.

[3] Nakane, C., *The Japanese Society*, C. Tuttle, Tokyo, 1982.

[5] Nakamura, T., *The Postwar Japanese Economy*, University of Tokyo Press, Tokyo, 1981.

[6] Sato E. was Prime Minister for seven and a half years from 1964. During that time he accepted 3 plans, i.e. had them developed.

[7] Mentioned during my talk to Mr Shimpo S. (head of section in EPA, 24th July 1984)

[8] Interview with Niimura Y. (EPA research group, June 1984)

[9] Economic Planning in Japan (EPA August 1979)

[10] Kiglics I.: 'Is it the End for Economic Guidance?' (in Hungarian: Tervgazdasági Fórum 1988/4)

[11] Yamazawa I.: Lecture on Japanese economy, under the sponsorship of the Japan Foundation (September 1984)

[12] From the famous slogan of the end of the 19th century 'Fukoku Kyóhei' (Rich country – Strong Army). The 'Kyóhei' (Strong Army) concept was abandoned by the Constitution after the WW2.

[13] Interview with Kaji M. (Professor from TODAI, January 1985)

[14] GS = Gyósei Sido = Administrative Guidance methods applied by government offices for direct informal influence on economic subjects. Its role is decreasing. Its use is controversial as it has no explicit legal base but is instead built on legal loopholes and guidance traditions. This type of intervention is more frequently used in Japan compared with the practice of advanced industrial countries.

[15] See e.g. *Maekawa Report*, EPA, Tokyo, 27 April 1987.

[16] Kiglics, I., *Some Experience of a Privatization Wave in Japan*, of TGI Nemzetközi Füzetek, Budapest, July 1987.

[17] On car export restriction: Daily Yomiuri, 22.01.1984; On petroleum restriction: The Japan Times, 20.07.1984.

Eva Kigyóssy

Some aspects
of macroeconomic control in the
Federal Republic of Germany

1. Some characteristic features of economic policy and planning

Let us clarify at the beginning that there is no central control in the form of proper planning in the Federal Republic of Germany. Global regulation and structural political instruments are the key tools of macroeconomic interference with the so-called magic triangle – namely, economic growth accompanied by balanced foreign trade, employment, and stability of currency.

An anti-planning 'social market economy' policy was adopted by the Adenauer administration in the early 1960s. This rigid policy of non-interference was waived after the 1967 decline. The new economic policy concept found its 'Magna Charta' in the 1967 Act of stabilization and growth (see [1]).

Typical objectives of this global approach of control:
- revise or partly or fully eliminate the price/profit mechanism as a regulator;
- preempt cyclical crises, cushion their impact and overcome their harmful implications;
- support the scientific-technical revolution and economic growth;
- use instruments of financial control.

In the 1970s the characteristics of economic policy and planning changed in the FRG, as in many other advanced industrial countries.

For instance, new values were expected from economic policy. The institutions of parliamentary democracy were subjected to growing criticism and non-parliamentary opposition, i.e. the so called 'basis democracy' increased its weight. In the context of the criticism of capitalism, a containment of growth was proposed as a way to promote human self-assertion. Inquiries into the natural limits of growth gave rise to remarkable movements emerging in the spheres of environment and energy problems.

National economies radically changed and uncertainties increased in a stormy external economic environment. New cross-border economic problems surfaced. The medium-term growth rates of industrial countries declined after the mid-1960s, resulting in simultaneous unemployment and high or growing

165

inflation rates. Expectations were badly shaken by the workings of these factors on the micro and the macro spheres alike.

The old economic policy based on a historical understanding of income regulation financed through state debts was no longer viable. Tax rates were steadily raised and met growing resistance. Certain forms of the shadow economy proliferated, indicating the limits of this form of financing. Consequently the Federal Republic of Germany began to 'reprivatize the risk of employment' and to return to a 'market defined structure' (cf. [2]). Protectionism came back as an economic policy instrument.

However, inflation was unmistakably the focus of economic and political effort. Plan estimates concerning certain segment sectors, e.g. state investment projects, were regularly frustrated by recurring steep price rises. The growing internationalization of markets became another obstacle to planning. Economic policy resorted more and more frequently to instruments of global control in order to restore international competitiveness or to stabilize the local currency. However, these manoeuvres were limited to correcting unforeseen disequilibria as soon and as effectively as possible, and thus did not show the quality of planning.

The course of development outlined above indicates that the intensity of planning endeavours runs counter to the cycle of growth. In this way the capacity of macroeconomic planning to reduce uncertainty was clearly limited. When uncertainty passes beyond a given threshold then planning itself is captured in the net of instability and is unable to keep the increasing unpredictable crises under control. On the other hand when acute problems come to an end and growth begins, then planning attempts are withdrawn, instead of transforming macroeconomic regulation into planning.

2. The system and tools of macroeconomic influence

The historical actors and processes of economic policy have lately shown a reallocation of spheres of influence. Political decision-making has become difficult as the roles of various lobbies have grown. Politics and bureaucracy have to face increasingly more intricate rules of procedure. Courts play increasingly more important roles, partly as middlemen between companies on the one hand, and initiatives of citizens on the other. From the formal point of view there has been no change in the legal status of the institutions that count in economic policy. However, the autonomy of business actors has been somewhat reduced by the growing international intertwining of economic policies.

Several special programmes have been enacted since the second half of the seventies, according to economic policy objectives. Significant special programmes were focused on growth and employment, such as:
-   programme of promotion of building type and other investments (1975);
-   since 1977 so-called future oriented projects focusing on urban reconstruction, sewage systems, energy rationalization, etc.;
-   promotion of economic growth (1978).

The German system of state budget provides for administrative control. On the other hand the budget is valid for a relatively short time-horizon, which is an impediment to the efficient and consistent performance of the function of financial regulation. As far as the political function, and especially the so-called program function of the budget, is concerned, the budget system is unable to discharge these adequately, for reasons which include the following:

- lack of adequate interfaces between financial and political planning because most of budget planning is beyond the scope of both the Chancellor and the cabinet and is the responsibility at best of a desk officer. Another reason is the fact that important decisions on budget magnitude and use are transmitted 'bottom-up' by politically unauthentic organizations. The 'top-down' approach of tackling political objectives is nearly entirely absent.
- Furthermore, the budget plans expenses and not services and its orientation is towards inputs, instead of outputs as the program function should require.

The budget policy changed direction in 1981. Unemployment benefits and retraining support were sharply cut by the 1981 Act of 'Labour market promotion and consolidation'. The budget was further disburdened within the framework of 'Action '82'. Services in the social sphere were restricted by the 1983 Budget Act. The same line was adopted the 1984 Budget Act. At the same time these Acts provided for accelerated depreciation and lightened the tax burdens of companies.

All in all, the range of classic economic policy instruments show the following shifts of accents:

- reduced importance of income policy;
- replacement of growth programmes with stabilization strategies;
- corresponding efforts to reduce the budget deficit;
- upgraded role of financial policy vs. other political measures (objectives concerning the volume of money have been formulated since 1974; the workings of the financial policy often enhance cycles);
- in fact, unchanging exchange rate policy since the introduction of common floating in 1973;
- insufficient growth is not accompanied by any action to offset the drop in real income.

Sectoral economic policy concentrates on a few sectors, i.e. the agricultural sector, state railways, coal-mining and housing. Since the mid-1970s, energy rationalization, aircraft and spacecraft production, ship building, metallurgy and the steel sector have been subsidized. As before, subsidies (financial support and tax relief) continue to be a key tool of state economic policy. Reductions in subsidies and reprivatization have long been at issue. Substantial state funds are nevertheless committed to growing support of the steel sector as well as of R&D activities.

From the point of view of asserting economic policy, public resistance is considered a 'new restriction'. Analysts report increasing tax fraud and 'illegal' business activities. The growing concern for the environment has been noted above. Increasing public concern is also shown over military strategy (stationing of Pershing II) or data protection (census) as well. Strikes have recently focused on the weaknesses of the economy. Public resistance action is completed with isolated cases of refusals to pay for electricity (protest over poor power plant capacity utilization) and isolated cases of refusal to pay tax (protesting over armaments).

3. Behaviour of the State and macroeconomic development

The following regional correlation emerges between the behaviour of the State and the economic development of federal states. When government purchases of goods and services are compared to GNP, an increase from 21% to 24% is found in the period 1970 to 1983 on the level of the Federation (cf. [4]). State consumption increased by over 4% to 20%. On the other hand, state asset investments were almost halved, dropping to 2,5%. The following is a possible interpretation of this trend: investment-intensive infrastructural development was replaced in the early 1970s by a person-oriented development stage. Production of new value by the State sector was surging: it increased its share in the production of new value by the overall economy from 10% in 1970 to 23% in 1983. Still more remarkable growth was shown by transfer expenses. Their value vs. GNP increased from 5,5% to over 23% (cf. [5]). This growth was the product of the pressing financial burdens of a high unemployment rate and of family allowances raised in the 1975 tax reform.

In the past decade budget policy has lived in a permanent dilemma. It hoped to promote macroeconomic development via central impulses and at the same time it tried to halt the debt process. Huge demand impulses launched from the state during the 1974/75 decline played a decisive role in reversion towards growth. Of course the downtrend of the economy had been accelerated before by the rigid restrictive policy of the State itself. At the same time the stimulation of demand on level of the national economy entailed a rapid growth of state debts. The budget policy consequently gave absolute priority to dismantling the deficit and this could only be done by curbing the boom. So the budget policy decision-makers changed course once again in 1977. The objective of expenditure restriction was waived and various measures were adopted to promote growth (future oriented investments, energy programme, tax reliefs).

In conclusion, the budget policy with its productive potential enhancing trend encouraged the prosperity of the end of 1970s. The built-in tax and transfer system operating as a stabilizer triggered expansive reflexes even during the 1980-81 decline. However, these impacts were much less powerful than in 1974-75. As in 1976-77, the main aspiration of the year 1981 was to deal with the deficit caused by the decline of the state budget. As before, macroeconomic development was once again slowed down by the aggregate impact of state behaviour.

4. Industrial policy as illustrated by electronics projects

The accepted meaning of the term 'industrial policy' covers the efforts of the governments of certain industrial states aimed at adjustment to the intricate processes of the times and at intervention in market events. In a highly articulated list of objectives, industrial policy may be a segment of sectoral structural policy or it may seek to improve the conditions of innovation, quality and services or to enhance the adaptivity of the production pattern (cf. 6). Another approach stresses the role to be played in the market of factors of production and goods produced. In still another approach industrial policy is instead a structural policy aimed mainly at developing the tertiary sector and in this mainly information activities and telecommunications (cf. [7]).

The orientations of industrial policy are always to be assessed in terms of their dynamics. Efforts at increasing future earnings are given preference over the regional balance of present production. This aim has been served for example by the 10% subsidy on investments introduced in the FRG in 1982.

However, R&D is the only component of state purchases of goods and services in the strict sense that one can claim really serves industrial policy objectives. This is also true with respect to development projects of electronics.

Electronics is one of the domains in most industrial states where the development process is subsidized by the state, usually because market self-regulation is a long and unreliable process. References are made to a general and structural lack of innovation, which the state must overcome for the sake of growth and employment (cf. [8]). On the other hand, it is claimed that the risk of own R&D is too high in some high technology spheres such as electronics (cf. [9]). According to an additional expectation, the state is supposed to encourage development in such fields of high technology, because these fields will eventually become key resources of growth chances on an international scale, and because of the spin-offs from their overall economic impact into supplier and user sectors. It is widely feared that a failure to give these impulses to an internationally competitive high technology sector might reduce the overall competitiveness of the economy. However, the example of the Federal Republic of Germany shows that this is not an absolute argument. Despite several lags recorded in high technology areas (cf. [10]), the top positions achieved by the FRG in certain sectors (e.g. engineering) or its overall foreign trade figures of recent years should be a warning against jumping to conclusions.

It is hard to summarize and evaluate the activities of the state aimed at the development of electronics. The volume of direct and indirect support of R&D projects can be estimated only where it is effected by fund transfers and not in the form of tax allowances. Moreover, although there are a number of state measures which are directly or indirectly aimed at the development of the electronics sector, direct quantification of impacts is impossible. This is affected by the scope of basic and applied research work done in government (or in autonomous but state financed) institutions, as well as by governmental purchases, state regulation of business, the policy of structuring the market and competition, restrictions of foreign trade, etc. For the time being the long range impact of state actions in assisting the achievement and maintenance of power positions are considerably more effective than actual support (in terms of cash).

In the Federal Republic of Germany, the development of electronics is concentrated on microelectronic applications mainly in R&D processes of new or development products. The goal is mainly to strengthen the innovative potential of small and medium companies. A special program between 1982 and 1984 with a total volume of DEM 450M provided funding not only for wage costs but also for development costs, consultancy fees paid to third companies (up to 40% of costs) and associated projects (up to 20% of costs). Development of competitiveness and positive employment implications were priority objectives of this program. Reports summarizing the findings of this special program note that the above objectives were actually achieved through specific product development projects up to the degree of maturity, and by expansion and streamlining of product ranges (cf. [11]).

In addition to the support given to the widest use of modern technologies, the federal Government provides financial support for R&D projects in three fields. In the field of electronic components production, a special 'Microperiphery program' sets tasks for the development of sensors and active parts as well as integrated optics. Computer aided design (CAD) of integrated circuits and other microelectronic components is given financial support, and the development of submicro-technologies and new panels is encouraged. The focus of EDP is on the computer aided design of hardware and software, the development of new computer configurations mainly for scientific purposes, and the development of shape scanning and data processing software. Last but not least, in the sphere of industrial automation, the development of computer aided production and manufacturing systems (CAD-CAM) and the application of robots are supported.

The programs outlined above were scheduled for the period 1984 to 1988 at an estimated value of 2,5 milliard DEM. Part of the planned support was given to autonomous research institutes, or cooperation between industrial companies and research institutes instead of channelling it directly to the company sector. Although the state organizations of the Federal Republic of Germany are strongly market-oriented and try to avoid intervention (let us not consider here the state of affairs prevailing in telecommunications), the development of electronics is powerfully influenced by the support given to research and development. The obvious aim is to eliminate the lags behind the USA and Japan in key technology areas.

As far as another facet of industrial policy, namely, its international implications is concerned, it is clear that as in most industrial countries and despite certain recent part achievements in combating the proliferation of protectionism, trade has clearly become increasingly restricted. This restriction has mainly shown a non-custom type discriminative quality. Since national industrial policies are strongly determined by historical, social, institutional and political conditions, there is no 'general success formula' nor any 'safe bid'; there are only part components to adopt. These components must be selected with due consideration of the fact that national industrial policies are often tailored to substitute for or to neutralize the multinational commercial policy approach in the European environment.

5. Technology policy

The scope of the technology policy of the state is known to cover research activities conducted by the government on its own; state assignments of private institutions and individuals; financial contribution and tax benefits given by the state to private research activities without chargeable services; as well as legal regulations of developments, especially standardization law. Research is assisted by several further state measures including training or laws of general taxation which reduce the risk of research work.

Although the ratio of state funding vs. contribution of company funds has diminished in recent years in the sphere of research as well, the participation of the state budget is still considerable. This technology policy is driven by the fact that the national benefits of certain processes are considered to be more precious than the individual gains of companies actually engaged in research. It follows that the external returns of R&D beyond the company (research centre) is the main thrust of technology policy. In the last analysis this means that state subsidy is justified where the private and national returns of research are substantially different, a frequent case in basic research.

However, instead of external returns, the issue of subsidy and 'counter subsidy' is the focus of discussions on current technology policy. Several measures have been adopted claiming that a given area is already subsidized abroad. It is also proposed that that all the involved countries could eventually earn national and economic benefits if subsidies were discontinued. From the point of view of the international dimensions of state support to R&D and the objectives of subsidy (market entry), direct export subsidies appear to be more cost efficient (cf. e.g. [12]). However, such and similar measures are prohibited by GATT, so the countries must choose the alternative of financing research activities.

The share of the Ministry of Research in FRG R&D inputs funded by the state is more than 50%. Governmental R&D activities are coordinated by this Ministry on the level of the Federal Republic. However, this institutional system of state technology policy may not be necessarily seen as evidence of an all-embracing technological concept.

The study of correlations between research inputs and international competitiveness reveals that high research inputs are not an absolutely necessary precondition to attaining world market leader positions in research intensive products. When research and production can be geographically separated without any appreciable loss, locations of production can be selected irrespectively of the choice of research locations. On the other hand when research should be close to production, specialization of research is followed by trade specialization. An empirical analysis of the FRG arrived at conclusions that were largely or wholly in line with theoretical assumptions (cf. [13]).

The competitive edge of research intensive products is not guaranteed by high research intensity rates (i.e., relatively high ratio of R&D inputs to GDP). The technology policy does not have much chance of enhancing the international competitiveness of local companies in areas where the role of international transfer is predominant. In more and more cases the subsidies granted to research cannot in fact influence company choices of manufacturing locations. While the technology policy gives preference to domestic research work it does not necessarily encourage the production of research intensive goods.

When technical knowledge is mobilized internationally, the importance of producing research intensive goods probably diminishes. Instead, labour is considered an important factor of production. Future locations of production will probably be selected according to the need for qualified or non-qualified labour for the process and the regional availability of such labour. Consequently, high research intensity as well as high skilled work intensity will be typical of future exports of advanced industrial countries. Any economic policy targeting to maintain a certain level of per capita income must concentrate on the development of training standards, i.e. of human capital. In this sense an adequate training policy seems to be a profitable alternative to technology policy.

References

[1] MÖLLER, A., *Kommentar zum 'Gesetz zur Förderung der Stabilitaet und des Wachstums der Wirtschaft'*, Hannover, 1968.

[2] CHALOVPEK, G. and TEVFELSBAUER, W., *Gesamtwirtschaftliche Plannung in Westeuropa*, Campus Forschung, no. 523, 1987.

[3] STAEGLIN, R. and STILLE, F., Laenderstudie 'Bundesrepublik Deutschland' in CHALOVPEK, G. and TEVFELSBAUER W., 1987.

[4] GEPPERT, K. et al., *Die wirtschaftliche Entwicklung der Bundeslaender in den siebziger und achtziger Jahren*, Deutsches Institut für Wirtschaftsforschung, Beitraege zur Strukturforschung, no. 94, 1987.

[5] Statistisches Bundesamt, Fachserie 18, Reihe 1, *Konten und Standardtabellen*.

[6] FRANZMEYER, F. et al., *Industriepolitik im westlichen Ausland – Rahmenbedingungen, Strategien, Aussenhandelsaspekte*, Deutsches Institut für Wirtschaftsforschung, Beitraege zur Wirtschaftsforschung no. 92/I-II, Berlin (West), 1987.

[7] WESTPHAL, J., *Brauchen wir eine neue Industriepolitik?* Kieler Vortraege, Neue Reihe no. 109, Institut für Weltwirtschaft an der Universitaet Kiel, 1986.

[8] BERG, H. and MAMMEN, G., 'Alternative Strategien staatlicher Technologieförderung: Eine Analyse der Projekte "Concorde" und "Airbus" ', *Jahrbuch für Sozialwissenschaften* 32, 1981.

[9] PAVITT, K. and SOETE, L.L.G., International Differences in Economic Growth and the International Location of Innovation, in Giersch 1982.

[10] Der Bundesminister für Forschung und Technologie (ed.), *Informationstechnik – Konzeption der Bundesregierung zur Förderung der Entwicklung der Mikroelektronik, der Informations- und Kommunikationstechniken*, Bonn, 1984.

[11] VDI-Technologiezentrum (ed.), *Sonderprogramm 'Anwendung der Mikroelektronik' des Bundesministers für Forschung und Technologie*, Zweiter Erfahrungsbericht, Berlin (West), 1985.

[12] SPENCER, B. J. and BRANDER, J. A., 'International R&D Rivalry and Industrial Strategy', *The Review of Economic Studies*, vol. 50, 1983.

[13] KLODT, H., *Wettlauf um die Zuknuft. Technologiepolitik im internationalen Vergleich*, Kieler Studien no. 206, J.C.B. Mohr (Paul Siebeck), Tübingen, 1987.

Bruno Dallago

MACROECONOMIC PLANNING IN ITALY: EXPERIENCES AND FAILURES [1]

1. Introduction

That planned development of the Italian economy was both opportune and necessary was already apparent in the years immediately after the war, at which time the new constitution of the Italian Republic was in the process of being drawn up. In fact, article 41 section 3 declares that the law will determine the programmes and controls as may be appropriate for public and private economic activity to be directed and coordinated to social ends [2]. Even then this definition gave rise to different interpretations: on the one hand, there were those who claimed that it appeared to imply that the implementation of global planning was possible [3]; on the other, there were those that maintained that the intention of the Constitution was more simply to refer to the need to adopt pogrammes and appropriate controls so that public and private economic activity could be directed towards social ends. This indeterminateness and ambiguity of the interpretation of Constitution has been a constant feature of the Italian planning experience and gave origin to a long-lasting debate between the two interpretations.

In actual fact, and despite the broad granting of power, the Italian Government has made scant commitment to any planning activity worthy of the name. The principal features of planning in Italy have been therefore the incoherence of such measures as have been attempted, in the absence of a generally accepted frame of reference; its close dependence on political events, which have always led to the rejection of any such general framework or to the practical impossibility of implementing it; the time lags in the implementation of pogrammes for the restructuring of the domestic economy and its foreign relation; the confused nature of technical solutions and the weakness of the institutional measures adopted. As a consequence, planning has rarely been able to condition – even less to direct – these transformations to any serious extent. Instead it has been a consequence of them, little more than a recognition of their occurrence and of the necessity to deal with the disequilibria that they have created. In the best of cases planning has been, as at the beginning of the 1960s, an instrument at the service of a reformist Utopia backed by insufficient determination or, better, political clout.

2. Tendencies of macroeconomic planning in Italy: a brief historical outline

The history of economic planning in Italy may be divided into four principal phases. They are distinguished in the first place by a change in the role and content of planning from one phase to the other.

a. The country's early experiences in planning, although they may be interesting in historical and scientific terms, were sectorial in character and the work of non-governmental bodies. These comprised plans drawn up by the allied authorities or in association with them in order to organize the use of the international aid provided for the war-damaged economies ('Piano di primo aiuto': First Aid Plan) and, under the Marshall Plan, the 'Programma di ricostruzione dell'economia italiana per il periodo 1948-1952' (Programme for the Reconstruction of the Italian Economy for the Period 1948-1952); plans designed to tackle the problems of economic recovery and reconstruction; the 'Piano del lavoro' (Plan for Labour) of the CGIL trade union.

b. From the 1950s onwards planning attempts became more substantial, and there was a growing recognition of the need for "global planning". The main achievement in this period was the drawing up in 1954 of the 'Schema decennale di sviluppo dell'occupazione e del reditto in Italia nel decennio 1955-1964' (Ten-Year Scheme for the Development of Employment and Income in Italy in the Decade 1955-1964), also known as the "Vanoni Scheme". This set itself three principal objectives: the creation of 4 million new jobs in non-farming sectors, the reduction of the gap between North and South, and bringing the balance of payments into equilibrium through increased exports. Although the conditions required to achieve these objectives (5% annual growth rate, increase in the propensity to save, change in the territorial and sectorial distribution of investments) all existed, thanks to the spontaneous development of the economy, the plan largely failed in the attainment of its first two objectives.

The vicissitudes of the Programme highlighted the lack of success of the planning policy followed during the 1950s. The causes of this failure were mainly political in nature, and manifested themselves in the economic field as a sharp division between planning and conjunctural economic policy, which continued to predominate. There was therefore a lack of the necessary coordination between the medium-long term objectives set by the Programme and conjunctural policies, which should have served to complete the medium-long term policies, although these in fact did not exist. This state of affairs was made evident by the fact that, in the course of the 1960s, the drawing up and implementaton of economic policy was entrusted to the traditional bodies (Bank of Italy, the Treasury, the Ministry of Public Works) rather than to the bodies responsible for designing the Programme itself. And this led, due to the predominance of the former over the latter, to the adoption of measures which were in contrast with the philosophy of the Programme and which therefore led to its failure.

c. From the end of the 1950s onwards there was a certain revival in the debate over economic planning and in early 1960s the political climate, more favourable to planning, was ripe. In 1961 a commission of experts, the Commissione Papi, was set up with the task of elaborating a macroeconomic model of development that would serve to provide estimates for planning purposes [4]. However, the Commission interrupted its work before it could use the model for a real programming policy. Three major events made 1962 an outstanding year in the history of Italian planning, a period when a new attitude, more favourable to macroeconomic planning than in any other period of post-war Italy, arose within the government. In 1962 the Socialist Party entered the Government and in the same year the "Nota aggiuntiva" (Adjunct note) by the Republican Party leader and Budget Minister Ugo La Malfa was presented [5], in which the need to give greater powers to macroeconomic planning was stressed. Also in 1962, the Commissione Saraceno was formed, with the task of studying the initiation of an incisive process of planning [6]. The outcome of these separate projects was the "Bozza di programma quinquennale per gli anni 1965-1969" (Giolitti Plan) [7], which was never implemented because of yet another government crisis. The subject was taken up again by Pieraccini [8], who had replaced Giolitti as Budget Minister; the Bozza (Outline) became the "Programma economico nazionale 1966-70", called the Pieraccini Plan [9], which set out to solve the main structural problems of the Italian economy (full employment, development of agriculture, of the Mezzogiorno and of collective services), but which met with almost total failure. These failures and a changing political climate led to an increasing lack of faith in multi-year global planning. In such circumstances, a major project, the "Progetto '80" was drawn up in 1968-69, which constituted both a document providing forecasting and planning for the major decisions in economic policy to be taken during the 1970s and a preliminary report for the 1971-75 programme. However, it kept the form and content of the Pieraccini Plan, and therefore came up against similar difficulties, which led to its substantial failure. 1971 saw the 'Documento programmatico preliminare per l'impostazione del programma 1971-75' (Preliminary Planning Document for the Drawing up of the 1971-75 Programme), and at the beginning of 1973, the 'Rapporto sulla programmazione' (Report on Planning) [10]. This latter, a very ambitious and broad-ranging document, foresaw the need for planning in order to respond to "fundamental challenges – i.e. those radical changes, as opposed to current tendencies, that appeared necessary for achievement of the plan" [11]. Growing social tensions (widespread strikes during the "autunno caldo"- the hot autumn), the rapid deterioration of the international economic situation, the first oil-shock and continual government crises led to the fall of the centre-left govenment, and this originated a radical change in planning strategy. Multi-year global planning was abandoned and its place taken by annual and sectoral plans. These, in a highly unstable period with acute sectoral problems, appeared more realistic. The weakness of such a solution is stressed by the fact that the radical changes occurred in this period in the domestic and world economy (in the cost of labour and the relative price of energy and raw materials in the first place) and the solution of still unsolved traditional problems (unemployment and North-South dualism in particular) would have required a comprehensive, planned approach for the structural accommodation of the domestic economy. The new political climate, the weakness and slowness of the planning apparatus, the lack of resources to afford parallely all the structural problems induced the government to concentrate on a few priority areas with sectoral programmes and leave the rest to the autonomous decisions of the private sector and the consequences of increasing foreign competition.

d. After years in which the word 'planning' had practically disappeared from circulation, the end of the 1970s saw its revival, coincident with the Communist

Party joining the political majority and at the height of the most serious domestic and international economic crisis since the war. The fundamental problems were the same as they had always been, in particular unemployment and the backwardness of the Mezzogiorno. To these, new ones were added like inflation, new oil and raw materials shocks, growing competition from newly industrialized countries in traditional Italian export sectors (textiles, shoes, garments). Therefore the principal objective of this new attempt at planning was management of the crisis. As a result, with the revival in the economy during the 1980s it too began to peter out, despite a certain amount of pressure to make room for planning in order to give a more orderly and lasting character to the revival.

In 1978 the Budget Minister Pandolfi presented his draft three-year plan for 1979-81, which was definitively approved in January 1979 [12]. The plan proposed, in respect of the government accords of the period of "national solidarity", to "...set the Italian economy on the road of development with stability", by placing itself "... in an intermediate position between a government programme and a traditional programme for development". The Pandolfi Plan was the last genuinely global plan considering the overall macroeconomic tendencies of the economy. However, on the Plan's own admission, this general character did not concern policies: it in fact "...does not directly involve the generality of policies that comprise a global plan for the country, but hinges on the factors and instruments of economic policy". In fact, it was an attempt to enclose the various forms of sectoral and regional planning currently under development (urban and rural planning, health planning, planning at the local district level, planning of state participation) within a framework of financial compatibility that ensured a common perspective and tied planning to an incomes policy aimed at creating prospects for accumulation and employment while respecting the open nature of the Italian economy.

Therefore this period saw the use mainly of instruments of administrative decentralization and sectorial planning. As a consequence, the importance of the Budget Ministry diminished and in 1977 the institutional centre of gravity passed to the Ministry of Industry. The Budget Ministry would only recover its proper institutional role with the La Malfa Plan, originally drawn up for the period 1981-83 and then updated to 1982-84, although it never came into effective operation [13]. This, however, was not a global plan in the true sense of the term, since it dealt almost exclusively with the components of supply.

The Plan led planning activity back into the ambit of government of the public budget, aimed at encouraging development by means of new investments able to raise the average productivity of the economic system and to render it less dependent on the foreign component. The chief aim became one of combining and controlling in a single flow all the various tributaries through which public money entered economic activities [14]. Planning therefore continued to be predominantly sectoral in nature, although it sought to harmonize the various sector programmes with the aims of a mainly financial plan.

Persisting sectoral problems (mainly the large and growing state budget deficit and widespread unemployment) and the conflictuality characterizing the renewed cooperation within the government between the Christian Democratic and the Socialist parties (which led the ministries controlled by different parties to compete fiercely against each other) led during the 1980s to the abandonment of the idea of establishing global plans and the concentration on sectors. The most significant examples in this regard were two in number: the Goria Plan, taking the name of the then Christian Democratic Treasury Minister, and the De Michelis Plan, taking the name of the Socialist Minister of Labour. The former was a financial plan developed in order to reduce the deficit in the national budget for the five-year period 1986-90. The latter, entitled 'La politica oc - cupazionale per il prossimo decennio' (Employment Policy for the Next Decade) was drawn up in 1984-85 and, given the crucial importance of the employment problem in Italy, included most of the standard themes of short-term economic policy. Despite the interest of the analytical section of the document and a number of novel proposals therein, the document was poorly articulated among it various parts and was particularly unsatisfactory with regard to the measures recommended to deal with what its analytical section identified as the fundamental long-term problem to be solved – unemployment in the Mezzogiorno.

3. The organization of planning

There are various bodies in Italy responsible for planning as a whole or for one or more phases. As we shall see below, the real organizational problem of Italian planning lies in the limited powers of implementation available to these bodies. In fact the implementation of economic policy is in the hands of other bodies, and this leads to a breakdown between the planning and implementation stages, which is one of the chief causes of the failure of economic planning in Italy.

a. Parliament and Government. According to the Italian Constitution, Parliament is empowered to take important decisions over economic planning. It takes the plan proposed by the Government and transforms it into law. But, as we have seen, the Constitution refers not to one single plan but, more in general, to programmes which direct and coordinate public and private economic activity for social ends. It is instead up to the law to formulate programmes and exercise controls which are applied through the intervention and direct action of the public administrations, which are responsible for the execution of the law [15].

This system is unwieldy and is a serious impediment to the efficiency of planning. The two-chamber nature of the Italian Parliament, in fact, makes a lengthy delay in the progress of any law through Parliament inevitable, even more so in the case of complex laws such as those to do with planning, which affect the economic interests of various pressure groups in various ways. Also, simply to coordinate the duration of the legislature with the period of time envisaged by the plan is difficult to achieve, because of the complex nature of the electoral process. Neither is Parliament able to verify with any precision the timing and modes of implementation of the plans. In fact, the instrument that it has at its disposal, the annual government reports [16] seems too generic to be effective.

The role of the Government also seems to be an ambiguous one, because of the multi-sectoral nature of planning legislation. In the absence of a body responsible for the drafting and implementation of the plan as a whole, the joint participation of all components of the Government in the establishment and execution of the plan is necessary. This entails the laborious and difficult work of coordinating the various ministers undertaken by the President of the Council of

Ministers and by the interministerial committees [17].

b. The interministerial committees. The most important is the 'Comitato interministeriale per la programmazione economica' (Interministerial Committee for Economic Planning) (CIPE). This was set up in 1967 to replace the old 'Comitato interministeriale per la ricostruzione' (Interministerial Committee for Reconstruction). It is chaired by the President of the Council of Ministers and comprises various ministers [18]. Apart from establishing goals for national economic policy and coordinating them within the EEC, CIPE sets out, in association with the Minister for the Budget and Economic Planning, the general lines for the national draft budget proposals, as well as general directives intended to implement the national economic programme and to promote and coordinate for this purpose the activity of the public administration and the public corporations. Here one notes a division of duties between the Council of Ministers and CIPE with respect to economic planning; it is the Committee's responsibility to introduce the general guidelines for formulation of the national economic programme and the draft budget, while it is the Council's duty to approve the proposed plan and budget [19].

The 'Comitato interministeriale per il coordinamento della politica industriale' (The Interministerial Committee for the Coordination of Industrial Policy) (CIPI). This was set up in 1977 along the CIPE and coordinates various ministers [20] and its meetings are attended by the Secretary General of Planning. The committee applies to industrial policy the functions assigned by the law to CIPE, within the ambit of the directives that the latter intends to adopt. In particular, the committee determines the directions that industrial policy will take. In the same 1977 year also the 'Comitato interministeriale per la politica economica estera' (the Interministerial Committee for the Foreign Economic Policy) (CIPES) was established. It comprises various ministries [21] involved in foreign relations and its aim is to define and coordinate the general guidelines of foreign trade policy, of insurance and credit to export, of international cooperation policy (in particular with developing countries), of supply policy and of any other economic activity with foreign countries and check their implementation [22].

c. The Ministry for the Budget and Economic Planning. In 1967 the old Budget Ministry was reorganized, the intention being to make it better able to preside over planning activity, and it was given a new denomination – Ministry for the Budget and Economic Planning. The reorganization also provided that the Ministry should collaborate with the Treasury Ministry over the draft budget, with a view to the general aims of economic planning. It comprises two general deparments: one of them, the 'Segreteria generale per la programmazione economica' (Planning Office) is of particular importance for planning. This is responsible for preparing policy documents and delivers the technical directives concerning the preparation of these policy documents to ISPE (cf. below). Here one notes a contradiction in the organizational structure: since the President of ISPE is the Budget Minister, it would seem the the law empowers the Secretary to influence the activity of the Minister. However, the technical directives of the Segreteria are subordinate to the general guidelines for the drafting of the general economic plan as laid down by CIPE, and this places the liaison between CIPE and ISPE under the supervision of the Minister. But it is evident that the badly thought-out relationship between Secretary and Minister does not contribute to the preciseness of the organizational arrangement responsible for drawing up the plan and does not promote its efficiency [23].

d. The 'Istituto di Studi per la Programmazione Economica' (Institute of Economic Planning Studies) (ISPE). This is in fact a technical body external to the bureaucratic organization of the Ministry. It has a fact-finding function. Set up in 1967, it conducts surveys and research relating to economic planning in order to compile policy documents in accordance with the directives of the Ministry for the Budget and Economic Planning. However, the Institute has come to play a diminishing role in planning, both for political reasons since the end of the first centre-left government and because of its lack of autonomy and powers, which have made it entirely dependent on the Ministry [24].

4. The temporal and spatial organization of planning

Italian planning undoubtedly displays a considerable amount of confusion in temporal terms, especially as regards the coordination of plans involving different time perspectives. In effect, such coherence does not exist, and it is short-term planning that tends to predominate. Moreover, as already seen, at the end of the 1960s there was a changeover from global to sectoral planning and more recently, the residual medium-term planning has actually meant decisions concerning the strategic allocation of public expenditure for investment. Sometimes it has merely meant the planning of public investments.

Horizontal planning (aggregate plans over varying periods of time, forecast and policy reports, financial laws, multi-yearly and yearly state budgets and sectorial programmes) have been supplemented by so-called vertical planning – i.e. regional planning with the relative instruments of regional finance. This completes the picture of planning in Italy, in which programmes by sector and regional programmes are synthesised into aggregate plans and in particular, in accordance with the law on national accounting (law no. 468/78), in the forecast and policy report, in financial law and corresponding yearly and multi-year state budgets.

5. Aims, methods and instruments of planning in Italy

Traditionally, the priority aims of Italian economic policy have been an increase in employment and the development of the Mezzogiorno. These two aims are closely intertwined, insofar as most unemployment has always been concentrated in the South. Economic growth has therefore been traditionally seen, in planning documents, in terms of these two fundamental objectives. In practice, of course, the situation has often been very different, as demonstrated by the absence of significant results. Personal and group interests, economic, social and political, have shown themselves to be more powerful than declared priority aims. Thus one witnesses a classic case of the greater force of concentrated interests compared with those that are general and therefore scattered.

Given this situation, the crucial factor becomes the planning of public expenditure, in particular when it comes to making decisions that affect the interests of specific social groups, since resources are scarce and choices have to be made among different and often contrasting priorities and needs. For this purpose the

'Nucleo di valutazione degli investimenti' (Investments Evaluation Unit) was set up in 1982 under the control of the Planning Office with the specific task of distributing the 'Fondo investimenti per l'occupazione' (Employment Investment Fund) among the myriad projects submitted by the central and regional administrations.

The situation is even stranger (and eloquent of the political significance of planning) when one looks at planning methods. Indeed, the planning bodies have no formalized model to serve as the basis for the drawing up of programmes. In fact, when it drafts its plans the Budget Ministry draws on the estimates and forecasts made by other bodies (Prometeia, CER, OCSE), which use for the purpose econometric models developed by themselves. The Ministry therefore takes the results of the elaborations carried out by these institutions, matches them to its own decisions and political aims and uses them as the basis for the plan.

Among all the means that the Government has at its disposal for fulfilling the plan, those most broadly and regularly used, apart from the sectoral policies mentioned above, are budget policy and financial policy. Although other instruments are frequently used, these generally have purely conjunctural aims and are principally instruments for maoeuvering economic policy in the short and extremely short term. In theory, they may be used to steer the economy towards fulfilment of the plan, but manoeuvres of conjunctural economic policy have always prevailed over medium-term plans, and thus also partial instruments and policies serve in fact for conjunctural economic policy and not for achieving plan objectives.

Law no. 468/78 introduced two important innovations in terms of policy instruments; the multi-year state budget, which has a duration of between three and five years, and the 'Legge finanziaria' (finance act). Given the importance of the state budget in the Italian economy, it is important that it should be a flexible instrument. In this sense, the introduction of the 'finanziaria', which is annual, guarantees on the one hand the flexibility and the adaptability of the multi-year budget and, on the other, the linking of the multi-year budget with the economic programme. It is no coincidence that the law explicitly stipulates that the 'legge finanziaria' is to be presented in Parliament together with the 'Relazione previsionale e programmatica' (Forecast and Policy Report), which should provide the economic back-up for it. The Relazione describes the general economic picture and sets out the directions of national economic policy and the consequent policy objectives by demonstrating the coherence and compatibility among the economic situation, the amount and the distribution of resources, policy objectives and the financial commitments foreseen in the multi-year budgets for the state and the overall extended public sector.

To understand the relation between multi-year budget and medium-term plan, which should provide the explicit economic underpinning of the budget, one must remember that law 468 provides for two types of multi-year budget: one with constant legislation and the other relating to policy. The former is tendential, the latter should reflect what is desired. In fact, however, policy budgets have yet to be drawn up, while the tendential budgets have been nothing more than mechanical constructions reflecting the forecast state of the multi-year expenditure budgets.

The financial law is submitted to Paliament by the Treasury Minister jointly with the Budget and Finance Ministers and concurrently with the draft bill for approval of the state forecast budget. The law may make changes and additions to legislative measures affecting the state budget, the budgets of the state-run corporations and those of the bodies relating to local finance. In addition, the law sets the maximum level of recourse to the financial market; this amount contributes, together with revenue, to determining the available cover for all the expenditures to be included in the annual budget. Despite its flexibility and adaptability, however, the 'legge finanziaria' has seen an increase in the heterogeneity of the items included in the law, because of the lack of planning by sector and a weak assertion of the financial budget constraint. As a consequence there have been numerous difficulties over its approval and application, as well as many criticisms and calls for its reform [25].

6   A contradictory and inefficient system

Apart from problems of structure and of coordination among the various components of the planning process, the relations between it and economic policy and the type and degree of constraint placed by the plan on economic, social and political agents represent perhaps the most confused aspect of planning activity in Italy. It is evident from experience that the constraining role of the plan is very limited, if non-existent. And, in fact, its provisions have largely gone unheeded. This has been due, on the one hand, to the generally unclear distribution of duties among the bodies responsible for elaborating and implementing the plan and, on the other, to the complex structure of Italy's social, political and economic relationships. However, it appears that it is the latter that is the principal cause of the problem, [26] and they take concrete form in the large number of interests expressed in the process of developing and implementing the plan. These are impossible to coordinate because of their frequent incompatibility, with the result that none manages to gain priority. Apart from passive resistance to plan objectives and the instruments of implementation, active resistance is also a particularly striking feature of the Italian case.

Generally speaking, the plan should constrain at least the Government and Parliament to take action to ensure its implementation. However, there exists no law, norm or constitutional provision that obliges the Govenment to put the plan into effect. There are therefore no barriers in the way of the contingent political, social and economic interests that wish to nullify it. No mechanism exists to force the Government and Parliament to respect even the most elementary of the rules of public finance: to provide the financial cover of approved expediture laws if the funds made available by the state budget prove inadequate.

Nevertheless, in recent times there has been increasing determination to enforce more responsible behaviour in matters of public expenditure. This change in attitude has come about as a result of a growing awareness among the political parties that the irresponsible behaviour of the past cannot continue because of its inflationary consequences. It therefore seems that only a political agreement among the parties will be able to constrain the Government and Parliament to respect the provisions of a document that they themselves have elaborated and approved. Events of most recent years, however, show how difficult it is to arrive at and respect such an agreement.

The plan, moreover, is not binding on lower-level bodies (ministries and regional administrations in particular). These enjoy a notable degree of autonomy in economic matters, at least as far as the the utilization of the resources in their possession is concerned. Hence the only instrument able to impose an effective constraint on these bodies is the quantity of resources assigned to them. Since this is an essentially quantitative constraint, it acts in indiscriminate fashion and is not really capable of inducing behaviour that complies with the objectives of the plan.

7. Conclusions

As we have briefly seen in the above pages, planning in Italy has had generally disappointing results, even if attempts in terms of means and intellectual effort have been considerable. Nevertheless, the country has achieved results in the economic field that are certainly not negligible, although they are matched by still unsolved structural problems (Mezzogiorno, agriculture, collective services, etc.). These results point to the conclusion that planning may not be indispensable for the process of economic growth, although it certainly is for a balanced development of the economy and society.

Experience of over forty years proves that the present economic system, if left to itself, is unable to solve its structural problems; instead it tends to neglect those (geographical and industrial) areas which are already underdeveloped and concentrate reources in areas where development has been greater – that is, where the infrastructures are more modern and more efficient, and where there is a broader and more sophsticated market. Italy, in fact, does not enjoy the traditional advantage of cheaper manpower available in the more backward areas of the country, since the unification of the labour market is by now a well-established fact.

If this is the case, why has planning been a failure in Italy? And what have been the consequences of such a failure? Is there a possible role for planning in the future? Of course, in Italy, too, planning has encountered the difficulties typical of such an instrument: for example, its rigidity when faced by rapid changes in the international economic system. But there also exist causes for it that are deeply rooted in Italian reality. Causes that are of three kinds: political, technical and institutional.

The political reasons for the situation I have described are to be found in the traditional diffidence that the politico-economic forces dominant in the country (the parties and the centre and centre-left governments) have shown towards the planning instrument, and more generally towards every sort of coordinated intervention by the government in economic matters. The traditional form of state intervention has strengthened the patronage system, which rigorous planning should have eliminated, thus endangering well-consolidated politico-economic alliances, especially in the Mezzogiorno.

Technical shortcomings have been equally serious, although they derive in large part from political opposition to this instrument. As we have seen, plannning in Italy has never even had a specific econometric model of the medium-long term and, moreover, has never had a systematic series of interregional input-output tables with which to verify the impact of economic policies on the various regions of the country (29). In general, instruments have been exercised in generic terms (although, perhaps, given the situation of scant control over these instruments by the planning bodies, this has been inevitable), while objectives have often been extremely ambitious.

Finally, there have been equally serious institutional deficiencies. Initially there was a total lack of any permanent planning body. When these were created, they rapidly showed themselves to be wholly inadequate to the task, or else they were made so by explicit political decisions or, more frequently, by underhand transfers of responsibility between different government bodies. But even more serious has been the fact that planning has been entrusted to a body (the Ministry of the Budget and Economic Planning) which has extremely limited operational powers, while implementation of the plan has been assigned to bodies (Ministries of the Treasury and of Industry especially) which have had no hand in formulating it. Moeover, medium-long term policy has been the responsibility of numerous different bodies, which has meant that coordination of decisions has been extremely difficult, if not impossible, in practice.

In point of fact the above problems do not only affect medium-long term macroeconomic planning but also short-term economic policy itself. Traditionally, the Italian government has never deployed a complete set of short-tem economic policies, but has concentrated on monetary policy (especially in the narrow sense of the term), and has never been able to use budgetary policy to any great effect. If the Italian economy has enjoyed a relatively favourable – not even particularly chaotic – growth trend, this has been mainly due to the decision taken immediately after the war to integrate solidly with the world economy. It has been to a great extent this decision and the strong international competition afforded by the domestic industry to compensate for the lack of medium-long term macroeconomic planning. The relative stability that the world economy has long enjoyed has thus been translated into the relative stability of the Italian economy, but also, and inevitably as we have seen, into the country's failure to find solutions to its most serious structural problems.

In recent years, Italy's inability to institute medium-long term macroeconomic planning and to manoeuvre the set of economic policy instruments as a whole – and chief among these budgetary policy – in the presence of considerable corporative pressure towards a constant increase in current public expenditure, has significantly exacerbated the situation of public finance. The Government has consequently often had to resort to residual policy instruments in order to achieve financial compatibility.

In view of experience so far, one may justifiably ask whether medium-long term planning has any role to play in Italy. Past experience has shown quite clearly, as we have seen, that if left to itself, the economic system is unable to solve its structural problems. Even though this has not impeded relatively dynamic economic growth, it has caused imbalances in it, has aggravated social problems (in relative terms even if not on an absolute level) and made it often difficult to achieve compatibility in finance and external accounts. It is also certain that the strong international integration of the Italian economy makes it more difficult than it was in the 1950s and 1960s to implement effective national economic planning.

The most probable prospect for the Italian economy in the next years appears to be one of increasing integration into the EEC, where strategic decisions –

through explicit or implicit medium-long term planning – will be taken by the leader countries. The Italian economy will adjust to these – probably with the customary delay and with the usual minor subterfuges – relying on the enterprise of its economic operators and on the diligence of its workers, but not on the organization of economic activities and on the clarity of political and macroeconomic choices.

Notes

[1] The research on which the present paper is based was financed by CNR (CNR 88.03107.10). The author would like to thank Dr. Milena Sgarbi for her collaboration in carrying out this research and Dr. Maria Luigia Segnana for having critically discussed with the author a previous version of the paper. However, all the responsibility for the paper's content rests with the author.

[2] On the economic consequences of the social role of macroeconomic planning and intervention, see the paper "Così muore il piano" (This is the way the plan dies) delivered by the Secretary General of Economic Planning Enzo Grilli to the session held on 5 June 1984 as part of the fact-finding survey conducted by the Commissione bilancio della Camera dei deputati, reported in *Mondo economico*, 12 July 1984.

[3] Cf. R. Chiarelli, *Gli organi della pianificazione economica.*

[4] "Proposte per uno schema organico di sviluppo dell'economia e del reditto", a report submitted by Professor Giuseppe Ugo Papi to the Budget Minister Giuseppe Pella on 19 February 1962, in: Ministero del Bilancio, *La programmazione economica in Italia*, vol. II, pp. 1-85.

[5] "Problemi e prospettive dello sviluppo economico italiano". Note submitted to Parliament by the Budget Minister Ugo La Malfa on 22 May 1962, in: Ministero del Bilancio, *La programmazione economica in Italia*, vol II, pp 87 -134.

[6] "Rapporto del Vice Presidente della Commissione Nazionale per la Programmazione Economica" submitted by Professor Pasquale Saraceno to the Budget Minister Antonio Giolitti, in: Ministero del Bilancio, *La programmazione economica in Italia*, vol. II, pp. 135-413.

[7] "Progetto di programma di sviluppo economico pe il quinquennio 1965-1969", presented by the Budget Minister Antonio Giolitti to the Commissione Nazionale pe la Progammazione Nazionale in June 1964, in: Ministero del Bilancio, *La programmazione economica in Italia*, vol. IV, pp. 1-55.

[8] "Progetto di programma di sviluppo economico per il quinquennio 1965-1969", submitted by the Budget Minister Giovanni Pieraccini to the Consiglio dei Ministri on 21 Janary 1965 and approved by the Consiglio dei Ministri on 29 January 1965, in: Ministero del Bilancio, *La programmazione economica in Italia*, vol. IV, pp. 57-247.

[9] "Programma economico nazionale per il quinquennio 1966-1970", submitted by the Budget Minister Antonio Giolitti to the Commisione Nazionale per la Programmazione Economica in June 1964, in: Ministero del Bilancio, *La programmazione economica in Italia*, vol. V, pp. 55-231.

[10] V. Valli, *Politica economica. I modelli, gli strumenti, l'economia italiana*, La Nuova Italia Scientifica, Roma, 1986, pp.293-294.

[11] G. Ruffolo, *Rapporto sulla programmazione*, Laterza, Bari, 1973

[12] "Piano triennale 1979-81", *Mondo economico*, 27 January 1979.

[13] V. Valli, *op. cit.*, pp. 300-302

[14] M. Valentini, "Sogno di una politica di piano", *Mondo economico*, 9 Dec. 1981

[15] G. Abbamonte, *Aspetti funzionali e organizzativi della programmazione,*

[16] The 'Relazione generale sulla situazione economica del paese' (General Report on the economic situation of the nation), annually presented by the Budget Minister together with the Treasury Minister; the 'Relazione programmatica' (Policy report) of each of the state-run corporations (IRI, ENI, EFIM, EGAM) presented yearly by the Minister of State Holding; the 'Considerazioni finali' (Summing-up) by the Governor of the Bank of Italy; etc.

[17] Cf. R. Chiarelli, *op. cit.*

[18] It comprises the Budget and Treasury Ministers, the Ministers of Finance, Industry and Trade, Agriculture and Forestry, Foreign Trade, State Holding, Public Works, Labour and Social Security, Transport and Civil Aviation, the Merchant Navy, Tourism and Entertainment, and Special Intervention in the Mezzogiorno. The Under-Secretary (Vice-Minister) for the Budget, who acts secretary, also takes part. The Governor of the Bank of Italy, the Chairman of ISTAT and the Secretary for Planning may also be invited to attend its sessions.

[19] Cf. R. Chiarelli, *op. cit.*

[20] The Budget and Treasury Ministers, the Ministers of Industry, of State Holding, of Labour and Social Security, of Special Intervention in the Mezzogiorno. The Committee is chaired by the President of the Council of Ministers or, in his absence, by the Minister for the Budget and Economic Planning, who is vice-chairman of the committee.

[21] The Ministries for the Budget and Economic Planning, for Foreign Affairs, the Treasury Ministry, the Ministry of Agriculture and Forestry, of Industry, of Domestic Trade and of Foreign Trade.

[22] *Politica del commercio con l'estero e politica industriale. Problemi e esigenze di coerenza*, Laboratorio di politica industriale, Nomisma, Bologna, November 1983, pp. 19-21

[23] S. Cassese, *Il sistema amministrativo italiano*, Il Mulino, Bologna, 1983; R. Chiarelli, *op. cit.*

[24] G. Girelli, "De profundis per l'ISPE", *Mondo economico*, 11 March 1981

[25] R. Bocciarelli, "Legge finanziaria: tutto da rifare?", *Mondo economico*, 10 March 1986.

[26] A. Berettoni Arieri, "Programmazione e contabilità delle regioni", in Aspetti funzionali ed organizzativi della programmazione, Quaderni della Regione Umbria.

John B. Hall*

Macroeconomic planning and dependency reversal in the Republic of Korea

Who would have believed that South Korea's economic development program would ever succeed? In 1955 South Korea was but a resource poor country located on the mainland of Asia. Per capita income was low, even by Third World standards. The colonial era from 1910 to 1945 left a distorted economy. Industry was largely north of the 38th parallel. The agricultural south had been oriented towards providing rice for the Japanese colonial masters. The civil war fought at the beginning of the 1950s left the population on the brink of starvation. Infrastructure, towns and cities were largely destroyed. Though military dictatorships sought to cure the problems of postwar political instability, the instability did not end, for the dictators tended to meet their fates in military coups, only to be replaced by other military dictators.

In 1964 Mr. Park Chung Hee began a modernization program relying heavily on borrowed credits. By the end of the 1970s when Mr. Park was killed in a bloody coup, South Korea was the fourth largest debtor in the world, just behind Brazil, Argentina, and Mexico. During his regime, Mr. Park had clearly made the South Korean economy dependent on the United States and Japan for the import of foreign capital and technology, and the export of manufactured goods.

But this is now economic history. Dependency reversal is occurring in South Korea and is being led by macroeconomic planning policies which have promoted rapid industrialization and competitive exporting on the world market. That dependency reversal is occurring is fully supported by the empirical evidence borne out in the national income accounts. In beginning an analysis of this interesting subject, let us first start with a review of dependency theory, for this is the knot which must first be untangled.

1. The dependency controversy:

Early contributors to the dependency school (e.g. Baran, 1957; Frank 1966, 1967; Amin, 1977; Wallerstein, 1974; Emmanuel, 1972) developed an effective counter-argument to the Ricardian theory of comparative advantage. [1] To the early dependency theorists the growth of trade and foreign investment primarily served to strengthen the economies of the developed, core countries, while retarding growth and contributing to the underdevelopment of peripheral countries. Later contributions in this theoretical vein (e.g., Cardoso and Falleto, 1979; Evans: 1979; Lim, 1985) acknowledged that trade and foreign investment could actually lend themselves to economic growth and development in the peripheral countries; however, such development would characteristically be 'dependent' and thereby plagued with accompanying problems related to the fact that financial and political hegemony remained in the hands of the countries at the developed core. In effect, the dependency relationship would not be altered substantially even through growth and development.

Both the earlier and latter traditions of dependency theory provided significant contributions. Most importantly, the towering monument of the Ricardian tradition that had stood erect over the world as the unquestioned axiom of international trade theory since the early 1800s was effectively toppled. The theoretical tables were turned so that Third World countries could better counterpose policies that worked in their own interests. Modernization theory's legacy (e.g. Rostow, 1960; Gellner, 1969) fell with Ricardo; technocrats working at multilateral institutions were placed on the defensive; social science theory was unleashed to do something aside from justifying the status quo; and the complex realities of countries in Latin America, Africa, and the Middle East were brought into clearer light.

There is, however, a recognizable streak of pessimism inherent in the dependency tradition. This is related to the Dependistas' position (e.g. Frank, 1969) that only a transition to socialism could provide the preconditions for real solutions to problems associated with capitalist underdevelopment, for a socialist transition is thought to break the bonds of imperialist exploitation and allow a national economy to begin a development program based on national control over production and allocation of surplus.

The problem, however, arises that such transitions are not as easily achieved as theorized, especially given the historic power struggle in the world between the United States and the Soviet Union. The case of Chile under Salvadore Allende in the early 1970s is especially exemplary of a Latin American nation caught in the superpower struggle, and, consequently, its unsuccessful attempt of a transition to socialism which was clearly thwarted by U.S. interference. Moreover, the consequences of Chile's remaining in the capitalist camp and under Auguste Pinochet's monetarist program, has contributed to this nation's further deindustrialization, as evidenced by '...manufacturing and real productive sectors losing ground to services,' e.g. trade and finance (Schneider, 1984:224). Nicaragua under Sandinista rule serves as a contemporary example of a country struggling for most of this decade to escape from the capitalist camp and implement a development program inspired by Sandinista leadership. Whether the Sandinistas will ultimately succeed or even survive as the dominant political force in Nicaragua remains dubious at this point in time, especially given the determination of the administration currently in Washington and the internal problems created by Sandinista leadership itself.

The evidence of these two cases, in particular, leads me to conclude that the dependency tradition suffers from unsolvable pessimism consequent on the superpower struggle. In short, if a third World nation must continue to function as a capitalist country integrated into the capitalist world market, and there exist real forces that help perpetuate this, then trying to solve problems associated with capitalist underdevelopment can and will only prove futile. I am inclined to regard this perspective as a correct assessment for the Latin American cases around which this school of thought has achieved its highest degree of academic sophistication. Given the international capitalist framework, countries in Latin America such as Argentina, Brazil, and Mexico are not escaping dependencia's grip even through growth and development, nor are they able to make a transition to socialism because of USA intervention. But what about capitalist development in East Asia? There appear to be some cases in East Asia for which such pessimism is unwarranted.

Admittedly, Japan's developmental successes might be easily passed off as the reachieving of core status (Cumings, 1987) during the high economic growth period (HEGP) of the post war years (Kosai and Ogino, 1984). For Taiwan and South Korea, however, success is more recent though far more difficult to discern. It might not even be success at all, at least if we look through the eyes of dependency theorists such as H.C. Lim, F. Cardoso, and E. Falleto. But let us not resign ourselves so easily to pessimism before considering another contribution.

Alice Amsden (1979) challenged the systemic determinism of the dependency theorists' positions. She made a convincing argument that Taiwan is indeed on the road to reversing its historical dependency and achieving this through sustained growth, balanced economic development, and a reasonably equitable distribution of income. Amsden (1979: 342) confronts dependency theorists with the paradox that Taiwan '...is both more integrated in world capitalism than other poor market economies and more developed'. Her challenging perspective has precipitated some serious soul searching on the part of developmental scientists. Fredric Deyo's (1987a) recently edited book is largely a response to Amsden's challenge. Deyo et al. attempt to find some theoretical middle-ground between the naivity of the modernization school and the pessim-istic determinism of the dependency school. What makes East Asian success unique in Deyo's view (1987b: 228) is the evidence of a 'strategic capacity model of development in which there is effective ... success in promoting change in the domestic economic structure and in responding flexibly to change in external develop-mental circumstances'. In sum, Deyo supports Amsden's case: that dependency theory cannot be applied across the board to all Third World countries.

Deyo et al. do not attempt to hide their opposition when citing the authoritarian character of the East Asian states, but their collective opinion, nevertheless, expresses that these countries and city-states are indeed going somewhere. Though Deyo, in his conclusion (1987b: 227-247) advances an alternate, synthetic theory, he fails to specifically address the pressing question: Can the East Asian NICs, through their developmental programs, effectively escape the strangling grip of dependency? In the spirit of Amsden's paradox, I will argue in this paper that South Korea is also 'more integrated' into world capitalism than other peripheral market economies and also more developed. And like Taiwan, the consequence of a successful modernization program led by intelligent macroeconomic planning policies in South Korea is resulting in this country's growing out of its historical dependency.

2. Defining dependency:

Definitions of dependency tend to be general and varied, though there are some unifying themes. Variation is accentuated by the fact that developmental scientists trained in and across several disciplines, ranging from economics to political science and sociology, have made contributions to this tradition. Cardoso (1973: 163) argues that dependency is manifested as the accumulation, expansion, and self-realization of local capital has an external reliance on a dynamic complement outside of the national economy. The dependent country's linkage with this dynamic complement disrupts and distorts economic and political processes within the local economy. Caporaso and Zarae also think in this vein. Their 'holistic' definition (1981: 48) posits that '... dependency refers to a structural condition in which a healthy, integrated system cannot complete its economic cycle except by an exclusive (or limited) reliance on an external complement'. Their emphasis attempts to draw together external reliance, restricted choices, and domestic fragmentation into one definition. Caporaso and Zarae (1981:44) provide a more contemporary understanding of dependency by shifting the analysis away from unified nation states to more fluid and institutionally evasive units. They focus on alliances between local classes and international capital, banks, industries, firms, and the like.

Peter Evans's notions (1979) also follow in this vein; however, Evans has concentrated his efforts on dealing with the phenomenon of 'dependent' development. According to Evans, dependent development implies both the accumulation of capital and some degree of industrialization which comes through the alliance of international and local capital. Evans adds to his argument (1979: 31-32) that the state also joins the alliance as an active partner, and the resulting triple alliance of international capital, local capital, and the state is the fundamental factor in the emergence of dependent development.

3. South Korean dependency

The beginning of Korea's integration into the modern world is marked by the signing of the Kanghwa Treaty with Japan in 1876. By 1910, Japan had both economically and legally incorporated Korea into her late-forming colonial empire, effectively subjecting Korea to the 'iron heel' of imperialism. With the meeting of the State-War-Navy Coordinating Committee on August 10th and 11th of 1945 (Cumings, 1981: 120), the Korean peninsula was partitioned just below the 38th parallel, following Japan's bitter defeat in August of 1945 and the signing of the armistice ending the Korean War in 1953 at Panmunjom.

Korea's dependency under Japanese imperial rule was clearly observable during the colonial period, for the Japanese colonial administration ran the country according to the classical model. Essentially, Korea supplied Japan with raw materials, food stuffs, and semi-finished manufactures, while also serving as a market for Japanese finished products (Cumings, 1981: 4-10). Korean dependency in the postwar period since 1953 is more difficult to distinguish. The North's incorporation into the Socialist World and the subsequent lack of available information on trade and finance severely limits the researching and drawing of conclusions about North Korea's developmental successes and failures. There is reason to speculate that North Korea's indebtedness to her socialist neighbours is a pressing problem; however, the closed nature of financial relations among the planned, socialist economies leaves statements concerning the scope and severity of North Korean indebtedness and potential dependency resting, at best, on a loose footing. The South's integration into the capitalist world since 1953, on the other hand, has very clearly been dominated militarily and politically by the influence of the United States.

As a late arriver on the world scene, the United States has resorted to more obscure means for creating and maintaining dependency relationships with countries such as South Korea, at least in ways which are more subtle when compared to traditional colonial control.

This is related to the fact that the postwar world under the strategic umbrella of Pax Americana has since become increasingly integrated through such institutions as the military-industrial complex led by Washington, along with private sector interests evinced by the activities of international banks and multinational corporations that are built on the international division of labour and a complex system of capital flows that are integral to a modern-day financial system. Consequently, the mechanisms for bringing a country into and holding it in a dependency relationship have changed and still continue to evolve as the multinational linkages integrating the world system through strategic relations, international finance, production, and distribution evolve and change over time. Unfortunately, there is neither a handbook which a clearcut set of rules for judging South Korean dependency, nor a yardstick or scale for measuring it.

In his seminal work on the period of the Park regime, Lim (1985) argues his well researched case: that the period from 1963 to 1979 was indeed an era of dependent development in South Korea. Development was evinced (1985: 89) by capital accumulation and differentiation of the productive structure. Dependency, on the other hand, was evinced by exclusion and repression in the social, economic, and political spheres; and, by increasing foreign indebtedness, balance of payment difficulties, and trade dependence' (1985: 4).

The 'dependency' aspects of dependent development argued by Lim are readily verifiable in South Korea during the Park regime from 1964-1979. [2] It is also observable that problems associated with dependency continued after the military coup in 1979 which ended Mr. Park's life and brought Mr. Chun to power in 1980. However, the prospects for changes in the political sphere appear more promising since concessions were made in June of 1987 by Mr. Roe, when he was one of the presidential candidates running in the 1987 election. Though exclusion and repression may still remain, visible gains have recently been made through the restoration of an electoral process. In effect, this provides for a greater degree of participation in presidential and assembly elections by the South Korean public. In addition, key opposition leaders running in the December 1987 presidential election were integral in the drafting of a new constitution during August and September of 1987. These are two examples indicating that exclusion in the political and social spheres is lessening. Increasing democratization also means that citizens can use the electoral process to increase voter participation in the economic sphere: by voting for an electoral candidate, the voter essentially chooses an economic policy that is advocated by the candidate of their choice. Long suppressed rights of freedom of association and active engagement in collective bargaining by the labour force have been fully exhibited on a nationwide and industry-wide basis since the summer of 1987. Repression is clearly on the wane with respects to the rights of labour.

If we were to accept the first part of Lim's definition of South Korean dependency, and, if the problems of exclusion and repression in the political and social spheres were to end, or at least diminish, could we then speak of development accompanied by diminishing dependency? The point which I would like to stress is that dependency should not be viewed as a static condition. One should be able to judge, over time, whether dependency is intensifying (as Lim did, from the period prior to the beginning of the Park administration to 1979 when he was ousted) or whether it is diminishing, (as I will argue has been occurring in recent years). Finally, if we can verify that dependency is indeed diminishing in the present period, can we make realistic predictions with respect to its diminishing more in the near and distant future? I am inclined to think so.

Political concessions made in the summer of 1987 clearly indicate dependency to be lessening, and, in effect, reversing. However, because such information is not generally quantified, it remains difficult to develop a statistical argument that in the political and social spheres South Korean dependency is indeed reversing. On the other hand, a careful review of the national income accounts does provide us with some concrete evidence for constructing a case that Korean dependency is indeed reversing itself in the economic sphere. Such reverse is evidenced by current account surpluses, capital goods exports, changing employment composition, rapid growth in per capita income, substantial increases in the rates of savings and investment, and the like.

4. Dependency reversal: the statistical evidence

One dependency indicator (Caporaso and Zarae 1981: 49) is measured by how 'uniformly distributed' the external reliance is in completing a country's economic cycle. What is interesting about the South Korean case is that there has historically existed a dual dependency, with the U.S. and Japan clearly dominating with respect to participation and influence in South Korea's economy. We might say that the U.S. and Japan clearly have a dual dominance in the 'completing' of South Korea's economic cycle. Both are the most important countries as sources of foreign investments, as suppliers of imports, and buyers of South Korean exports.

The U.S. and Japan together provide the largest share of Korean imports, accounting for 67.3 percent of the total in 1970. This figure decreased to 55.1 percent by 1986. Such a decrease indicates some degree of diversification of Korea's import markets with respect to her trading partners. During this 17 year period from 1970 to 1986, the percent of U.S. imports remained less than half of the combined U.S.-Japan total, decreasing from 27.5 percent of the total of 67.3 in 1970 to 20.7 percent of the 55.1 percent in 1986. Japan's share of South Korea's import market, on the other hand, remained larger than half, changing slightly from 39.8 percent of the 67.3 percent in 1970 to 34.4 percent of the 55.1 percent in 1986 (measured in current $U.S.) (*Major Statistics of the Korean Economy*, 1987, p. 230, hereafter referred to as 'MS,1987').

Korean exports (MS,1987: 223) display a similar but reversed pattern. The dominant market share of exports is bought by the U.S. and Japan, and is diminishing over time as the Korean export market diversifies to include other nations markets. However, there is a reversed role here: while the Japanese sell to South Korea an increasing share of her imports, the U.S. is buying the larger share of South Korea's exports.

What is important to recognize is that the dominant role played by the U.S. and Japan decreased from a joint export share of 75.4 percent in 1970 to 55.6 percent in 1986. This means that the South Korean export market has been diversifying to include a larger share for countries besides the USA and Japan. While this occurred, however, the U.S. share increased significantly from 47.3 percent of the 55.6 joint total in 1986, making the United States the key connection for maintaining South Korea's export promotion program.

An examination of imports and exports by commodity groups presents a mixed picture requiring some inter-pretation. Machinery and transport equipment as percentage of imports measured in current dollars (MS, 1987: 215-216), increased from 29.7 percent of total imports in 1970 to 33.7 percent in 1986. Such an increase might be interpreted, at face value, as an indicator of South Korea's growing dependency on foreign technology. However, this growing percentage could also be viewed from a different perspective: that the transfer of technology achieved through importing machinery into South Korea is indeed taking place, and, at an increasing rate. If we likewise consider exports by commodity groups, we find that the percentage of machinery and transport equipment exported by South Korea also increased.

The evidence presented clearly demonstrates that the classical dependency model no longer applies to the South Korean case. South Korea is no longer in the position of a peripheral country, exporting food stuffs and raw materials, and relying on technological imports from the developed core countries. Machinery and transport equipment as a percentage of South Korean exports (MS, 1987: 215-216) increased from 7.36 percent of total value of exports in 1970 to 33.6 percent in 1987, while the traditional exports of food and livestock which played an important role during the colonial period had actually decreased to 4.5 percent of the total value of exports by 1986 (MS, 1987: 212). This trend might be related to the peculiarity of the South Korean case: for a country with a small internal market, limited land base, and shortage of natural resources, exports from the processing sector provided the only possibilities for development in this country. As early as 1970, South Korea's manufactured goods (MS 1987: 212) accounted for 83.6 percent of exports. By 1986, manufactured goods had increased to 94.6 percent of exports. The increasing percentage of exported manufactures must be seen against a backdrop of a seventeen year average annual growth rate in GNP of 9.97 percent (measured in constant won against 1980 prices from the years 1970 to 1986, MS,1987: 3). Likewise, per capita GNP (measured in current $ U.S., MS 1987: 3) increased from $ 252 in 1970 to $ 2,200 in 1986. The merchandise trade balance in current dollars has shifted since 1985 from deficit to surplus, showing (MS, 1987: 207-208) a positive balance of $ 4.2 billion for the year 1986, and this trend is likely to continue, provided that exchange rates remain close to what they were at the end of 1987. Foreign exchange holdings continue to increase and now total an amount equal to almost eight billion dollars in 1986 (MS, 1987:207-8). The unemployment rate (MS, 1987:23) has consistently fallen from 4.5 percent in 1970 to 3.8 percent in 1986, according to the official measure. Meanwhile, there has been a real and constant increase in the percentage of the labour force working in manufacturing and mining, increasing from 14.3 percent of the total labour force in 1970 to 25.9 percent in 1986 (MS, 1987:25). Those employed in the sector of 'social overhead capital' have increased from 35.5 percent of the work force in 1970 to 50.5 percent in 1986. Meanwhile, those employed in agriculture, forestry and fisheries decreased as a percentage of the work force, diminishing from 50.4 percent in 1970 to 23.6 percent in 1986 (MS, 1987:25).

Another important measure of South Korean development is that the national savings as percentage of GNP (MS, 1987: 57) has effectively doubled in the last seventeen years: from 16.2 percent in 1970 to 32.8 percent in 1986, making South Korea's national savings rate, measured as percentage of GNP, the highest in the world. Similarly, the 1986 investment ratio of 30.2 percent in 1986 was also the highest in the world (MS, 1987; 57).

The statistical indicators referred to here serve to support a strong case that growth and economic development have, and, are, taking place in South Korea - - and at an extremely rapid rate when measured against most other countries in the world. With respect to changes in employment, savings ratios, rates of investment, and composition of imports and exports, the South Korean case is, without question, an exemplary case of economic development based on an upward structural mobility of its industry and a rapid advancement with respect to its international position in the product cycle, combined with reduced dual country dependence on both the U.S. and Japan for import and export markets.

5. The role of planning

Macroeconomic planning has clearly played a role in this process of transition from a dependent Asian country to one exemplifying rapid per capita income growth based on dynamic industrial development. Planning in South Korea has included indicative planning supported by a comprehensive incentive system, explicit planning through actual five year plans, and even heavy-handed interventions.

South Korea is a late industrializer in the Gerschenkron (1962) sense. While industrialization in Britain in the 18th century originated with and was led by invention, and industrialization in the 19th century in the United States and Germany was based on innovation and especially the advances made in introducing mass production into the factories, South Korean industrialization (Amsden, 1988: 38) has been based on learning and borrowing foreign technology. Consequently, the relative costs of industrializing have been reduced and the pace increased.

In late industrialization the State and state-inspired planning have played a crucial role. While South Korean firms have largely remained in private hands, banks were nationalized and the allocation of credits have been under State control. The basic strategy of planning during the Park regime (Lim, 1985: 93) was to rely more on foreign loans as opposed to direct investments. This strategy effectively strengthened the national capitalists while simultaneously keeping the door partially closed to international exploitation through direct surplus transfers by foreign owned firms. From 1962 to 1969, during the period which is argued to be characterized by deepening dependency, Lim (1985: 19) notes that

'...among the total of $16.2 billion of foreign investment in current prices between 1962 and 1979, the amount of public and commercial loans accounted for about 15 times that of direct investment.' In addition, the South Korean *Chaebol,* unlike the *Zaibatsu* in Japan, does not operate its own banking institutions; rather, the state has maintained a tight grip on the banking institutions for capital and credit management. This has further strengthened centralized control over the development of a protected national capitalism in which both the state and national bourgeoisie have cooperated hand in glove.

Firms were compelled to comply with state planning because they were dependent on receiving credits and other forms of preferential treatment necessary for their expansion. Preferential treatment of firms has generally involved subsidies in various forms. For example, as part of the export promotion program, South Korea's policies have selectively placed tariffs on some imports while others come in free. Those that come in free are characteristically raw materials and semi-finished products which are to be further processed in Korean industries.

Between 1962 and 1986 the Economic Planning Board (EPB) introduced five-year plans. The first three were overfulfilled, the fourth underfulfilled (Johnson, 1987: 142). In South Korea explicit plans have served the purpose of defining strategies and outlining the methods for achieving them. Unlike in Japan where the Economic Planning Agency (EPA) formulates indicative plans and asks firms to comply, the Economic Planning Board (EPB) in South Korea can force firms to comply with the fulfilling of plan targets by direct interventions.

One point distinguishing the explicit plans in South Korea from the sorts of five year plans customarily found in Soviet-type economies is the emphasis placed on the development of infrastructure. South Korea differs from the traditional planned economies and even from other Asian countries by the high rate of investments in transportation, communications, and education. Moreover, the building of these large public investment projects has served as the starting point for the development of South Korean construction firms which in the last two decades have achieved a noted reputation for competence and speed in fulfilling international contracts.

Macroeconomic planning in South Korea has fostered export promotion. This has been encouraged by an exchange rate policy undervaluing the won relative to the yen and dollar, combined with an incentive system which has given preferential subsidies to successful exporters. The home market has likewise remained protected from most finished products. The strategy has been to bring in raw materials cheaply, process them, and ship them out. The State has fostered this program by promoting the training of labour and implementing the longest official work week in the world, fifty-four hours. Up until 1987 labour was subjected to restrictions concerning the rights to association and striking.

What is to be noted about contemporary South Korea is that macroeconomic planning is no longer applied with such a heavy hand as was characteristic earlier. As the economy records annual trade surpluses and private firms become more and more autonomously directed with respect to improving product profiles, quality, and volume exported, the need for centralized State planning diminishes. While the EPB still plays a role in formulating plans, there is a decreasing need for strict enforcement. That the State and state planning is diminishing in South Korea over time confirms the correctness of the original conception of planning, its implementation, and enforcement.

Notes

[*] The author would like to express his thanks to the Alexander von Humboldt-Stiftung of the Federal Republic of Germany for research support during the years 1988-9 and to the Südost Institut in Munich for hosting me during my research visit in Germany.
[1] David Ricardo established the foundations for international trade theory with the publication of 'On Foreign Trade', a chapter of his book *On the Principles of Political Economy and Taxation* published in 1815-6. This theory still provides the core of ideas for neoclassical, international trade theory that is taught in universities throughout the world.
[2] In *Dependent Development in Korea, 1963-1979,* Lim analyzes the multiplicity of factors contributing to Korean dependency. These range from the problems created by the system of Japanese colonial education which left the country with too few trained leaders after 1965 to the damaging role of U.S. security interests.

References

Amin, Samir (1974), *Accumulation on a World Scale*, Monthly Review Press, New York.
Amsden, Alice H. (1979), 'Taiwan's Economic History: A Case of Etatisme and a Challenge to Dependency Theory.' *Modern China*, no. 5, pp. 341-380.
Amsden, Alice H. (1988), 'The Issue of Business-Government Control.' *The Columbia Journal of World Business*, no. 1, pp. 37-42.
Baran, Paul (1957), *The Political Economy of Growth*, Monthly Review Press, New York.
Caporaso, James A. and Behrouz Zarae (1981), 'An Interpretation and Evaluation of Dependency Theory.' pp. 43-56, in Munoz H., *From Dependency to Development: Strategies to Overcome Underdevelopment and Inequality*, Westview Press, Boulder.
Cardoso, F. H. (1973), 'The Consumption of Dependence Theory in the United States', *Latin American Perspectives*, no. 12, pp. 7-24.
Cardoso, F. H. and Faletto, E. (1979), *Dependency and Development in Latin America*, University of California Press, Berkeley.
Cumings, B. (1981), *The Origins of the Korean War:Liberation and the Emergence of Separate Regimes,1945-1947*, Princeton University Press, Princeton, New Jersey.
Cumings, B. (1987), The Origins and Development of the Northeast Asian Political Economy: Industrial Sectors, Product Cycles, and Political Consequences, pp.44-83 in Deyo, 1987a.
Deyo F. C. (1987a), *The Political Economy of the New Asian Industrialism*, Cornell University Press, Ithaca.
Deyo, F. C. (1987b), State and Labour: Modes of Political Exclusion in East-

Asian Development, pp.182-202 in Deyo (1987a).

Emmanuel, A. (1972), *Unequal Exchange: A Study of the Imperialism of Trade*, Monthly Review Press, New York.

Evans, P. (1979), *Dependent Development: The Alliance of Multinational, State and Local Capital in Brazil*, Princeton University Press, Princeton, New Jersey.

Frank, A. G. (1966), 'The Development of Underdevelopment,' *Monthly Review*, September.

Frank, A. G. (1967), *Capitalism and Underdevelopment in Latin America*, Monthly Review Press, New York.

Frank, A. G. (1969), *Latin America: Underdevelopment or Revolution*, Monthly Review Press, New York.

Gellner, E. (1969), *Thought and Change*, Weidenfeld and Nicolson, London.

Gerschenkron, A. (1962), *Economic Backwardness in Historical Perspective*, Harvard University Press, Cambridge.

Johnson, Ch. (1987), Political Institutions and Economic Performance: The Government-Business Relationship in Japan, South Korea, and Taiwan, in Deyo (1987a), pp. 136-164.

Kosai, Yutaka and Yoshitaro, Ogino (1984), *The Contemporary Japanese Economy*, M.E. Sharpe Inc., Armonk, New York.

Lim, Hyun-Chin (1985), *Dependent Development in Korea,1963-1979*, Seoul National University Press, Seoul.

Major Statistics of the Korean Economy, 1987, Economic Planning Board, Seoul.

Ricardo, D. (1912), *The Principles of Political Economy and Taxation*, J.M. Dent and Sons, London.

Rostow, W. (1960), *The Stages of Economic Growth*, Cambridge University Press, Cambridge.

Schneider, A. (1984), Supply-side Economics in a Small Economy: The Chilean Case, pp. 207-228 in Nell E. (ed.), *Free Market Conservatism: A Critique of Theory and Practice*, George Allen and Unwin, Boston.

Wallerstein, I. (1974), *The Modern World System: Capitalist Agriculture and the Origins of the European World Economy in the Sixteenth Century*. Academic Press, New York.

PART V
TOWARDS A NEW
PARADIGM

Janos Hoós

The planning reform
in Hungary

After the world crisis of 1929-33, and even more after the Second World War, the idea of planning became established in most of the capitalist and developing countries. The social division of work, technological development, changes in the settlement system, the circumstances of urbanization and its contradictions that increasingly complicate planning principles in modern industrial societies, entailed the mitigation or elimination of the adverse consequences of supposed or realized spontaneous market and economic processes by state intervention and by planning. Even during the early stage of industrial development the need for prognosis and prognostic methods had been established. During the past decades out of the 170 countries of the world 120 had worked out some kind of national economic plan. The belief had spread widely – especially in the 1950s and 1960s – that planning would make the world a better place and progress more harmonious.

Worldwide experience has accumulated over the years in the theory and practice of planning. Certain countries, however, have become alienated from planning because they failed to fulfil their initial unrealistic expectations. In the socialist countries the reform of planning, a reconsideration of its structure, role and methods are now on the agenda.

In Hungary the reform of the economic management system in 1968 stipulated a basic change of the planning system. The overall system of breaking down the plan was terminated. This was one of the most important elements of the reform in its time. Directives stipulated the termination of sectoral planning and plans, the reinforcement of the strategic character of the planning, a major change in the content and function of the yearly plans, and the requirement that the planning should concentrate on the crucial questions of the economic policy. The basic concept was that the government would be able to control the economic processes more effectively if, instead of dealing with the details, it only planned the main correlations, while realization of the objectives would be ensured by indirect economic measures. Two decades later it can be said that the basic principle accepted and implemented in 1968 proved to be sound. This, however, does not mean that there is no need for modification or that there is no urgent demand for it.

An overall view on the operation of planning and its system-oriented reform is required because during the past two decades other elements of economic management – the price, tax and fiscal system and the institutions of the economic management, especially from 1984 – have changed considerably. On the other hand, internal and external development conditions have transformed during the past 20 years. The economy had to be put on a qualitatively new growth path to improve its adaptability to external market conditions. The economy would be more open and the influence of external commerce, trade, production and financing would increase. The adjustment to the world economy processes, as well as integration into the main-stream, require a new kind of behaviour (responsive and initiative) in management. This is the inevitable precondition for restructuring and developing efficiency.

Planning could predictably maintain its perceived or actual position if it is devoted to the development of new principles and practices in social and economic administration. This exercise requires the deliberate calculation of change in at least two conditions – namely, a market economy and the sociopolitical tasks of the administration in a plural political system.

1. A new balance between Market and Plan

Market functions will not be restricted to directing the business conduct of state companies and cooperatives. Business will involve new actors and organizations thatwere largely ignored in previous considerations of the Administration. Thus it is certainly not irrelevant that while these actors develop into actual market factors, because of their conditions of ownership their management and control are necessarily different from the traditional state sector.

Let us consider one example of possible cases. If, for example, individual citizens are in a position to act as real market factors – i.e. as producers and consumers – then in the indefinite (spiral) flow of production and consumption, it will become increasingly impossible to fit market decisions into the 'dream frameworks' devised by planners. If this is true for citizens it will be even more acutely true for external finance – i.e. for organizations with foreign participation. Influencing investor intentions will be limited to the regulations – specifically, Acts passed by Parliament – and the government level will no longer define yearly investment volumes for the national economy as a whole. Consequently, the assumption that the Administration has the right to take direct measures [1] to control purchasing power whenever midyear processes (data) indicate overfulfilment of plan figures will become untenable.

It is therefore supposed that in the future the behaviour of business actors will be directed by their own interests and not by 'higher' economic ideas, and that these behaviours can be oriented by various financial regulations (taxation, loans, etc.). However, it will not be possible to impose dictated limits. Hence planning and administrative control will automatically lose the right and duty to set tight manoeuvering frameworks on each actor in the economy.

The importance of money in the economy is uprated by the multi-actor system of real economic decision-making, the structure of ownership and the importance of global trade. (This is also true in the case of reverse inflationary impacts.) A new perception develops of the fiscal and banking spheres. This point is an important one, especially because the old methods of planning will be unable to develop successful programmes for change, and development because it will not be possible to outline the dreams of the future on basis of projected averages. Inevitably, the current system of planning with its given methodology, concentrating on sectoral equilibrium and central redistribution of resources, based on the state sector but covering the entire national economy, will have to be discarded.

If it is true that the development and output of the economy are governed by market conditions, then it must be a prime task of planning to understand market conditions and to forecast the predictable market changes. Avoiding dealing with the causes and correlations hidden behind averages and accounting for substantial changes is no longer as acceptable as it used to be.

2. Towards socio-economic planning

There is an increasingly strong requirement that the concepts in the plans should deal with social movements and with the reciprocal effects of society; human social objectives should receive the same treatment as economic tasks in the plan. Therefore, planning should became a type of socio-economic planning.

The new form of economic policy decided at the end of 1978 enforced restrictions on domestic demand. This approach imposed an unusual task on social and economic control, as well as on national economic planning: new (internal and external) additional resources had to be found to enable the economy to achieve a higher performance in volume as well as in quality. [2] Formally, the plans adopted this approach by specifying that 'economic development has to be directed along a new intensive path' or by postulating the requirements of 'intensive development', 'improvement of income-earning capacity'.

The new requirements of planning were based on the following assumption: society, different skills, companies, cooperatives, entrepreneurs, different regions, more precisely the people, had to understand that temporary declines (of 2 or 3 years?) were be inevitable as long as the performance of the economy failed to achieve a desired level. This decline also involved the standard of living. Moreover, it was also stated that the current period of transition would be accompanied by new and unusual differentiation and a certain degree of existential uncertainty – such as unemployment. Attention was addressed to social objectives, not only because of the growing number of justified social claims but also because the administration could not expect people to give their support to blueprints which they were unable to interpret in terms of objectives and tasks insofar as they felt that these plans had nothing to do with their lives – indeed, they simply did not understand the 'terms'! (It is relevant to ask what meanings are communicated to simple people by terms like 'equilibrium of the balance of payments', 'rebound of external economy' or 'restructuring' showered on them every day by the media.) There was the further fact that planning or, more precisely, administrative control has not been able to achieve much success in the last ten years. Even the accomplishment of plans has been a frustrating experience for drafters, approvers and society alike! This must serve as a lesson now that the future of planning is considered!

3. Tasks of strategic planification

The most important lesson of the past decades has been the inadequacy of our adaptive capacity. Hence there is a need for more flexible and faster reaction ability. Therefore, within the planning system, the importance of planning as a working process will grow relative to the plans as documents. Planning work will be a continuous activity and its rhythm will be determined by the economic policy tasks awaiting solution. Instead of the time breakdown of the traditional plan documents (short, medium or long-term), distinctions based on the character of their tasks and function will come into focus. In the continuous conceptual and coordinative work of the central government authorities, the importance of the preparation of plan documents and their publication will decrease.

In the economic sphere, the responsibility of planning, or, more accurately, of the government, can be best expressed in the development of research, training and infrastructure. State-financed investment projects are expected to be directed mainly to the energy sector. There is general agreement over this, although the methods of approach are still discussed. I shall not concern myself with in this here but move to discussion of the oft-quoted task of restructuring or innovation.

The requirements of structural change in production, the updating of technical standards or export development are different facets of the desire to achieve substantial improvements in resource utilization. The actual formula changes from time to time because our modernization lags far behind expectations, as well as actual opportunities in terms of orientation, degree and, especially, success. [3]

Factors contributing to the delay in restructuring include the present mechanism of social and economic control, a lack of real market conditions, scarcity of financial and technical assets, downgrading of intellectual work, poor R&D efficiency and, most of all, the general weakness of inventiveness and capability of the social and economic system. Related to these, the inconsistency of political commitment is another reason for the failure to achieve any appreciable economic modernization in the last decade.

The modernization process has been impeded by the fact that a substantial portion of our comparatively scarce resources were devoted to mistaken and very costly projects with slow rates of return (more than 10 years or never), reducing the opportunity to modernize of competitive sectors. A possible reason is the unnecessary emphasis laid by economic policy on energy and raw material supply security through domestic capacity development and through participation in foreign development projects. At the same time, by adopting the safe market concept, single-market projects were implemented simultaneously in industry and in the food economy – within the framework of CMEA relations – channelling a considerable amount of production and investment into forced trajectories. Central planners have (erroneously) supposed, that enterprises would be able to assume and meet tasks of modernization even in these circumstances, under the pressure of general economic regulation. Thus the task of restructuring has been treated in a rather inconsistent way by national economic planning.

To put it simply, restructuring must have no other meaning than a programme for 'Modern Hungary' updating the social and economic establishment in this country. This also entails that it will be impossible to achieve any significant improvement in economic performance and in technical standards without profoundly changing and updating the social and economic terms and conditions which determine performance. Assigning so-called 'driving sectors' is highly risky and of doubtful value; and is therefore not the right road to structural development. Now that encouragement is given to different types of business, it appears that only a few development projects of high capital requirement or exceptional risk will be implemented with state participation. Thus structural development is not a suitable title for the elaboration of programmes or the taking of individual decisions on what to develop and what not in the short term, i.e. 3-5 years). It would be more reasonable to develop a programme for business ventures which could adjust the efficiency of the social and economic system. (In this programme the economy could be one element – certainly not the only one – in the sense of introducing the integrating force of entrepreneurship and invention into this society).

4. Short term planning tailored for macroeconomic development

On the basis of the assumption that planning will be one of the professional tasks of the Administration, the central planning function is imagined in a dual role. While the primary function is supposed to include analysis in the context of the entire economy, fact-finding and forecasting, it is accepted that the decision support function will have to be maintained in a definite and narrow range where several central commitments may be rationally required. Thus the current system of yearly planning for the purpose of systematic regulation of macro processes would be replaced by regular studies, forecasts and information to the Government. The planning centre would report to the government at regular intervals on the conduct and predictable changes in the conduct of various actors (state companies, cooperatives, public companies and other organizations), of autonomous organizations and of certain strata of households (or of the population). This approach also proposes that electronic data processing could perform an effective function, especially as traditional techniques are insufficient to handle the enormous amount of computation required for the task of planning, information and forecasting. [4]

However, this approach can accommodate different new methods of analysis and forecasting as well. Aggregate analysis of different actors, their activities, etc. will be required by for the future administration to define the pilot processes and problems to be considered in forecasting the future and the problem areas. On the other hand, regarding the central information and forecasting function, this idea of ours would raise no objection to making this service available, apart from the Administration, also to the real actors of the economy including companies, banks, individuals, etc. Accordingly, planning in its present form (plan calculations) would be replaced by planning analysis information and forecasting: this function would become autonomous and would thus gain an independent quality as somewhat distinct from planning. It follows in turn that information and forecasting could also be the tools of operative administrative control.

In this approach, and already in the present stage – which is often named a 'period of transition' – yearly plans could be abandoned because their functions could be discharged as part of central budgeting or of information and forecasting. The old function of yearly plans, i.e. purchasing power control, has been transferred to the budget and the financial administration. Moreover, if adopted, the general practice of codifying the major regulations of economic control in Acts of Parliament would eliminate the need to effect proposed revisions through directives, instructions (or eventually publications) of the Council of Ministers or of Ministries. Another argument against yearly plans is that it was a mistake to invest yearly plans with decision-making capacity on strategic type tasks. (On the other hand in a context where yearly plans could be the tools of implementation of medium and long-range plans, the abolition of yearly plans cannot be claimed to mean a loss of function, since the role of such plans in the implementation of strategic plans was merely formal.) Our conclusion is therefore the following: with the given principles and approaches of control, yearly macroeconomic plans can be eliminated from the set of tools of the administration without any devaluation of planning: furthermore, yearly planning should be reasonably replaced by the function of analysis and forecasting.

5. Conditions for the realization of plans

Under the conditions of plural social and political control the methods used to gain public support will be necessarily different. Therefore it is assumed that wide public commitment to the implementation of national modernization projects will be an integral component of the success of central development programmes. So if we consider the realistic chances of catching up with the advanced world in a historically short period of time or at least to eliminate our lag, it will be necessary to develop social and economic development objectives and programmes which, in the longer run, give priority to social objectives and tasks over economic tasks.

Up until now Socialism has been of little service to the human being, to the needs of the people, despite the declared ideology. These models have been strongly economy-oriented. Physical output has been considered to be the key element in the established system of control (and planning) and man has been downgraded to a servant of production, a 'factor of production'. We have to reverse the present order, i.e. to assert the priority of man as served by production. A reassessment of so-far overemphasized ideological thinking and an acknowledgement of economic rationality instead of the prioritization of political orientations are further integral factors in the new approach of planning.

The financial inputs required by the first steps to be taken towards this new approach are negligible, but the requirements concerning political effort and revision of management and planning attitudes are enormous. The monolithic political and economic pyramid has to be transformed if the new function of administrative control and within that of planning is to be assured. This requires a multifactor political system where a multicentre and, in the broadest sense, mixed economy can come to life, provided that the laws of economy prevail and that there is sufficient capacity and energy for defining the goals and tasks of society.

Realization of the plan is a social process that unfolds through the continuous expression of interests, their confrontation, conflicts and conciliation. If the interest structure is ignored, then it is almost certain that the plan will fail. Different groups in society have their opinions and desires; better understanding and mutual information requires a wide involvement of the society in this context. For this public opinion should be more closely involved in planning as well.

Planning is changing and developing everywhere. It is important to integrate the main results of this process into domestic practice and use it. For this reason, research work is absolutely necessary which will scientifically and practically clarify what kind of additional development is needed in the planning system, or what the international experiences can help and how. This should be based on a research and development program that systematically works to collect experiences of our planning practice, to adopt international experience and through this prepare planning for new and newer challenges.

References

Csikós-Nagy, B., 'Overall renewal of socialist planned economy', *Tervgazdasági Fórum*, no. 2, 1987.

Báger, G., 'Public discussion of the new medium range draft plan', *Tervgazdasági Fórum*, no. 1, 1985.

Hoós, J., 'The new path of growth and the tasks of development of macroeconomic planning', *Közgazdasági Szemle*, 1985. No.1.)

Mrs. Huszár, J., 'Planning and democracy', *Tervgazdasági Fórum*, no. 3, 1987.

Kulcsár, K., 'Shaping of society, planning, science', *Tervgazdasági Fórum*, no. 2, 1988.

Lóránt, K., 'Search for solutions in national economic planning', *Tervgazdasági Fórum*, 1988.

Drecin, J., 'Planning is not a witchcraft', *Tervgazdasági Fórum*, no. 4, 1988.

Notes

[1] This logic cannot accept the following repeated exercise of recent years. On more than one occasion the government took measures regulating the future and at the same time as retroactively effective, as if such rules had been passed several years earlier, and as if such measures could be considered lawful.

[2] This was expressed by ideas published in various political resolutions such as in the stabilisation program and in the plans themselves – 'higher efficiency', 'streamlined structures of production, employment, and foreign trade' – while the philosophy of planning did not change its perception of its role in economic control and while the planning methods and processes were left unchanged.

[3] The idea of restructuring and modernization was adopted about 10 years ago. On the other hand it is undeniable that ever since we have national planning, that is, since 1947, for more than 40 years! structuring was one of the main tasks of planning. The slogan of 'Iron and Steel Country' then

some subsequent engineering priorities and central development priorities can be considered restructuring ambitions similar in tune to our present claims about structural limits.

[4]   Note that up till now the planning approach has been actually unable to tackle the task of utilizing the established and regularly modernized EDP network. Namely, according to the accepted – and applied – idea, it was more effective to roll through the frequent changes and revisions manually than by computer. As a side effect of this approach the application of modelling technique has been limited to analysis and evaluation at best.

Ottó Gadó

Planning, regulation and deregulation

My task is to present Hungarian planning, regulation and deregulation. I want to devote the time at my disposal in expounding the third issue and, therefore, I shall say only a few words on the first two topics and on their interrelations.

I start from the probability that the notion of the further development of Hungarian planning is becoming clear to those present. Therefore, it should be sufficient to say that economy-wide planning is undoubtedly necessary in order to establish a macroeconomic policy. The annual plan should be elaborated in strict harmony with the annual budget and with respect to the balance of public finances, both in order of time and in order of work. It is possible that gliding three-year plans should be elaborated for the medium term.

The national economic plan has to take into consideration the effects of the existing economic regulators (tax system, etc.), though naturally this does not exclude that some regulators will eventually have to be modified under the effects of the plan or in conformity with the aims contained therein. This has, however, to signify a mutual consideration of the effects and may not result in a one-sided subordination of the regulators to the plan. I believe that these are basic issues which should be enforced in an economic management system that takes into consideration the effects of both the market and the plan.

On the other hand, regulation should as far as possible be normative, though this does not necessarily mean uniform regulation of the whole national economy. It definitely does mean that uniform regulations are valid for economic units belonging to different sectors and that exceptions should only be made in very rare cases. It also means that preferences built into the regulatory system should apply to activities and not to single units.

The building of a market economy and the extension of the entrepreneurial field of manoeuvring are the conditions of what has been said so far. And the work of deregulation, which started in 1988, is closely connected with these preconditions. This work is oriented partly towards a revision of legal rules, partly towards a reduction in the administrative obligations of economic units. There are already some initial results, as a product of reports and measures prepared so far (e.g. the repeal of the regulation on public utilization of motor vehicles, or the replacement of the administrative prescriptions relative to the entertainment expenses by economic regulators), but we cannot speak of substantial changes as yet.

Deregulation can be really effective only if the reduction of legal constraints as well as of administrative measures derives from the essence of the economic policy. Since the main cause of governmental over-regulation is the distortion of market-like ownership, it is a precondition of deregulation that it should develop market relations and, in accordance with them, ownership relations, and also to modify the interests of economic units and the aims of the state management.

In a broader sense, deregulation means supervision and reduction of the range of state interventions in market processes. Here I want to investigate how results may be attained by repealing legal prescriptions which hinder the self-accommodation of economic entities or, in some cases, prescriptions in contradiction to newly adopted acts. (On the other hand, naturally, legislation reflecting the logic of market-economy has to be continued).

On the basis of these aims the principles of a deregulation process may be outlined as follows:

a) the law should regulate the functioning of legal entities in its capacity of public power and not as proprietor. It is not the state-owned enterprise, but an economic association – the latter corresponding much more closely to entrepreneurial conception – which should serve as a basic type of legal regulation;

b) the rules affecting other entrepreneurs should also affect the state-owned enterprises, while exceptions – deriving from the state property – should only prevail (as already stated in my introduction) in a very narrow circle (e.g. in the case of enterprises under governmental supervision, etc.);

c) the state should not regulate problems typically belonging to the entrepreneurs' sphere of activity and interests (e.g. internal organization within a management structure, etc.);

d) an effective and consistent information system has to be established at the national economic level which imposes, however, fewer burdens on enterprises; on the other hand, when establishing administrative (management, accounting) obligations in legal rules, the burdens of the enterprises should be lightened as far as possible and attention should be paid to this aspect when forming the regulators.

The main problems in the area of which forward steps are needed and possible are, in my opinion, the following:

1. In the regulation of property, since it follows from the Constitution that social property and within this state property, as well as the exclusive economic activities of state organizations, play a leading role. Therefore the majority of the legal rules assign a determining part of the means of production to state, i.e. society ownership (e.g. significant factories, mines, the Post office are state properties, while foreign trade is considered to be an exclusive state activity). Therefore, after the Act on Economic Associations (Company Act) came into effect a lot of contradictions and constraints remained (e.g. how state owned enterprises may enter into contracts on the operation of some of their parts).

Private activities are also restrained or hampered to an unjustified extent by several – sometimes even contradictory – legal rules (e.g. small scale industry, restrictions on the turnover of land, etc.).

A definition of the ownership system which is more suited to a market economy therefore becomes necessary while, at the same time, several constraints on activities or turnover should be revoked.

2. Problems connected with legal rules affecting enterprises and cooperatives are as follows:

a) Legal rules often constrain economic units also to carry out activities other than those closely attached to their entrepreneurial activities (e.g. developing the general education of their employees, meeting their welfare, social and cultural needs, etc.). It may be said that in the case of cooperatives such duties derive from their belonging to the movement, but this cannot serve as an argument in the case of enterprises. On the basis of such legal rules the state-owned enterprises are obliged, among other things, to organize a youth parliament, socialist emulation, to promote the general education of their staff, to grant social and cultural benefits, to support housing construction by their staff. Though these are very different kinds of tasks, a conceptual decision is needed: whether in the future the enterprises should be obliged to carry out (and if so, what kind of) obligatory social tasks (e.g. support of housing construction) or whether they are entitled to outline such tasks themselves, eventually in the framework of the collective agreement.

b) The economic units are also obliged by legal rules to perform duties which are partly or completely tasks of the State (e.g. the administration of social security or personal income tax affairs of the staff, the handling of notifications or complaints of public interest). The simplification, elimination of (or perhaps remuneration for) such work would also be necessary.

c) The economic organizations are obliged to issue a number of internal regulations and their internal organization is determined by detailed legal rules (e.g. enterprises are obliged to prepare more than 20 internal statutes).There is good reason to revise such legal rules and to discontinue some of these tasks (e.g. draw up a medium term personal plan, or keep some oblig-atory staff – such as a person responsible for socialist emulation).

3. In the absence of real ownership interests, the State wants to replace them – in the interest of protecting social property – with legal rules in several cases. A large number of these rules had been repealed by the end of 1988 (as already mentioned), but in other areas constraints are unchanged (e.g. permission for service trip abroad by the enterprises manager, handing over a product for a workshop test, etc.). These rules concern marginal affairs, yet they bear down hard on enterprises. Their repeal should be managed, parallel with the building up of ownership interests, in such a way as to simultaneously prevent possible misuses.

4. Several licensing procedures are also connected with ownership relations and constraints on activities (e.g. the licence to import industrial fodder from abroad, or to modify the line of cultivation in the agriculture.) It would also be necessary to revise – in relation to the state duties to be carried out in the framework of market management and the building-up of a more up-to-date State administration – the sphere of licensing and the procedures of the authorities affecting the economy in general.

5. Supplying of data according to external requirements represents at pre-

sent about 30 per cent of the administrative tasks of economic units. In my opinion, more than the half of such requirements could be simplified. Therefore, all obligations to provide information not in harmony with the information needs of a market economy, as well as all parallel supply of information, shoud be abolished. In the future social organizations should not be entitled to demand any information from enterprises, apart from those continuing to exist by central regulations, while information of a trade union character should be regulated within the collective contract. Should any data be required outside regularly supplied information, a cost refund should be paid to the enterprises, in accordance with the servicing principle.

6. Simplification of the book-keeping system may also be included in the notion of deregulation. Very useful proposals have already been made in this respect by the Union of Hungarian Auditors. It is, however, evident that several rules of book-keeping have no internal origin, but derive from other decisions (e.g. tax rules). Therefore, modernization of the book-keeping system requires that tax and other aspects should be better harmonized with an ownership attitude and the requirements of book-keeping should be brought up to date.

Some of these tasks of deregulation may be realized during this year, but some only gradually. Apart from the cutting down of legal rules and administrative management requirements it is, however, necessary to prepare and establish rules conforming to changing relations. A revision of the rules in force at present may simultaneously extend enterprises' room for manoeuvre, even under the present circumstances. Within this it becomes necessary to review all existing legal rules and administrative management prescriptions. This would, properly speaking, be the task of all ministries or organizations with nationwide authority, concerning the legal rules or prescriptions issued by them. Since it is difficult to expect self-rationalization by individuals, it would be useful to establish an inter-governmental commission, made up of a group of experts independent of the state administration. This commission could then elaborate the propositions on deregulation, cooperating with the ministries and the interest representing organizations. Final decisions should naturally be taken by the government or in some cases by parliament.

Gusztáv Báger

Coordination and coherence in national planning

Coordination and coherence reflect the idea of the plan as a promoter of order in a situation which is supposed spontaneously to tend towards trial and error improvization, or even anarchy: anarchy of economic life if decentralized decisions are only coordinated by the price sistem. Although coherence is a pragmatic concept, it is often presented as a maximalist demand by saying that the plan will draw up a 'societal brueprint' in a more or less marked discrepancy with the trends supposedly at work within society, a view which is congruent with the search for deeper concerted actions within the framework of a 'national plan'. Therefore coordination and coherence should be taken into account when dealing with concrete planning practice. Hungarian planners, first of all, attempt as much as possible to maximize:

- coherence between policies (amployment policy, investment policy etc.) conducted in parallel, to avoid too many conflict between various actions aimed at the adopted objectives;
- coherences in time – that is to say, continuity of a certain policy beyond the short term (e.g. in the case of a large individual investment project).

1. Ordering phases of planned work

To ensure coordination and coherence in the operation and development of national economy, claims distinguish activities, which have to be adjusted to well-identified sequential phases or stages of planned work in a national framework. These phases can be characterized as follows:

As empiricial evidence shows, one needs to distinguish two different phases: 'P' for the planning phase, and 'I' for the implementing phase. Both may be further differentiated depending on the nature of the work object, product, abilities, etc. In the framework of a national economy, practical ordering capacity may be gained from the following four phases: 'P' planning, 'A' accepting, 'I' implementing and 'E' evaluating phase. It will also be useful for our consideration of the rationalities and interests in national planning to differentiate in each phase the planning practice further, and in greater variety. We must note that over a longer period of planned economy we may perceive a series of P-A-I-E cycles in shorter or longer form, relating hierarchically to each other in time. It is agreed that national planners must think in terms of the whole P-A-I-E cycle, and of a series of such cycles. The chief characteristics of this cycle are as follows:

PLANNING PHASE:
(a) An analytical-synthetic fact-finding phase exploring the society, economy and the multiple surroundings
(b) The phase elaborating possible future alternatives
(c) The phase for elaborating plan guidelines or a conceptual plan
(d) The phase for elaborating the detailed plan

ACCEPTANCE PHASE: This phase of the cycle is hard to define as the segmentation is not as clear-cut as it is in the planning phase.

This is the phase of adjusting, modifying and reshaping the plans (this admittedly depends on whether the accepted plans should be adaptively modified for whatever reason and the whatever stage of implementation. This phase generally blends with the next phase).

IMPLEMENTATION PHASE: The phase of direct implementation.

EVALUATION PHASE: This phase is not differentiated either.

Now the question emerges: is it possible on the basis of the criteria of this frame of reference to meet simultaneously the rational and interest-charged requirements in the operation of a planner organization? In certain conservative and ideologically biased views, there is no such possibility, nor necessity. There are also conflicting approaches that maintain that this task can be unambiguously and easily solved by an omniscient and omnipotent planning organ. It is more expedient to contrast these extreme approaches giving preference to heterogeneous, independent and random elements, on the one hand, and to homogeneous, hierarchical elements on the other, and to a conception of society and planned institutionalized creative work as an ensemble of heterogeneous elements in multidirectional interaction aimed at attaining common benefits (positive sum game assumption). A similar reply in the affirmative was given by the Cavallo Report (1979) and by Hajnal (1981). Their findings testify, in a very important interpretation, that the specialization and heterogeneity of interests are not necessarily disintegrating factors. If we manage to resolve the counteracting tendencies of isolation and interdependence, then they may become to one of th epreconditions for evolution.

2. Some characteristics of Hungarian plans and planning

Important features of national plans and planning can be revealed through analysis in terms of a number interrogative words:

Operational objectives of the planning organization -why?

Result of the planning   - what?

214

Raw materials for the plan	- what from?
Activities necessary for plan design	- what kind of operations?
Logical order, programme of plan design	- how?
Chronological order and pace of plan design	- when?
Institutions conducting planning	- who?
Scientific results, process, technical means, etc., used for planning	- what with?

Why ?

Long-term (twenty years), medium-term (three years) and short-term (annual) plans are prepared for the national economy.

The long-term plans outline the strategic programme for economic development. They serve both as a basis for decisions on long-term economic development and as a guide for medium term planning. The main issues arising in the long-term plan are:

- identification of societal objectives (norms);
- identification of development strategies; conditions and factors of economic growth;
- more efficient international economic cooperation;
- definition of development objectives important for technical progress;
- improvement of the living conditions of the inhabitants; education, professional training, culture, housing, local authorities, and society.

The medium-term plan forms the basic link in the planning system for different time scales. It specifies the long-term goals in a positive form for a three-year period, and has power over their implementation. Direct government decisions (Pda plan) and economic regulations (Pi^a plan) enable the implementation of the plan. The rate of development is based on calculations for the whole range of national activities.

The short term plan enables some of the medium-term targets to be made concrete in a given year. It allows the definition of problems to be solved and determines the operational measures required.

What ?

Taking into account the population (labour force), the resource base and the known technology, the medium and short-term plans for the Hungarian national economy are built on four basic elements, viz. production, final use, value added and disposable income for final consumption.

The plans foresee how the features of the national economy, and their interrelationships, should develop over different time periods. The interrelationships, should be seen as flows between production, final use, value added and dispos-able income. The flows between production and the components of final use are product flows, and the flows between the value added and dispos-able income are income flows.

Final use and disposable income constitute the market. The function of the market is to exchange production (product) for income by interaction of the sup-ply side (products) and the demand side (disposable income). There are five ba-sic markets in the plan:

- market I: private consumpiton
- market II: public consumption
- market III: investments
- market IV: inventories
- market V: foreign trade [1]

The equilibrium or disequiilibrium situations are dependent on the intensity of the two main types of flows as a consequence of planning decisions. In the chart, the flows interconnect the basic elements with the five markets and form a structure of the two subsystems which are built from the two main types of flows presenting a network. Its branches and nodes show a model of relation-ships taken into account at the macroeconomic level in the planning. In planning practices and/or in economic growth analyses, this plan model is, of course, de-composed so as to separate the individual branches into spectrum components, e.g. age groups, strata, branches, industries, product groups and regions, thus resulting in a much more complex model (or models) of the relationships consid-ered.

Direct government decisions are made for those goals achievable in the form of a product (Pd^a plan). In the plan, these direct decisions concern

- state investments (individual 'large' investments, 'aim-grouped' investments and 'other' state investments), which have a considerable bearing on the structure of the national economy. These are government approved;
- central development programmes and their means of execution aiming to solve basic structural tasks. These programmes are also government ap-proved;
- actions (including the provision of subsidies) to ensure fulfillment of inter-national commitments.

Apart from the direct decisions, the incentive system consists of economic regulators – prices, wages, fiscal, trade and credit policies – which indirectly in-fluence the course of economic activity (Pia plan). Economic regulators within the plan model control certain flows of the income subsystem. These are not connected directly to the real economic sphere [2], but, on the one hand, through the direct flow linking up value added and production and, on the other, through the market.

The plan model contains the planners' idea of the national economy and its functioning. The connexion between the regulators and the plan model can thus be formally expressed by determining which of the regulating branches has a di-

216

rect influence on it. Clearly, one or other of the direct effects also spreads over the next branch and finally over the whole system.

What from – what kind of operations – how, when, who?

The detailed methodological guidelines of the National Planning Office contain those activities needed for planning, its logical order and rhythm, data system and the division of labour among the planning institutions.

What with?

Over the last 40 years, a so-called traditional method of planning – involving tabulated, quantitative descriptions of past and future economic trends – has evolved. It may be characterized by the following essential features:
- it can satisfactorily consider details of actual economic trends and partial correlations; to a certain extent it simulates social phenomena connected with economic trends, and the origin of group interests and products;
- neither the content nor the form of the quantitative correlations is declared in an explicit manner. The overall flows are simplified and the main method of synthesis is the balance sheet. The main resources used are the human brain, the slide rule, and the desk calculator;
- the actual form and content of the tabulated plan system are subject to constant movement and change, as a function of changing economic reality.
As an innovation, various mathematical models (input-output models, linear programming models, etc.) and computing techniques have been applied to the planning process within the last fifteeen years. They tend, however, merely to complete existing methods and to become gradually part of the traditional approach.

3. Problematic areas in planning practice

From what has been said so far, it is clear that there are complex mutual relationships tying together the systems of goals and means in the planning model and the organizational-institutional system. Although the system of goals is the decisive factor, the other two strongly influence it. If these mutual relationships are not applied to a sufficient degree, the effectiveness of planning and plans is decreased, so that the systems of goals, means and organization must be coordinated. However, in our planning practice the lack of coordination or coherences repeatedly appears in the following four problem areas:

a) *Intersectoral and sectoral development realized through central development* programmes and state investment are largely influenced, alongside economic policy goals, by the following:

(i) achievements of scientific and technical progress;
(ii) international economic relations;
(iii) intersectoral and sectoral technical and economic correlations.

As a result of these and a lack of coordination, partial development tendencies may conflict with overall economic policy objectives. For instance, sectoral developments require more resources and produce relatively or absolutely less as a result (e.g. a smaller net inflow of convertible currency). For this reason the national economic balance is repeatedly less favourable than planned.

b) *Policies and regulators* – There are still more complex correlations between economic policy objectives and the results achievable through the influence of economic regulators. The difficulties of attunement to economic regulators stem above all from the problem of knowing how to measure directly and exactly the overall effect they will have on economic processes. We are still unable to estimate adequately what will be the impact of the main elements in the system of regulators – for instance, this or that price system and financial regulator – on economic development, and so it is hard to select the appropriate regulators.

c) *Spheres of institutions and organizations* – The institutional and organizational system is one of the relatively inflexible elements in regulation. Here there is still less chance of measuring exactly beforehand what changes will occur than there is in the case of changes in economic regulators. But progress in this field is currently gaining importance, since significant changes are taking place. For instance, since 1980 some large horizontally organized trusts have been broken up in moves to increase competition, creating around more than a hundred new companies in the process.

d) *Development and regulators* – Lastly, problems arise in a peculiarly comprehensive way in the case of the correlations between intersectoral or sectoral development and the system of means, most of all the economic regulators. Even in an ideal situation individual coordination with economic policy objectives will not ensure full correspondence between these spheres. So what should their relations be?

One solution is to try and extend the goal-means relationship to the chosen development paths, for instance by giving preference to the technical development goals decided upon. In this case, comprehensive attention must be paid to the extent of the development spheres chosen and supported centrally, and to the dimensions and methods of subordinating economic regulation to the development objectives of the economic sectors.

The other solution is for development objectives to be selected by market forces, and influenced by the regulators and by the interests of the company concerned. This assumes that the bulk of the regulators are well-orientated (not just as an average but over a wide area), so that short term fluctuations in economic activity can be filtered out and trends over an extended period measured.

The two approaches are put into action by different means and in various ways. In practice, up to now both alternatives of principle have been applied in combination. However, in the future it will be the purpose of making changes that will favour the second solution.

This statement accords with the further development of the economic system towards a stronger coordinating (stimulating and forcing) role by the market.

4. The explanations for problem areas

What kind of causes can be identified in explanation of the fragile coordination and coherence of the four areas in our national planning? The following three explanations must be mentioned, at least:

a) *Overambitious goals* – High-level political decision-making has often led to overambitious economic policy goals. It is true that the ruling party has not had a professional branch within its central machinery to work out detailed proposals for economic policy decisions, but even so its resolutions have overwhelmingly dominated economic policy decision-making. E.g. in the 7th five-year plan too many economic policy objectives were adopted, the realization of which appeared to be badly founded. The methods applied to counterbalance the dominating role of the monolithic party's decisions-making proved not to be efficient enough.

b) *Plural rationalities and interests* – National planners represent a special expert subculture, which may be regarded as an important source of special non-homogeneous rationality and interest.

Looking at the participants and the contributors in national planning work, one can easily discover what kinds of views and interests guide their activities. The main types of planners or contributors may be identified as follows:

(i)   policy decision-makers (government, politbüro);
(ii)   national planners: National Planning Office, ministries, etc.;
(iii)   council (local, municipal) planners;
(iv)   company planners;
(v)   bodies representing interest groups (trade unions, Chamber of Trade, etc.);
(vi)   public organizations of a political nature (e.g. Patriotic People's Front)
(vii)   scientists and scientific institutions, universities;
(viii) population (strata of population, individual citizens).

In most cases conflicts arise because the congruity between comprehensive and fractional examinations are unattainable (or only through extremely long procedures). This conflict generally emerges between the National Planning Office, the Central Statistical Office and the functional ministries on the one hand, and the sectoral ministries, company planners and council planners on the other. The conflict may find expression in a number of forms.

Typical case: fractional branch rationalities and interests make the production bottlenecks obstructing their advancement appear more serious than they really are. Allegations are often made nowadays as to the shortage of imported items, above all those purchased for hard currency, investment funds and labour. In these pronouncements the underlying motivation is evident: edging towards an advantageous position over other planners in arguing for a larger slice of central allocations and subsidies.

Another typical case is the way that results are massaged. Some planners make their achievements appear greater than they really are, for considerations of interest or prestige. Examples can easily be found in the fields of energy and materials conservation related to central programmes of economic development. The rational motivation impeding harmony is conspicuous here, too.

National economy planners and scientists often clash over the implementation of new methods of analysis and indices. In these situations the scientists' 'implement-everything-henceforth' attitude conflicts with the reluctance, if only initial, of the planners.

c) *Inappropriate planning tools* – The third cause of the lack of appropriate co-ordination and coherence is the unsatisfactory use of formalized tools (models) in planning. Sometimes the planners' need for new information can be satisfied with even more intricate indices, which casts doubt on the improved analytical proficiency as compared with increased costs. For example, the controversy over the method of computing growth rates adjusted to worsened terms of trade is far from over, even at present.

But it often happens that the new methods recommended for implementation are typically simple (linear) in their functional approach even if the interdependences between the phenomena examined are more intricate.

The generation of prognoses is of special importance for forecasts of changes in the world economy, due to the fact that Hungary has an open economy and high debt service payments in convertible currency. In this field, however, it is a recurrent contingency undermining the rationalizations that forecasts of external conditions (e.g., price forecasts on external markets) are not reliable enough. Hence, it is expedient to enhance their reliability through new scientific methods, prompt supply of information and the continuous adjustment of forecasts. Breakthroughs are also expected from having the planners, including the economics research institutes of the Hungarian Academy of Sciences, elaborate parallel forecasts which will be compared by an open forum of experts. The openness of the forum places increased responsibility for the forecasts on the specialists. In these cases we might speak of the different rationalities and prestige-interests of specialists.

With respect to forecasts relating to international markets, an especially interest-charged debate has evolved between the representative organizations of a political nature, on the one hand, and the national economy planners, on the other. It so happened that due to insufficient command of information the former group considered the forecasts of world economy as too pessimistic and, hence, the curtailment of domestic consumption – above all, the decline in investments effected in order to improve the external equilibrium and solvency – as too drastic. These cases might be interpreted as examples of attitudinal rationalities and interests.

Beyond the abovementioned plural rationalities and interests, several others might be identified. Their great number makes it difficult to arrive at a final plan which is a product of coordination, harmonizing and fine tuning. To achieve this, two approaches are available: wider social participation in planning, and the democratic political process. At present, as it is well known, there are several promising innovations in Hungary in both respect.

In Hungary the leading politicians and the leaders of administration are aware of the existence of plural rationality and interest. A few ranges of new activity stem from this recognition, e.g.:

a) extending societal participation in the elaboration of policies, development goals, strategies and plan concepts;
b) drawing different scientific and practising experts, corps, representatives into the planning work;
c) continuous strengthening of the role of parliament in acceptance and legalization of national plans, and in evaluating the realization of these plans.

Today some other innovations (restructuring the political and institutional systems, etc.) are to be introduced, beyond the activities mentioned above. But in closer relation to national planning work, the first steps appeared only as 'societal debates' on the preliminary forms of the 7th five-year (1986-1990) plan. Different organizations of a political kind, trade unions, Academy of Sciences etc. (their leading boards or commissions) discussed the elaboration of the plan in its different phases. Many of their criticisms, considerations, propositions were accepted, so they enriched and improved the products of the National Planning Office. This practice of societal debate has suggested some important conclusions for the future, although we are only at the beginning of a long and continuous innovating process. This issue needs scientific examination and research as well as evaluated practical experiences (Bager, 1985 and 1988).

5. Some conclusions and future orientations

Coordination and coherence – as specific requirements the national plans and planning – have proved to be useful sensitizing terms in critical consideration of Hungarian planning practice. I have critically reviewed characteristic insufficiences from both points of view. The coordinating work and activities designed to deal with real coherences have to be – but are not – adjusted to claims determined by the nature and sequence of the phases of planned work within the framework of national economy. Further insufficiences have been revealed through analysis of some specific features of plans and planning; Hungarian planning practice is lacking in such features. Other problems have also been discussed in deeper and more concrete form. These problems belong to special areas of the economy: (a) to intersectoral and sectoral developments; (b) to relations between policies and regulators; (c) to the spheres of institutions and organizations; (d) to the correlations between development and regulators. Behind the problems – raised by unsatisfactory coordinations and neglected coherences – specific causes seem to emerge within these areas, such as overambitious policies, plural rationalities and interests among politicians, planners, municipalities etc., and inappropriate planning tools.

It is part of my criticism that most leaders and planners are not aware of such insufficiences. Comprehensive examinations and new planning methods and tools are necessary in order to eliminate these shortcomings. It seems self-evident that the unsolved problems cause serious disturbances in the development of our society and national economy. Looking forward, we need to recognize the problems that have been discussed. We need to alter our thinking, our approaches, our problem-sensitivities, and consequently we need to search for new kinds of solutions. Such classic notions as 'coordinations, coherences' are also going to become obsolete. (I applied them because of their widespread use among planners in socialist countries). Nowadays new paradigms and new conceptualizations are increasingly emerging to replace obsolete ideas of plans and planning.

There are promising innovative ideas such as 'organismic thinking', 'systems thinking', 'integrated development', 'proper interdisciplinary models and techniques' and conceptualizations combined from previous ideas such as 'systems approch to planning integrated development', which suggest important improvements. Instead of discussing them in detail, I recommend a UNESCO publication (Socio-Economic Studies, no. 14), in which Hajnal and Kiss review critically the state of the art of planning integrated development and point out how a systems approach is necessary to take into account the multidimensional nature of development in planning' (Hajnal and Kiss, 1988). Apart from surveying almost a hundred references, they suggest an original conceptualization which has greater ordering strength than that of the classic 'development' paradigm. Hajnal (1985) elaborated a new conceptualization and technique for handling national health care within the framework of national planning. His technique can be interpreted and extended to any other issues in which the result of work are human beings (as newly-born; as educated, socialized, cultivated; as cared for by social workers; as families altering according to the stages of the life-cycle of the individuals and of the family). An important component of this technique is that it replaces the concept of pure 'resource allocation' with the concept of 'economizing' with human values, in the sense of long range social discount.

Another important possibility for planners is the use of national plans and planning work as a framework for uncovering, making overt, comparing and reconciling different views and interests concerning a desired future (Bager, 1988). One may look at national plans and planning work which might decrease trial and error and might strengthen the effectiveness, efficiency, adaptivity of development in the short and long term as well, instead of viewing plans as the means to increase central political power at any expense. If one accepts the first case, the suggested function of plans and planning in fostering consensus seems a real possibility. As mentioned earlier, Hungary has taken the first steps to realizing this possibility (social debates on alternatives of national plan concepts and policies through discussion with different groups of interests, or corps of representatives, etc.). But many other steps have to be taken if we want to exploit the possibilities. New plan-images are needed which are more appropriate for making overt the different views, rationalities, interests and values, the different problem sensitivities and standpoints of how urgent it is to solve problems; the widely used macroeconomic categories have proved to be quite distorting and mis-leading and therefore are inadequate for such a function. Consequently, the new plan-images can not be only lists of statistical indicators, because 'statistical-classificational schemes directly destroy the organismic-systemic nature of living societal entities' represented by plan-images (Hajnal and Kiss, 1988). Many of the diseases of socialist economies have 'iatrogenic' origins (becoming ill through care), i.e. are caused by the deficient plan-schemes of planners. It is also easy to perceive that such requirements cannot be satisfied without adequate new planning methodologies and techniques. And of course, national planners must be able to use these new plan-images and planning techniques. But any necessary innovations inevitably remain lifeless and useless if political decision makers do not learn how to think, infer and decide according to the new requirements.

All these thoughts about future trends have to be regarded as only drafts. Discussing them in detailed form is another issue quite beyond the scope of my lecture, which has been restricted only to critical notes about present Hungarian national planning practice. To innovate national plans and planning – that is the main question of our survival and development.

Notes

[1] There is also an intermediate consumption market, not explicitly mentioned in the model.
[2] An exception is price regulation, which enters the whole system of economic flows. This effect is not made explicit in the plan model however.

References

Bager, G., 'Social discussion of the 7th five year plan concept', *Tervgazdasagi Forum*, no. 1, 1985.
Bager, G., 'Planning culture – policy culture', *Kîzgazdasagi Szemle*, no. 2, 1988.
Cavallo, R.E.(ed.), 'Systems research movement: characteristics, accomplishments and current development', *General Systems Bulletin*, Special Issues (Summer), vol. IX, no. 3, 1979.
Hajnal, A., *Knowledge, method and culture in the systems research movement – Notes on Cavallo Report*, Institute of Economic Planning, Budapest, 1981.
Hajnal, A. and Kiss, I., 'Systems approach to planning integrated development', in *Innovative approaches to development planning*, Socio-economic Studies, no.14, UNESCO, Paris, 1988.
Hajnal, A., *The health care in national socio-economic planning*, Institute of Economic Planning, Budapest, 1985.

Andrzej Karpinski

Changes in the role of planning in Poland

The profound economic reforms presently being implemented in the socialist states require substantial changes in the approach to planning at the national economy level. Planning will have to be adjusted to the new conditions arising from the introduction of the market mechanism, as well as to those due to the greater degree of autonomy of state-owned and cooperative enterprises and the expanding scope of the private sector. This will require not only changes in organization and methods applied in central planning but also an utterly new 'philosophy of planning'.

The essence of this change is expressed by a different way of perceiving the principal function of the central plan. So far its function has been to set targets for the economy as a whole and for particular economic subjects. Under the reform, however, the main function of planning should be to provide conditions and premises favourable for the development of economic initiatives and activities of enterprises that are necessary in order to fulfil social tasks and priorities listed by the central plan.

On the basis of present practice and experience, and recent discussion as well, some general lines of the changes in central planning can be traced. They can be treated as the probable elements in a future new model of central planning in the mixed economy which is emerging through evolution. At least six of them should be taken into account from this point of view.

The first of them is the shift of the focus of attention from the process of elaborating a plan, i.e. from its formal aspect, towards the shaping of an overall economic strategy as the main function of central planning in the new conditions. This tendency coincides with those observed in planning done by the western corporations [1].

Under the reform, in the conditions of self-management by enterprises, the domination of planning in the development of the economy as a whole can be ensured by the centre only if it has a general strategy of its own for the development of the country and acts for its consistent implementation.

Therefore, central planning should take on the characteristics of strategic planning at a macrolevel. As the principal function of strategic planning is to adjust a given entity to the external situation and future needs, central planning must become the driving force for the restructuring and modernization of the economy as well as of overall technological and cultural progress.

Strategic planning in this sense should contribute to the implementation of the accepted economic and social development strategy by measures and means belonging to economic and social policy.

In contrast with earlier approaches to national planning, strategic planning should concentrate only on those elements of the national economy which have a key importance in the implementation of the general strategy, since market mechanisms should be the main regulator in the short-term perspective.

The essence of this system could be expressed as linking strong market mechanisms simultaneously with strong state intervention in the areas of strategic importance. For scientific and technological progress is a factor of strategic importance and planning in the future should play the role of the main driving force in these fields, and contribute to civilisation's progress. At the same time strategic thinking should not be limited only to the central planning body or other agencies of state administration. Any kind of monopoly in this field is undesirable. Therefore there are very important arguments in favour of a multicenter model of strategic studies in the country and a substantial share of different social forces acting in this field besides state administration. For example, in Poland some efforts are being made to create such centers for strategic thinking in the Polish Academy of Science, universities and social organisations, for example the Polish Union of Economists (PTE), the Supreme Organisation of Technicians (NOT) and so on.

Central planning can play a very important role in devising a general strategy for the country's development:

a) By providing more information on social aspirations and on the social response to certain solutions in order to define priority targets which could be accepted by society. We will call this process the 'socialization of planning'.

b) Planning must identify the areas of potential success, i.e. the domains offering the highest overall social and economic efficiency, equivalent to the so-called 'high value added sectors' in western terminology. Resources should be shifted towards these areas in order to optimize the structure of resource allocation. At the same time, this gives an enormous advantage to central planning, which can accelerate the transformation of the economic structure towards the optimum model more efficiently than the market mechanism alone.

c) Central planning can formulate the directions, resulting from strategy goals, which should strongly influence scientific programs of science and research institutions and accelerate in this way the process of adaptation of some new technologies and products in the national economy.

d) Planning should provide information on the social effects of particular processes in technology and culture in order to ease the social tensions that usually accompany intensive structural changes, such as the closing down of enterprises and limitations on the development of whole branches of industry.

The second element in the new model of planning is its increasingly structure-creating role. In the past, in spite of numerous declarations, those matters were not given adequate attention. Because of the high supply of factors of extensive

226

development, such as raw materials, labour and free ecological space, the rational allocation of resources was neglected. Now, under the self-management of enterprises, an appropriate allocation of resources has become the key issue.

It is expected that the optimization of the production structure can be carried out more efficiently in strategic goals-oriented development. This assertion is confirmed by the experience of Japan and other Pacific Rim countries. In this situation, central planning has to face completely new issue, namely the problem of resources reallocation. This would mean a process of withdrawing resources from the declining branches of industry, whose products have lost their international competitiveness and redeploying these resources to branches with the highest economic efficiency, these being the branches of advanced technology. Hence, the future of central planning is inextricably linked with the process of macrolevel restructuring.

The state will inevitably have an active role to play in this process. This role, however, should have an economic not a formal or administrative nature. Central planning must function through the market and not against it. This will mean that more favourable premises (and especially credit) for development will be provided first of all to those branches that have already attained confirmed success on the domestic or international market.

Therefore, investment policy should remain one of the principal functions of the central plan. This policy should take into consideration various sectors of national economy. In a way, this is a return to the planning formula adopted in Poland in the 1940s and called 'planning through investment'. This formula, however, must be put into effect by new methods, such as the proper setting of priorities for credit policy. The process of restructuring of the national economy should naturally be carried out first through negotiation rather than by direct involvement of the state. But there is a need for a central programme of restructuring within the framework of the central plan. It is especially necessary in contacts with foreign capital and 'joint ventures'.

The third element in the new model of planning, which concerns the methodology of planning, is the shift in the focus of attention from the planning of quantified objectives to the shaping of developmental mechanisms and to the establishing of principles designed to regulate the functioning of enterprises under self-management. It is important that those enterprises should function in conformity with the priorities and trends laid down by the central plan.

Regardless of the system of planning and administration, conformity of the functioning of enterprises with the assumptions of the central plan has always been and will continue to be an important criterion in assessing the efficiency of this planning.

From this point of view, especially important is the method of plan preparation, which in Poland has gained the name of 'detailed breakdown of targets towards adjustment mechanisms'. This means that in the plan each quantified target is matched by appropriate quantified central resources allocated to its realization, as well as by planned, real changes in the principles of enterprise regulation that are going to serve the same goal.

Given the necessity of profound economic restructuring, more importance is being laid on the assessment of particular development areas (branches, products) from the point of view of their economic performance and especially export efficiency. This must mean at the same time a differentiated approach laid down by the central plan for given branches, groups of goods or directions of development in the regulative system (credits, taxes etc.).

Such development is increasingly more important as a method of industrial planning. This entails the necessity to apply the Domestic Resources Cost (DRC) method in central planning. This method examines the costs of domestic factors of production in relation to world prices. Together with other similar methods, it may be used to compile ranking lists of enterprises, branches and economic ventures according to the efficiency of their development.

The application of 'marketing methods' to planning also becomes important, especially as regards markets and the external environment of the economy.

Under the reform, new methodological problems appear that have never been solved before. One of them is the question of how to incorporate into macroeconomic calculations the effects yielded by the rapidly developing private sector, as well as the influence of joint ventures and other forms of foreign capital. This issue has not been examined theoretically yet. In a mixed type economy such as the modified socialist system this issue is of enormous importance.

The fourth element in the new model of planning concerns its scope. Instead of elaborating targets for the whole economy, the new planning focuses upon the issues that bear strategic importance. To achieve this situation, it may be necessary to abandon numerous issues that have so far been subject to central planning. This concerns chiefly those problems which:

a) can be more efficiently dealt with by market mechanisms,
b) permit an easy change of factors of production or of product range,
c) concern the domains in which short-term changes due to changes in fashion or to accelerated technological progress occur so rapidly that central planning would not be able to respond to the needs fast enough.

If these three criteria are taken into consideration, the scope of central planning in Poland would be reduced by some 30 to 50 per cent.

Among the strategic issues that have to be dealt with in the plan, extremely important are those that may be better solved through planning than by the market mechanisms.

Those issues include, among others, the protection of the environment – in which market mechanisms usually fail [2] – and the control of aggregate demand which, if left to the free play of market mechanisms, leads to distortions in market conditions and causes inflation. Thus, demand management must remain one of important functions of central planning. Other problems are the optimization of the economic structure, mainly of the fuel and energy balance, as well as setting programs for scientific research according to economic needs and the educational system, and managing international economic relations. A plan constructed in this new situation should focus on the issues stated above, i.e. it should concentrate upon matters that can be best solved by the state according to formula 'what does the state do best?'. This is one very important premise for determining the scope of the new planning.

The fifth element constituting the new model of planning is the shift in the focus of attention from annual plans to long-term plans accompanied by medium-term operational plans of various time ranges, which ensure the fulfilment of the long term targets. In discussions the need is stressed to work out a new class of medium-range plans covering periods longer than one year but shorter than the presently adopted five-year interval. It is declared that the most efficient would be a three year strategic plan which could be adjusted to the current situation. Such a plan could respond to any necessity to change the policy (if the policy proves to be a failure) and it could be adjusted if the conditions for its implementation change. In Polish practice it is called 'Policy-corrective plan'.

It cannot be assessed yet to what extent such plans based upon long-term plans could or should replace the five-year plans that have so far dominated the Polish economy.

There exist important formal and substantive arguments in favour of five year-plans. From the point of view of international cooperation within the CMEA it is extremely important that plans prepared for equal periods of time can be coordinated. Thus it is hard to predict which model will prevail in practice: the traditional one, providing for 3 kinds of plans (long term, medium term, i.e. usually five-year and annual plans), or the new one, providing for 4 kinds of plans, namely for the long-term, five-year, three-year and annual plans.

No matter which model is chosen, significant modifications will have to be introduced into the traditional kinds of plans.

As regards the long-term plans, the following changes will have to be introduced:

Under the reform, the principal function of a long-term plan should be to prepare the economy for future needs and *not* to just try to guess the future. This entails abandoning the currently accepted way of planning, i.e. the one-variant vision of the economy at the end of the term covered by the plan. This should be supplanted with numerous variants of the future situation each accompanied by appropriate ways of acting. The long-term plan should play a key role as regards the development of those domains that determine the position of the country in the world and its ability to compete on the world markets. This applies especially to the development of the 'avant-garde' (i.e. of high technology) industries, which are usually started from scratch, as well as to the spread of those tendencies at a macro scale which represent the most advanced stage of civilisation. Thus, the main function of long term planning should be to foster the development of high technology industries, to promote macrotechnologies and the technological progress necessary in order to accomplish the restructuring of the country's economy. Therefore a program of development of the most crucial high technology industries should constitute an integral part of the long and medium-term central plans.

In order to fulfil its social function, the plan – and especially a long-term one – must first try to determine the respective targets of the country as regards the most advanced branches of industry which will define its situation on the world markets. [3]

It is also necessary to define the way in which these targets are to be achieved. It is vital that planning should focus on these issues, even if it entails a restriction of its scope.

Therefore, the key function of long-term planning, as well as its distinctive feature, should be the determining of the direction of the structural changes in economy and the ways to bring forth those changes. This means that a long-term plan must at the same time constitute the programme of the restructuring of national economy.

In the past, Polish long term planning covered as many as fifteen to twenty years. Presently, because of the rapid pace of technological development, it is believed that long-term planning should not exceed the ten year range. To reach further ahead would substantially increase the margin of uncertainty, which in this kind of planning is already very large. It is suggested, however, that it would be useful to develop more preparatory studies and forecasts covering periods longer than ten to fifteen years and have different scopes and time horizons, depending upon the problem studied.

We should reject, however, the views presented in certain western publications which state that planning in general should be restricted to long-term planning only.

Even in the countries with market-oriented economies, priorities are modified over periods of time shorter than those covered by long-term planning.

This can be illustrated by the example of Japan, where medium-term plans are developed. Those plans are characteristic for their variable temporal range as their well as variable priorities and they cover periods of 3 to 5 years. [4]

For the 5-year plans, the principal directions of change within the new model of planning should be as follows:

a) stronger links between the targets and the underlying regulations of economic activity of enterprises connected with the goals of the economic strategy. This is a follow-up of the principle stating that each target in a plan should be accompanied by quantified, definite means serving to fulfil it and also by regulations serving the same goal,

b) a substantial increase in the role of the synthetic financial balance sheets, a reduction of the scope of planning in physical output terms in favour of planning in financial terms. Planning in terms of financial results should be treated as equally important and serve to verify the financial feasibility and attainability of targets specified in physical output terms,

c) a substantial increase in the importance of cost-benefit studies and of calculations of the feasibility of particular ventures.

In annual central planning there is a drive towards restricting planning in physical output terms. The latter is to a large extent left to the decisions of enterprises. Physical output targets in central plans are limited to the scope and volume of the Government orders which are assigned to meet the most urgent social needs and to eliminate shortages. Such orders entail certain privileges assigned to the enterprises, in areas such as procurement of raw materials and financial resources.

The chief function of annual central plans is thus more closely related to the creation of a current economic equilibrium. Therefore the demand managing function of the central plan should be increased. As this is eventually expressed in financial terms, the annual plan would focus rather on the question of financial balance. In this manner the main content of such plans should consist of synthetic, principal financial balances, such as the financial balance of the state, the budget, balance of payments, the balance of the citizens' revenues and expenditures, the credit plan. The need arises for a large-scale improvement and development of a common balance of revenues and expenditures of state-owned and cooperative enterprises.

As a result of this, we observe the drive to replace the traditional annual plan dominated by physical output goals by a plan defined in terms of both financial and physical output. In such a plan the estimates of the physical output volume would serve merely as general indicators of the volume of production and turnover upon which the financial calculations are based. This plan would also provide for a direct and strong relationship between the policy objectives and targets and their physical and financial expression.

The effort put into drafting an annual plan would concentrate upon the elaboration of changes in the currently existing regulations that determine the functioning of enterprises. Such need would arise if the regulations require adjustments in order to ensure the fulfilment of medium term targets.

The sixth element of the new model of planning is the change in the position of the central planning agency in relation to the financial planning bodies.

The Act of 23 December 1988 declared the liquidation of the Planning Commission at the Council of Ministers, which had so far fulfilled the duties of the central planning body. In its place the Central Planning Office was set up. This new body of central planning is to be freed from dealing with current, operational decisions and will constitute a centre for strategic studies on economic and social development.

At the same time a Social Council of Planning will be created at the Central Planning Office and connections between the central planning body and different social organisations like consumer organisations, professional organisations (i.e. Economists, Technicians, Trade Unions) should be increased.

In this new situation the following division of tasks within the central planning is possible:

The central planning body would develop long term, two-year and five-year plans. The Ministry of Finance could at the same time elaborate a so-called 'Annual physical-financial central plan'. The role of the central planning body in preparation of this plan would be limited. This organ would compile the materials necessary in order to work out the annual plans, assess the conformity of those plans with medium-term policy and help to prepare future changes to be introduced in the system of regulations concerning the functioning of enterprises. In a way, such organisation of central planning would represent a return to past attempts to separate long-term planning from operational planning (such ideas were elaborated in the USSR and other countries). Such proposals are being advocated in discussions conducted in Poland, although they have not yet gained official acceptance.

To conclude, it is worth stressing that in spite of the limitation of the scope of planning in the socialist economy under reform, this scope must remain much broader than is the case in market-oriented economies, where national planning, if it exists, tends to be 'indicative planning'. The principal difference would be a far more active role of the state in resource allocation and in the processes of economic restructuring. Thus, in a socialist economy, the role of the state in shaping investment policy would be generally more important and would also include the private sector. Similarly, central planning would have a larger influence upon the organizational structures in the economy, i.e. upon the creation of new enterprises and the liquidation of others.

As regards the national income distribution, the scope of central planning would exceed the influence usually exerted by indicative planning, mainly in the following areas: control of the distribution of revenues among the principal social groups according to the principle of social justice, giving shape to the structure of social-cultural expenditures (collective consumption), setting of priorities and of volume of subsidies for the economy. This is due to a wider conception of social objectives in such economy.

Those differences do not rule out the possibility that a socialist economy under reform may borrow certain solutions worked out in market-oriented economies. This provides both sides with favourable premises for a mutual exchange of experiences.

Notes

[1]   The Economist, 5.11.1983, p.81.
[2]   See e.g. The Economist.15.10.1988, p.15.
[3]   Andrzej Karpinski, 'Method of Constructing a Long-term Plan and the Challenge of the Future', *Gospodarska Planowa*, vol. 1, 1988, p.6.
[4]   Hiroichi Iyemoto, 'The Japanese Macro-economic Planning and Economic Planning Agency', Nanzan University, p.8.